THE FUTURE OF CREATION

Jürgen Moltmann

THE FUTURE OF CREATION

Collected Essays

FORTRESS PRESS   PHILADELPHIA

Translated by Margaret Kohl
from the German
Zukunft der Schöpfung: Gesammelte Aufsätze
Christian Kaiser Verlag Munich 1977

Translation © SCM Press Ltd. 1979

First American Edition by Fortress Press 1979

———————

Library of Congress Cataloging in Publication Data

Moltmann, Jürgen.
  The future of creation.

  Translation of Zukunft der Schöpfung.
  Includes bibliographical references.
  1. Eschatology—Addresses, essays, lectures.
2. Hope—Addresses, essays, lectures. 3. Theology
—Addresses, essays, lectures. I. Title.
BT823.M613 1979   236   79-7388
ISBN 0-8006-0627-2

———————

7707I79   Printed in the United States of America   1-627

CONTENTS

Contents

PREFACE

Nine years ago I published a collection of essays under the title *Perspektiven der Theologie* ('theological perspectives'). The essays in this second volume are grouped thematically round the subjects 'future' and 'creation', and I have therefore decided to gather them together under the title *The Future of Creation*. These essays do not merely represent stages in my progress from *Theology of Hope* (1964; ET 1967) to *The Church in the Power of the Spirit* (1975; ET 1977). They are also intended to illuminate the factual and methodological basis for the eschatological trend of this progress. My discussion about alternative views on eschatology and my ideas about the relationship between eschatology and the foundations of Christian ethics are to be read in this context. The essays on the theology of creation are designed to open up an eschatological concept of creation which will take in both 'creation at the beginning' and the promised 'new creation'. On the other hand they also aim to relate the eschatological hope to created reality. In these essays it is not my desire to defend the position I have taken up in the past, either apologetically or polemically. I hope, rather, that they will serve to deepen and crystallize eschatological thinking, and will show how open-minded and how ready to learn that way of thinking is.

I should like to thank Dr Michael Welker for the discussions which accompanied the book's preparation, and for his work on the proofs.

Tübingen   JÜRGEN MOLTMANN
10 *May* 1977

I

THE FUTURE AS A NEW PARADIGM
OF TRANSCENDENCE

1. *The Idea of Transcendence*

Transcendence is a relative term, for wherever we use it we mean the transcendence *of* something for the sake of something else. We generally use the word 'transcendence' for whatever exceeds the immanence that is present and open to our experience – for whatever goes further, into what is beyond immanence. We use 'immanence' for what projects into our experience, for the present, for this world. Just as the beyond is always the beyond of something here and now, in this world, so the here and now is always 'this side' of something beyond. The two terms therefore belong together. They define each other mutually and are reciprocally related to one another. Our understanding of transcendence is always dependent on our experience of some reality as immanence. Conversely, there is no concept of immanence which does not imply an understanding of transcendence, as the reverse side of the shield, as it were. There is no dichotomy between immanence and transcendence. There is only a distinction and a relationship in the experience of 'the boundary'.[1]

If something is experienced as limited and finite, the possibility of negation emerges at its boundaries. Transcendence may then be defined negatively, as the in-finite and the un-limited. On the other hand if something is experienced as being finite and limited, what emerges at its boundaries is the possibility of its growth or enhancement into what is endless and limitless. Transcendence is then analogously defined as the super-finite.

In history, 'the boundary' has been experienced in very varying ways. But it was always the boundary that first made it possible to talk about transcendence and immanence If. there ceases to be any experience of 'the boundary', transcendence is denied, and then it is no longer possible to talk about immanence either. Then the difference between the two, which we experience 'on the boundary', disappears. Everything is one, and Yes is No.

It has been rightly asked – notably by Karl Barth – whether the theological application of the terms transcendence and immanence to the God of biblical history and historical faith is an appropriate one. If it is purely a concept of relation, expressive of 'the boundary', then the expression transcendence does not comprehend God's independent and underived existence – his aseity – or his subjectivity. Anyone who only thinks of God as the transcendence of a particular immanence, has thought of him merely as a predicate, not as a subject. He has thought 'God' for the sake of something else, not as yet for his own sake.[2] All the same, the word transcendence can appropriately be used for God's relationships to something else – for his relationship to the world and history. For it allows us to express what God is and what he is like in his relationship to the world and to men and women by means of the experience of 'the frontier'. It does not allow us to say who we may say God is, however. Historically, Christian theology has always linked the historical transmission of the 'name' of God, and the history in which his name is revealed, with man's present experience of 'the boundary' and of transcendence. The *sacra doctrina* was linked together with the *prima philosophia*. Let us leave on one side the special theological question about the divine revelation, name and history, and turn to the question of people's experience of the boundary and of transcendence at the present day. Like the experience of the boundary, transcendence and immanence are comprehended in the history of their changing relationship. If we investigate this history we come across 'the transformations of God' (in Bultmann's phrase). We shall thereby take as our premise that the Christian faith is due to the word of Christ, and we shall ask solely about the boundary at which faith has to be present today if it wants to participate in the transcendence of God's presence. In this respect there are 'transformations of faith' too.

The following account and comparison of patterns of transcendence is necessarily simplified and reduced to typical cases. Our aim is not exclusiveness; we simply want to find our bearings in the present.

2. *Patterns of Transcendence*

(i) *Physics and metaphysics*

Greek metaphysics grew up as concept or *theoria* on the basis of the ancient Greek cosmic religion, which is reflected in Thales' saying: πάντα πλήρη θεῶν (Everything is full of the gods). The metaphysical idea interpreted the whole of experienceable reality in the light of its origin or its widest horizon. According to Parmenides, the world is a sphere. Transcendence is the furthest, all-comprehending periphery of immanence in its finite perfection. When, later, the Stoics called the cosmos the visible body of the invisible God, they were thinking of the divine and transcendent as being the reverse side of everything worldly and immanent, corresponding to it in the order of logos and nomos. The divine is the transcendence of the divinely ruled cosmos; the cosmos is the immanence of the invisibly divine. But where do we find 'the experience of the boundary'? Here metaphysics is the answer to the fundamental metaphysical question about all being. Everything that exists is threatened by its finitude, transience and impermanence. That is why all being longs for – and the being that is endowed with consciousness begs for – an infinite, non-transient and permanent existence. 'Being refuses to be badly administered. The rule of the many is not healthy; let there be only one ruler', says Aristotle.[3] If on this 'boundary' immanence is experienced as being finite, transient and threatened by chaos, the transcendence that corresponds to it takes the form of the infinite and non-transient, the ordering power and the one. Through participation in infinite existence, finite being acquires its transcendence and, correspondingly, this transcendence acquires its immanence. The physics of finite existence and the metaphysics of the one, ordering and moving Being correspond to one another.

Now, for many centuries Aristotle's *Metaphysics* counted as being the very embodiment of 'the transcendent'. But his metaphysical concept of transcendence was only valid as long as, and to the degree in which, Aristotle's physics put its stamp on people's experience of the world and their experience of the boundary. Any change in the physics – that is to say, in the understanding of reality – was therefore bound to alter the metaphysical understanding of transcendence as well.

(*ii*) *Existence and transcendence*

Modern man no longer interprets himself as being part of the world, or a part of finite being. Although this understanding has not completely disappeared, man increasingly sees the world as the field of constructive potentialities for his own spirit. For him the world is no longer a 'house of being' in which he dwells. It is increasingly becoming the material which he investigates so that he may make it his own possession. He no longer feels part of the eternal cosmic order; he feels himself to be the lord of nature, which confronts him as something different from himself. The more the world becomes man's object, the more he becomes in himself a subject transcending the world. But then he ceases to find transcendence in the furthest, all-comprehending periphery of the cosmos. He finds it in himself; for he has made himself the centre of 'his world', a world which is becoming his property to an increasing degree. It is no longer the heaven of metaphysics which opens up the physics of the earth to him; his world is revealed to him through his own transcending subjectivity. That is why in modern times transcendence is increasingly experienced in the inward dimension of human existence, in its capabilities, which are to be defined transcendentally. Man can objectify everything and make it his own property; it is only his own self that transcends all the objectifications of his spirit. The boundary between immanence and transcendence runs through man himself and is experienced there. He experiences both finitude and infinity in his own existence. He knows himself as God present on earth. And so in place of the old correlation between physics and metaphysics, the modern correlation between existence and transcendence steps into the foreground. We find this in the history of Cartesian and Kantian influences in their many variations.

With this transformation in metaphysics, a whole traditional view of God collapses. It is forced even further into the background by way of criticism of religion, criticism of that naive 'metaphysics for the masses' (Nietzsche's phrase), demythologization and 'atheistic' theology. Critical thinking tells us that transcendence can no longer be expressed in objectifying language, because its 'objective' (the world) has lost its ancient metaphysical framework. It is the existential interpretation which for the first time links relevantly the Christian tradition as kerygma with man's new experience of transcendence.

It is true that men and women always feel that 'God is dead' whenever they lose a picture of God with which they have been at home. It is true that they like to talk about the end of metaphysics whenever they lose the traditional feeling for transcendence. But what they fear only seems to be so. In reality it is a question neither of 'the death of God in modern times', nor of the end of metaphysics in general, nor of the age of secularization and atheism. We are merely being faced with transformations of transcendence and transformations in the boundary experience of immanence. The experience of transcendence, the experience of the boundary, and religion in the general sense of the word are just as relevant today as they ever were. It is just that we no longer find them in the places where they used to be.

(iii) *Alienated transcendence in the realms of play: release through modern society*

Today even the modern pattern of existence and transcendence is losing its power to mould our thinking. It is true that man still transcends nature outside him and in his own body. It is true that by means of reflection he is increasing his potentialities for being 'superior' to the world. But instead he is surrounded by an ever denser web of his own works – social institutions, political organizations, giant industrial firms – like a new quasi-nature.[4] The natural cosmos, which man sees through and dominates more and more, is being replaced by a new cosmos of his own objectifications; and this cosmos is increasingly hard to see through, and harder still to dominate and control. In this artificial cosmos of his scientific and technical civilization the old conditions are returning, ironically enough, on a different level – the very conditions from which man once freed himself: the irrationality of the forces of nature returns again in the irrational compulsions of his civilization; the impenetrability of fate finds its correspondence in the impenetrability of the tangle of bureaucratic manipulations; the part once played by natural disasters is now played by social and political ones. Man, who in his society rules nature, is becoming the slave of his own works. They are taking on autonomous form, are running away from him, acquiring power over him. Consequently the problem of man's liberation from the paramountcy of his own works has been the theme of 'applied' philosophy since the beginning of the Industrial Revolution.

Because of this men and women are arriving at a new experience of the boundary. It is no longer the experience of their own inner subjectivity, which transcends the objective world; it is the experience of their own helplessness in an ironclad shell of objectifications, which have taken on independent life, and their impotence in a 'closed society'. Since the beginning of the industrial world transcendental subjectivity has been aware of its own impotence. Its own world is becoming a stranger to it. This consciousness is easily transformed into the ivory tower of romantic subjectivity. 'At the centre of this fantastic superiority of the subject [i.e., over the world] is embedded the renunciation of any active alteration of the world as it is.'[5] The switch-over from confidence in the cosmic world to fear of it – a change which took place in the later years of the ancient world – is repeated in the gnosticism of recent Western civilization.[6] There is a growing feeling of alienation, because of the materialization of social conditions, where people are viewed as things, and because of the political impotence of the individual; and the suffering inflicted on man by his own world, which is enslaving its creator, is producing new, ecstatic forms of the search for transcendence and transcendental experience. Where can we find a transcendence which, instead of being a form of alienation, liberates us from alienation?[7]

People are seeking for this freedom beyond the realm of necessity and compulsion in many of these new forms of religiosity and search for transcendence. Then the alienation which makes men and women conscious of 'the boundary' is seen, not as alienation at all, but as release.[8] The old relationship between immanence and transcendence is overturned. The immanence of man's own world, which is hardening and becoming autonomous, is closing round him in an ever tighter net; and this releases a freely hovering transcendence of the soul that has ceased to feel at home in its own world. Since modern subjectivity is no longer in a position to dominate its own world, inner transcendence is becoming the play of an impotent escapism.[9] The 'unhappy awareness of the noble soul' (in Hegel's phrase) has fled from a confining and alienated reality that seems to it meaningless, into the dream worlds of the deyond, into the unassailed realms of play, with all their unreal potentialities. Yet it is precisely this flight from reality which surrenders the real social and political world to senseless and inhuman forces. The abstract negation of the real world makes every kind of cynicism possible in the reality that has been abandoned. That is why the new mysticism is often coupled with nihilism. These forms of modern romantic religiosity can initially be understood as the secondary phenomena of modern existential transcendence, for they are due to the release of the soul through a stabilized immanence. Immanence then ceases to be understood as the immanence of a transcendence. It ceases to be moulded, impelled and changed by the transcendence that goes beyond it. It becomes instead the basis which sets free those abstract transcendental realms of play.

When this happens the characteristics ascribed to immanence and transcendence change as well. In our modern immanence, where food-production is automated and the automation can be cybernetically regulated, 'transcendence' has lost its job. It is becoming the play of the spirit that is freed from necessity. The sphere of the kingdom of play, culture and transcendence rises on the foundations of 'the kingdom of necessity'. The more stable the immanence is, the more unstable and open the possible interpretation of transcendence. Earlier, transcendence had to be viewed as being the stabilizing factor leading to order – as 'being's loftiest star', in Nietzsche's phrase; but, in a stabilized world, transcendence can turn into the inexhaustible fascination of new possibilities, just because its openness is unlimited. The perception that in the modern world Bonhoeffer's 'working hypothesis called God'[10] is really 'out of work' only sounds negative to the world of work and necessity where men are not free. But if the 'kingdom of necessity' is automated and left to self-regulating processes, it loses man's interest, simply by itself. What does not offer any resistance, thus forcing people to acquire it creatively in the pain of labour and self-denial, is no longer experienced as being 'real'. That is why the unreal increasingly attracts the interest of men and women – the sphere of what has not yet been realized and of what cannot be realized, the possibilities which are actually absurd; and this is experienced as a 'boundary'.

In the realms of play where modern society provides release, there can therefore be a rebirth of experience of transcendence. Since wide areas of neighbourly love have been socialized, we can arrive at the rebirth of the love of God, free of any ulterior purpose.

For a long time people needed 'God' in order to enjoy the world, or at least to cope with it; but God will by no means disappear from a world where he is no longer 'needed'. On the contrary, we shall arrive at the Augustinian reversal that we 'need' the world in order to enjoy 'God'. Now that the economy has been automated and politics have been cyberneticized, theology can become man's new theme, in the form of man's eternal dialogue and play with God and God's with man. If the world is becoming emancipated from 'God', God is also emancipated from his function as 'emergency helper' in the world. He becomes free for himself, so that he can be contemplated and loved for his own sake. In Herman Kahn's 'post-industrial society', industry becomes uninteresting and theology in hitherto unknown form can become the game men and women play in deadly earnest. For then doxology and nihilism will be directly confronted with one another. Work on the finitely negative (which reconciles the two) comes to an end. Then men and women must seek directly for forms whereby they can exist between God and nothingness, without any reconciliation. First signs in this direction may be found in modern literature and art.

In human civilization people live from anticipations of 'life' like this. In play, in feast and in laughter they free themselves from the rational sequences of work, with all their purposeful expediency, and are liberated from the moral compulsion to alter conditions and improve society. If it were not for these anticipations of the kingdom of freedom, play and laughter – even, it may be, in inadequate form – people would not suffer so painfully over the negative and the pressure of necessity.

Yet this culture in the realm of freedom, which is based on release from the realm of necessity, is none the less an alienated transcendence. It is only a by-product of the realm of work, not as yet victory over that realm. But if it is understood as an anticipation of the transformation of labour into self-activity, the metamorphosis of morality into play and the change of the prayers sent up in time of need into the prayers of free adoration, then out of it spring the forces that can change the world. Man still experiences 'the boundary' everywhere in the finitely negative. That is why Hegel's criticism of Schelling has lost none of its truth:

> The life of God and divine intelligence, then, can, if we like, be spoken of as love disporting with itself: but this idea falls into edification and

even into insipidity if it lacks the seriousness, the suffering, the patience and the labour of the negative.[11]

But at the moment it is Schelling who seems to be in the ascendancy.

(iv) History and the eschatological future

Since the pattern of 'existence and transcendence' has lost its power, a new, realistic understanding of immanence as *history* would seem to offer itself. History was not of pre-eminent importance in the ancient world's ideas about metaphysics. It was the incalculable and chaotic factor. Only the cosmos, with its cyclic orders, and the determinations of destiny possessed transcendence. In the patterns of transcendental subjectivity, history took on the significance of personal decisions and encounters. Today social, technical and political history is becoming the field of mediation between man and nature. It is only in this field that man acquires his identity, and it is only in the medium of this mediation that he comprehends nature and that, for him, nature becomes nature. If this medium of mediation acquires an autonomy hostile to man, the reciprocal relationship between man and his own objectified world increasingly becomes the theme of history. 'The boundary' of transcendence no longer lies only in the finitude of all things and all being; no longer does it lie merely in the subjectivity of man, who surpasses nature; it is found in the fossilized, dead forms of his own objectifications and in the power of his works over him himself. In modern society, human subjectivity and the materializations of man's works and relationships have drawn apart from one another in such a way that now the creations dominate their creators, and rationalized conditions exercise an irrational dictatorship over people. This is a new 'boundary' at which people reach out for transcendence. It is a transcendence of an existing system. It is therefore directed to 'the future'. The present situation is experienced as a state of being torn apart between subjectivity and the materialization of what is really non-material.[12] The impotence of the individual and the paramount power of conditions, which behave according to their own laws, determine this situation. If this is the historical present in its torn totality, then it is clear that transcendence can be found neither on the subjective level nor on the objective one. It can only be found where this antagonistic state of affairs discovers a qualitatively different, transforming and new future. If the 'boundary' of present immanence is experienced in the fact that man is alienated from his world and that this world is alienated from man, transcendence will be experienced at the point where critical perspectives open up for our present conflicts, where new possibilities emerge for a meaningful incarnation of man, and new potentialities for a humanization of his alienated conditions – in short, where a future of reconciliation and alteration wins the upper hand over this situation.

Our understanding of 'the future' is also subjected to the divided consciousness of modern men and women. On the one hand, 'future' in industrial society was identified with progress and development within the existing state of things. 'Future' was objectified into the rate of growth of the national product and the acceleration of man's objective potentialities. As long as the industrial system was being built up, objective progress therefore enjoyed the magic of transcendence. It promised to overcome man's dependence on nature, to fulfil human longings, to conquer economic alienation and even to bring about the kingdom of peace, politically. But modern post-industrial planned society de-futurizes this type of transcendent future. Progress in industrial society lost the magic of transcendence to the degree in which society's structure was completed. A planned and programmed future has no longer anything to do with transcendence.[13]

On the other hand 'the future' was personalized, becoming (as it did in existentialism) the inner extension of human existing, openness of heart and futurity of decision. Yet on the other hand such personalization of the release from responsibility for our present history is due to the objectifying of the future. In this context the personalistic understanding of future as potentiality of existence is just as much a product of the cleft in the modern mind as the objectifying of the future in the automatic progress of society.

In what sense, then, can 'future' become a new pattern of transcendence? Only when it becomes the embodiment of the transcending of present conflict and lack of freedom in something qualitatively new. The magic of true transcendence is inherent in the future if that future promises something qualitatively new, which stimulates people to change the 'system' of the present radically; and if in this future something different can be expected which will lead to the altering of the foundations of the present, antagonistic condition of immanence. That means, in present-day language: if it becomes the condition that makes possible a revolutionary consciousness which tries to transform an antagonistic society into a non-antagonistic one, and an enslaved society into a free one. In this way (in a further step along the road of previous transformations in the concept of transcendence), transcendence will cease to be a noun and will become a verb. Transcendence becomes the embodiment of the actual historical transcending of the actual historical 'boundary'. The noun then means the forecourt of the open future into which the historical transformations enter. This implies that future transcendence will no longer be understood as the quantitative expansion and development of the present, but as a qualitative alteration of history, which will be experienced in conflict. The 'wholly other' of transcendence will then be understood as 'what makes wholly other' and the 'crossing' of the boundary will be seen as the transformation of history in the light of its qualitatively new future.

The power of what actually exists, which only wants to reproduce itself or to adapt itself to the times by means of particular reforms, will be confronted by the forces of a qualitatively new future and by a fundamental transformation. Transcendence is being sought for, and also experienced, in many quarters today at this 'boundary' or 'front' of history in the present. For Marxists this is the leap from quantity into new quality, and from the realm of necessity into the realm of freedom; for many other people it is the changing of an unfree into a free society, or from a repressive into a human one; Christians consider it to be the qualitative difference between history and eschatology, anticipated in specific faith under the conditions of history.[14] It is just at this point that we find new experiences of the 'boundary' and transcendence in political responsibility. These experiences differ from man's experiences of suffering over finitude and his suffering over himself, though they do not displace them entirely.

3. *The Language of Transcendence*

In the patterns of metaphysical transcendence reality was determined and ordered in definitions. In viewing the physical world, the act of perception was joined with the remembrance of eternal Ideas. In the synthetic act of *theoria*, the mind reconciled the mutable with the immutable, the image that appeared with its true

Idea. The defining concept became the image of true reality. If transcendence is the most perfect reality, then the concept of transcendence is correspondingly the definition of all definitions and the quintessence of all concepts. The hierarchy of being corresponds to the hierarchy of defining and subsuming concepts.

In the patterns of subjective transcendence, we find a different kind of definition of transcendence. Here the reflection of the subject links objective experience with its own transcendental conditions of possible experience in general. The things that are perceived are no longer associated, in *theoria*, with the Ideas that form their essence. They are related in their appearance to the perceiving subject. This means that objective definitions are replaced by concepts of relation, which express the relationship of things to the human subject. Correspondingly, transcendence can no longer be apprehended in definition either, but now only in relation to the inner ground of the subject.

Cognition and language change yet again in the pattern 'history and the future'. The perceiving of a thing or a relationship not only establishes its reality; it links this with the expectation of its future possibility. Things are known in their history and associated with the future of history that is sought for and hoped for. Things do not appear on earth against the background of the transcendent heaven of their fixed ideas. Nor are they merely grasped in the searchlight of the perceiving subject. They are comprehended in their meaning for the whole in the foreground of history's open future.[15] Language does not merely establish facts; it knows as well that merely by establishing what is, it is intervening in and changing the open process of history. Where knowledge and language become aware of their own historicity, together with the historicity of things, language as a statement of existing facts becomes a critical language; for everything that is historical is accompanied by its own negation. On the other hand this historical language becomes a 'performatory' language – a language that makes something happen.[16] By putting things in history into words, it alters history and the things in history. Language must therefore be clear about its purpose – what it is putting things into language *for* and what it is altering them *for*. This means that the objective, subsuming concept of 'species' gives way to the dynamic concept of function, and the subjective concept of relation is replaced by the concept of work and production, as well as by the idea of redemption, which redeems a thing or person from his immobility.[17]

4. *Representations of Transcendence*

The connection between philosophical metaphysics and theology in the ancient world shows how political monarchy could correspond to cosmological monotheism. We find parallels of this kind wherever the polis saw itself as being the human correspondence to the cosmos. These parallels are not necessarily always inevitable, because human life often shows inconsistencies. Yet there are affinities and alliances here. We have already mentioned the much quoted sentence out of Aristotle's *Metaphysics* XII: 'Being refuses to be badly administered. The rule of the many is not healthy; let there be only one ruler'; and this could be understood as the justification of an imperialistic peace policy. The hierarchical structure of the metaphysical world was often interpreted as being the transcendent background of the political world's hierarchical structure. Conversely, the 'one God' was represented by the 'one ruler', as in the imperial ideology.

On the other hand, the modern form of 'existence and transcendence' could no longer find its reflection in the old hierarchical and authoritarian patterns of rule. It is represented by the sovereign irreplaceability of every individual. That is why in modern times religion is no longer understood as the hallowing of authority in church, state and society, but as the inner self-transcendence of every individual. As a result the democracy of free individuals, directly related to God without any mediation, becomes the new way of representing transcendence. The divine crown no longer rests on the head of the ruler; it belongs to the constitution of the free. Transcendence can no longer be represented on earth 'from above'; its only possible earthly representation is now the web of free relationships of free individuals. The relationship to God or to transcendence is no longer reflected in the relationship to hallowed authority; we find it in the free recognition of, and respect for, our neighbour, in whom transcendence is present.

In the growing autonomy of the human world of things, this democratic way of representing transcendence is apparently losing its power. Consequently, in the pattern of transcendence called 'history and the future', the representation of transcendence in the

democratic network of interpersonal relationships will be transformed into new, revolutionary forms of transcending. In a society
that has its eyes fixed on its status quo, this democratic transcendence (if it is not to fade into a hollow ideological sham) can
only be realized by liberating the repressed and alienated groups in
society and giving them an autonomous part in the shaping of
society's future. Particular societies only show their transcendence
within themselves, by excluding others, or by outvoting them. In
these cases transcendence finds its representation in revolutionary
groups which ally themselves with the people who are at present
alienated, oppressed or perhaps just frustrated. It is for that very
reason that revolutionary movements in societies of this kind carry
with them the magic of transcendence. But wherever they pick up
the old hierarchical forms of transcendence again, by way of party-
political machinery and so forth, or wherever they merely try to
stabilize their own identity, they betray this new experience of
transcendence. Their end, in bureaucratic hierarchies of official
functionaries, is a retrograde step. It is not an advance compared
with the democratic form of transcendence.

5. *The Future as a New Paradigm of Transcendence*

In closing, let me give a brief outline of some reflections about the
possible identifications of future transcendence.

Here we understand by history the experience of reality in
conflicts. It is not simply the experience that everything is
transient. Nor is it merely the experience that everything is caught
up in the river of time and that the present stands between the 'no
more' of the past and the 'not yet' of the future. Nor, either, is it
simply the experience that men and women are continually forced
to make decisions. For history is rather the impression that man,
together with his society and his world, is an experiment; and that
not only is he himself a risk – his world is a risk too. At the crises
and focal points of his life he has the same impression as Hamlet:
'To be or not to be, that is the question.' Involved as he is in the
experiment of history, he has to conceive the vision of a successful
solution, even though he is seized by horror at the thought of not
succeeding. These visions too have the character of risk and are
only provisional designs. They must prove themselves through the
critical energy they bring to bear on present reality, and through

personal involvement. They do not take the form of an objective 'insight into necessity'. They are more like a draft, reaching out into the possible in order to avert the present need. And what I am about to say should be understood in this sense.

'The future' has as yet nothing to do with transcendence as long as it simply means a historical future. It is true that a vision of the future can only be evolved out of history. That is why this vision is as transient as history itself. An endless transcending is not as yet true transcendence.[18] Yet in intention future history can undoubtedly be distinguished from the idea of history's future. Only a future which transcends the experiment of history itself can become the paradigm of transcendence and give the experiment 'history' meaning. The 'utopia of the beyond', properly understood, bursts apart all the worldly relations and cohesions we know. It can therefore be interpreted as the fundamental and ultimate experience of transcendence. This experience of transcendence, which even transcends historical transcending, is generally expressed in religious symbols. If we can talk about reality 'as history', we can also talk about 'an end of history'.[19] What eschatological symbols we can use when – in the midst of history and under historical conditions – we talk about such an 'end of history', is a different matter. Here we can at least say first of all that a 'future of history' cannot already be a quantitatively new future; it must be a qualitatively new one. The future can only be identified with transcendence if in using the word future we are thinking about an alteration in the conditions of history itself. It is only if the conflicts which cause us to experience present reality as history are abolished that the future has anything to do with transcendence. It is only where, in history, these conflicts are transcended in the direction of their abolition or reconciliation that something of this qualitatively new future is to be found. Other outlooks on the future soon show themselves to be only apparently transcendent. They promise more than they perform and quickly surrender the magic of transcendence to resignation. Conversely, however, the vision of a qualitatively new future of history can become a transcendent horizon which opens up and stimulates the process of transcending towards a new historical future. If the relation between history and eschatological future shows itself to be this, then we come up against the relationship between distinction and analogy. The future of history is something qualitatively different and new compared with what we here experience as history. But as the future of this particular historical reality, it already puts its stamp on the way history is experienced and moulded here, in the present. It therefore offers correspondences, analogies, directions and trends in the qualitative difference. It is not these analogies and trends that cause the 'leap' into a different quality; but the vision of this necessary leap does undoubtedly influence the way we form, and also endure, history here.

In order to make the dialectic clearer, let me mention two attitudes which are one-sided and mistaken. If we overstress the qualitative difference between history and the eschatological future, we arrive at an abstract negation of the world and its history. The great failures in the experiments of history then become an indication of the senselessness of all happening and action in history. The world is a 'vale of tears'. It is dominated by what is fundamentally evil. The end is resignation. If, on the other hand, we stress the relation of correspondence between history and the eschatological future, down to the point of asserting continuity between the two, then transcendence is the very quintessence of history itself: a continual revelation of the future in the present, a permanent over-stepping and surpassing of what is actually present. The result is again resignation, because every transcending creates in its turn a present that has to be transcended. And why should the future succeed any better than the present? There will only be a meaningful reconciliation when the transcendence that surpasses history is linked with actual historical transcending; when, even in the midst of the critical difference, people believe in the possibilities of correspondence, but when, on the other hand, in the possibilities of correspondence we keep in mind the qualitative difference. Then 'system-transcendent criticism' and the keeping open of a qualitatively new future are linked with specific steps opening the way to a qualitatively better correspondence.

For the Christian faith, the two things – history and the future – come together in the Christ in whom that qualitatively new future is present under the conditions of history. That is why faith talks about the historical Christ eschatologically and finds in him the end of history, present in the midst of history. This 'end' does not supplant history, making it a matter of indifference to the believer. Because he can hope for the new future through faith in Christ, he begins to suffer over the unredeemedness of the present and feels at one with all who suffer, consciously or unconsciously. But the end does not disappear in history either, making this future a matter of indifference to faith. Because faith can hope for this future, it begins to resist and to change the scheme of this world and the systems of the present. For a long time the Christian faith interpreted the transcendence it believed it had found in Christ metaphysically; later it understood transcendence existentially; today the important thing is that faith is present where the 'boundary' of transcendence is experienced in suffering and is transcended in active hope. The more faith interprets Christian transcendence eschatologically, the more it will understand the boundary of immanence historically and give itself up to the movement of transcending. But the more it interprets this eschatological transcendence in Christian terms – that is, with its eyes on the crucified Jesus – the more it will become conscious that the qualitatively new future of God has allied itself with those who are dispossessed, denied and downtrodden at the present day; so that this future does not begin up at the spearheads of progress in a 'progressive society', but down below, among society's victims. It will have to link hope for the eschatological future with a loving solidarity with the dispossessed. The future of the new existence which ends history is linked for faith with the dialectic of the negative in the historical present. The transcendence of the future of a 'Wholly Other' begins for it dialectically, in the lifting up of those who are 'the others' in a particular present and in particular societies. This is the link which is for faith 'the power of change'; and this is the way faith experiences, in the midst of history, the power of the God who transcends history.

II

TRENDS IN ESCHATOLOGY

1. *The Beginnings and Later Stagnation*

About the turn of the century, a Christian world committed to belief in progress and cultural optimism was shocked by the exegetical and historical findings of Johannes Weiss, Albert Schweitzer, Franz Overbeck and others, with their recognition of the apocalyptic character of Jesus' message about the kingdom and the early church's proclamation of Christ. People, it is true, had enough historical honesty to accept this unique feature of the early Christian message: 'In Jesus' view, the kingdom of God (is) a totally supernatural power . . . which is absolutely opposed to this world.'[1] Yet men and women found it impossible to revolutionize their own Christianity in accordance with early Christian apocalyptic. 'We no longer pray, "Let grace come and the world end." We live in the joyful confidence that this present world will increasingly be the scene of a "divine humanity".'[2]

Since that time the pendulum has swung backwards and forwards, both in historical research into New Testament eschatologies, and in systematic justification of the Christian hope today. On the one hand Albert Schweitzer and his followers developed what was known as consistent eschatology. With its historical assertions that Jesus and the early church shared the apocalyptic expectation of the imminent end, this was really only designed to furnish the systematic proof that Jesus' crucifixion nullified his own eschatology and that the delay of the parousia revoked the eschatology of the early Christians.[3] Indefinable history makes every expectation of the end of the world obsolete. On the other hand, C. H. Dodd and Rudolf Bultmann developed different forms of what has been called presentative or realized eschatology.

This is a partly Platonizing, partly existential interpretation of the early Christian message, which stresses the presence of salvation in the Spirit, in the proclamation and in faith. It attempts to eliminate early Christian apocalyptic as being a mythical view of history belonging to its own time. Presentative eschatology swallows up history.[4]

At first glance both lines of approach are to be found in the New Testament writings; there seems to be no discussion about the eschatological future without a qualification of the present, and nothing is said about the present qualified by Christ without a determination of the future. Consequently mediatory eschatologies have emerged in both exegesis and dogmatics. Oscar Cullmann tried to link the two in an 'eschatology of salvation history'.[5] Emil Brunner combined the two trends into 'the paradox of the primitive Christian, the truly Christian life; it is characteristically both a "now already" and a "not yet".'[6] Even if in the New Testament the stress on the 'now already' and the 'not yet' are differently distributed in the different writings, all the Christian witnesses have this in common, says Brunner: that both the 'now already' and the 'not yet' are valid, and that the Christian ethos develops out of the duality of possession and expectation. We have Walter Kreck to thank for a reawakened understanding of futurist eschatology in the sphere of the German tradition (which is characterized by an existential interpretation). In discussing the trends we have mentioned, Kreck worked out a 'simultaneously' from the 'already' and the 'not yet' – apparently in a reminiscence of the Lutheran *simul justus et peccator* – laying claim to biblical testimony in doing so.[7] For him 'the basic question of eschatology'[8] is the determination of the relationship between the 'already' of the salvation conferred in the gospel and the 'not yet' of its expectation. If we take as final the exegetical findings which tend towards a futurist and a realized or presentative eschatology, then the only remaining question is, how and where can the two stresses (on salvation's present and its future) be reconciled. This 'paradox' and 'simultaneity' can be described in terms of theological history (Cullmann); it can be depicted against the dialectic of existence between faith and hope, between being-in-the-world and being detached from the world (Brunner, Althaus and Bultmann); it can be christologically based (Kreck). But we should not pin down the exegetical findings of this kind of dialectic between realized and futurist eschatology to their present form, and then systematize them. We should enquire, both exegetically and systematically, about the unified centre which binds the two together and thus relativizes them. Otherwise it is all too easy for a biblicism to emerge, as the common-sense view, which canonizes the 'paradox' and the 'simultaneity': a new orthodoxy, comparatively Chalcedonian in spirit. This combats supposed one-sidedness in the direction either of a 'purely eschatological' theology or of a 'non-eschatological' theology by thinking that it can combine the opposites dialectically; but in actual fact it is itself unable to formulate the combining 'centre'. At present theological work on eschatology is stagnating in a biblicism of this kind, based on existing exegetical trends, and in this type of orthodoxy, which gathers everything together dialectically.

2. *Does the Present determine the Future, or does the Future determine the Present?*

The alternative between presentative and futurist eschatology has only seldom arisen in systematic work on eschatology in recent years. The basic methodological question about the beginnings of Christian eschatology has rather been, whether one should start from 'the future of the present Christ' (or faith) or from 'the presence of the coming Christ'. Does the future determine the present, or does the present determine the future?[9] Is the theme of Christian eschatology 'the future of what has already come' (Kreck) or 'the presence of what is still to come' (Iwand)? Is the future theologically the 'revelation' of the present (apocalypse) or is the present the realized anticipation of the future (fulfilment)?[10]

(i) *Paul Althaus and Georg Hoffmann*

Since it appeared in 1922, Paul Althaus's work on 'The Last Things' has determined present-day eschatological discussion; while as a result of this discussion the book itself underwent fundamental alterations, which led to a complete revision of the third edition in 1933. Althaus began with a presentative eschatology which (following Windelband) he called 'axiological eschatology'.[11] The discussion increasingly led him to integrate futurist eschatology into this, in the form of 'teleological eschatology'. But the way he began remained his point of approach: the presence of salvation includes the future of salvation. His earlier 'time-eternity dialectic'[12], which led to a criticism of all end-of-history eschatology, developed into a 'soterio-centric systematics'[13] which settled down to a harmonization of biblical statements about 'remaining in the here and now' of salvation and 'the coming of the end'.[14] 'Assurance rests both on the remaining and on the coming of the end.' This duality in eschatology is based on the hiddenness of God's revelation, the kenosis, or self-emptying, of God's Son, which is 'wooing' or 'soliciting' but not yet 'convicting reality'. Althaus therefore bases eschatology on 'the expectation of what is to come in the present salvation established through God's revelation'.[15]

> Firstly, hope grows out of the faith which lays hold on the promise of salvation as being salvation in the present; eschatology grows out of the certainty that salvation is already present. Secondly, faith inevitably leads to hope.[16]

The future is hence apocalypse, the revelation of the presence of salvation determined through Christ in faith. This presence determines the future, and the future is the public and visible outcome of this present. That is to say, it is a change of modality on the part of present salvation from hiddenness to revelation.

Georg Hoffmann objected to this 'indirect' explanation of the Christian hope in his book on the Last Things. According to Hoffmann, eschatology was, on the contrary, 'directly' founded on God's promise of salvation.

> The promise of the eternal future of full salvation is already implied in the divine Word, from which faith draws the power for its present existence.[17] . . . For that reason the assurance of the forgiveness of sins always already implies hope of eternal life, and on the other hand hope for eternal life always contains in itself the assurance of the forgiveness of sins. Hope maintains that there will be complete fulfilment of salvation in eternity; justifying faith claims an anticipatory partial fulfilment in time. This is what gives the eschatological aspect precedence over the relation of the present. The divine fellowship of justifying faith is not yet salvation; the fulfilment of it is only the expectation of complete fulfilment. It too already bears fulfilment within itself, it *is* fellowship with God, but only provisional fellowship, which points continually to the perfected divine fellowship which is to replace it. . . . Faith looks directly towards the salvation that is still to come and lays hold of the present at the same time as it grasps the future.[18]

Hoffmann therefore subordinates salvation in the present to the eschatological relation of faith. For him the faith that grasps the assurance of salvation spans the present too; whereas for Althaus the present assurance of salvation also spans the future.

Here we might put the following questions to Althaus. If we make the present our starting-point, then the future is the prolongation of that present along the line from present to future. But the present is claimed to be the presence of salvation in faith. Consequently the hoped-for future is the future in full revelation of the present in which believers now participate. That is why Althaus begins his eschatology with the heading 'Personal Fulfilment'.[19] But in that way it can hardly be maintained that the future of Christ is a universal future. It merely becomes the perfected future of believers. Consequently it is not clear how, or for what, we are to experience the hiddenness of present salvation as pointing to the future, or by what compulsion faith necessarily becomes hope. If no universal claim is inherent in the present existence of salvation for faith, then faith will hardly be aware of the contradiction in the face of which it projects itself towards hope. Through what are we to experience and assess the open, insufficient, contradictory and forward-pointing character of present salvation in faith? Why, then, does hiddenness desire to be revealed and made known to all? Surely because it is the presence of the future; or, to be more precise, because it is not merely the presence of salvation for the believing man or woman, but the presence of Christ in his rule, which prepares the way for the sole dominion of God over his creation (I Cor. 15.28). The presence of salvation therefore only has a future if God's universal future is present in it in particular terms.

Hoffmann makes one problem clear: that it is difficult to acquire and preserve a direct relationship to the future. Christian hope is certainly mediated hope – hope, that is to say, for the resurrection and eternal life through the cross of the risen Christ. Only a christological eschatology leads beyond the fruitless dialectic of presentative and futurist eschatology: resurrection and eternal life is mediated to those who have come under the power of sin and death through the crucified Jesus, who emptied himself into their alienation, and who, through his solidarity with the godless, reconciles them with God. But what is mediated to them through the crucified Jesus is the future in which God dwells with men and men with God. The 'partial fulfilment in time' and the 'waiting' for 'complete fulfilment' are therefore not unmediated and direct anticipation. It is the mediation of eternal life to those given over to death, and the mediation of righteousness to the godless in the cross of the risen Christ which opens up anticipation of that future in this present. The cross of Christ always already stands in the light of his resurrection – if it does not, it loses its universal significance. Consequently faith 'always already stands in the light of hope'.[20]

(ii) Karl Barth and Ernst Käsemann. Attempt at a Confrontation

Whereas Althaus still assigned Barth to 'purely eschatological theology',[21] Barth's doctrine of reconciliation (*Church Dogmatics* IV: *The Doctrine of Reconciliation*) apparently conveyed precisely the opposite impression.[22] Althaus appealed to one of Barth's statements: ' "The promise is fulfilled" does not mean: the promise comes to an end and is replaced by the actual thing that is promised. It means: the promise itself is now whole, complete, unambiguous and hence already in force.'[23] But nowadays this statement is apparently considered un-Barthian.[24] Both critics and friends accordingly largely concur in their impression that in his doctrine of reconciliation Barth's eschatology concentrates on the idea of apocalypse;[25] the future of Christ contains no new event in the creative sense, but – being the 'revelation' of what 'has already been completed' – is now a merely noetic event. Barth, it is said, has firm views about the presence of Jesus Christ in his future; but not vice versa – not about his future in the present.

Now this is correct as far as extensive sections of the *Church Dogmatics* are concerned.

> That which comes finally is not a second reality. . . . On the contrary, it is already the one reality which here and now still encounters us in concealment but there and then will make itself known, and will be knowable and known, without concealment.[26]

But if we were to pin Barth down to words like these we should be failing to recognize the differentiations in his thinking. Barth can also, conversely, term the anticipation of the parousia what in Christ is already completed and real (even if hidden) present salvation. 'The resurrection is the anticipation of His parousia as His parousia is the completion and fulfilment of the resurrection.'[27] In Barth's doctrine of reconciliation especially, the concept of 'the anticipation of the eschaton' takes on dominant importance. As 'the revealer of his work' – i.e., in the third aspect of the doctrines of reconciliation – Jesus Christ is 'still on the way', 'not yet at the goal'.[28] In this passage Barth shows that this *munus propheticum Christi* is not merely (as it has frequently been understood as being) the mere mediation of knowledge about Christ's saving work, it remaining an open question what then brings about the revelation, the disclosure and the knowledge (faith? the church?); the *munus propheticum* is the integrating ingredient of the *munus triplex* – Christ's *single* work and office.

Christ himself is the witness, the proclaimer, the revealer until the consummation through his appearance in glory. But if this third aspect of the doctrine of reconciliation actually belongs to the *work* of reconciliation itself, then it would seem difficult to distinguish, *in* the work of reconciliation, between the reality of reconciliation and its revealing, just as it is difficult to differentiate between the work in itself and the mere publishing of it. Consequently, the paired concepts 'hiddenness – revelation' are no longer sufficient to express the third aspect of the doctrine of reconciliation. We must also stress the creative character of work and decision in God's revelation in his Word. Otherwise the historical relationship between promise and fulfilment deriving from the Old Testament would in the New turn into the a-historical relationship between completed history and apophantic logos. The stress on the completed 'having happened' of reconciliation in Christ must not rob the word of reconciliation of its present force; it must not turn it into an unemphatic indication of something, a mere allowing-it-to-be-seen.[29] Barth gives us the occasion to think about this in his stress on the universality of the reconciliation of the world already brought about in Christ. Because for him the universalism of the coming glorification of God already lies in the incarnation and reconciliation, the coming glorification, consistently enough, only brings a revealing and nothing new. But is there really no longer anything 'secret' about 'God in Christ', as Hegel said in his criticism of Luther (*de servo arbitrio*)?

Contrary to this view Käsemann has objected[30] that Barth and his followers must be compared with the theology of the early Christian hymns. But Paul had to contest Enthusiasm of this kind all his life, just as he had to resist Judaism. In this struggle he replaced the pattern of Christ's incarnation and enthronement by the other scheme of cross and resurrection; he certainly let Christians participate in the cross in the present, but not directly in the glory of the resurrection; and he moved statements about the universal lordship of Christ not only into present hiddenness, but out of the perfect and present into the future (I Cor. 15.28), and consequently did not yet bestow the title of cosmocrator on Jesus. If this objection is justified, then the proclamation, the mission and the obedience of Christians cannot merely be seen against the background of revelation or disclosure. On the contrary, the divine dispute about truth and lie, obedience and disobedience, election and hardness of heart involves God's creative activity. In Rom. 11.15 Paul therefore gives not only the cross of Christ but also the rejection of Israel as reason for the reconciliation of the Gentile world: 'For if their rejection means the reconciliation of the world, what will their acceptance mean but life from the dead?' The eschatological arch of the raising of the dead spans Israel's historical obduracy and the historical reconciliation of the world in the apostolate. These real events cannot still be included in the notion of apocalypse. But here Barth's doctrine of predestination shows the beginnings of surprising changes in his eschatology. Barth stressed[31] that the distinction between time present and time future cannot be theologically comprehended through an analysis of the concept of time; and the still remaining 'not yet' of the future may not, in the New Testament sense, be understood as a 'gloomy minus sign' of suffering on the borders of this existence of unconquered misery – let alone as being the result of some insufficiency or incompleteness in the reconciling presence of Christ. Just as justification cannot be based on sin, so eschatology cannot be derived from present misery. Christian eschatology must have a theological foundation.

In what seems at first sight a similar approach, Käsemann stresses in his interpretation of I Cor. 15 that

> the anthropological hope [is set] from the very beginning in a wider context. The content of the Resurrection is primarily not anthropological at all, but christological. . . . Its meaning is not immediately and primarily our re-animation, but the lordship of Christ. 'Christ must reign': that is the nerve centre of the design.[32]

But if the rule of Christ serves the single purpose of the sole rule of God, then the significance of Paul's eschatological exposition is a theological one: its aim is the divinity of God. Barth, however, develops his theological eschatology in a temporal interpretation of the knowledge, given by the resurrection, that Christ is 'the Lord of time'.[33] He, who is alive for evermore, in fact demands this threefold witness that he was and is and will be. This 'verdict of the Father' shows him to be 'the first and the last.' He 'besets us behind and before' (Ps. 139.5) and therefore totally – to all eternity. That is to say, the eschatological cry does not come out of the depths, not out of the ground of the misery and the injustice of the world that cries out to high heaven; a burning eschatological longing looks towards Jesus Christ himself and therefore cries in doxology: Amen, Come, Lord Jesus! Christian eschatology is therefore the utter and complete confession of Christ as the 'Lord of time', who is hence the future one as well. It is therefore christological doxology in time. It is designed to unfold the finality proper to the action and revelation of Christ. For that reason Barth likes to let doxological phrases out of the New Testament speak for his eschatology.

Quite apart from the curious basing of eschatology on the totally un-eschatological 139th Psalm (which is a hymn to God's almighty power), here Christian eschatology is not, it is true, shaped with the help of a modern concept of time (progress – irreversibility – teleology); but the temporal concept of eternity, as we know it from Platonism, is called upon in order to depict eschatology as being essentially a development of God's sovereignty.[34] Because Christ has been raised into the eternity of God, he is, like God himself, 'the Lord of time', since he is also cosmocrator. So his lordship must be known in all three 'times', or temporal modes: he who is, and was, and will be. But the third of these temporal modes is not so expressed in Rev. 1.4. There this ontological concept of eternity is broken through by the expression 'who is to come'.[35]

Through the Old Testament expectation of the unique and final coming of God and his glory on earth, the 'future' gained the upper hand in the New Testament as well.[36] Who God was and what he was like – who God is and what he is like – is determined in the light of God's coming in his divinity. It is not for the sake of completeness that the 'future of Jesus Christ' is integrated in his eternity as his lordship over time. On the contrary, this future becomes the 'soul of time'. What time means is shown by his future. In Christian terms, 'the end of history' is not its completion

and revelation but 'its key, the very foundation for the understanding of it'.[37] A theological eschatology, if it is to remain
eschatology at all, cannot develop the future as the sphere of God's
existence on the basis of the temporal concept of his eternity, or the
impression of his sovereignty gained from the Christ event.[38] It
must rather see to it that – just as the kingdom of God is not the
mere 'accident' of his divinity or something added to it, but is that
divinity's quintessence[39] – so the future too is the mode of his being
that is dominant in history.[40] God shows his power as the power of
the future over every condition. He shows his grace as liberation for
his future from the fetters of the past (sin) and of transience
(death). If it is true that for Paul the lordship of Christ is limited
and passing, and merely serves the purpose of giving way to the
sole rule of God; if, for Paul, 'Christ is God's representative over
against a world which is not yet fully subjected to God',[41] then the
history of Christ and the presence of the Spirit must be understood
in the light of this future and as moving towards it.

Barth and Käsemann both maintain a theocentric eschatology.
The dividing line, however, lies in the question: is the incarnation
the horizon of the eschaton, or is eschatology the horizon of the
incarnation?[42]

(iii) Reconciliation and the Righteousness of God

If we now term the present 'reconciliation' and the future
'redemption', then the same question confronts us again in more
specific terms. Is the final consummation based on the present
reconciliation, or is reconciliation the beginning of a cosmic
redemption?[43] Walter Kreck has concerned himself particularly
with the first of these questions. 'The perfect tense of our reconciliation is at the same time the future tense of our redemption and
thus the present tense of our assurance.'[44] 'The promise of this
future event is inextricably anchored in the "already" of his having
come and his coming today.'[45] Hence we understand 'the future in
the light of the present, and the promise on the basis of the
fulfilment which has already taken place and has already been
proclaimed.'[46] 'The reconciliation aims at the coming consummation and implies it as its telos; but the consummation is based on the
reconciliation.'[47]

It is unfortunate that Käsemann's essay, 'Some Thoughts on the
Theme "The Doctrine of Reconciliation in the New Testament" ',

with its critical questioning of the traditional dogma of reconciliation, has not attracted more attention. It helps us to see more self-
critically the change of meaning which the words 'reconciliation',
'atonement', 'sin' and 'cross' have undergone from Paul down to
the present day.

> It is indeed a remarkable fact that the motif appears only in the general
> realm of Paulinism, though without having any significant meaning for
> Pauline theology as a whole, and that it can be used both casually and
> thematically.[48]

Whereas the idea of reconciliation derives from the doxology of the
Hellenistic congregation, and the idea of the expiatory sacrifice
from Jewish-Christian hymns, these concepts are found integrated
in the Pauline view of the victorious divine righteousness in which
God enters into his lordship over his creation (Rom. 5.9–11;
II Cor. 5.18–21 and Rom. 3.25). This gives rise to tensions. The
idea of the expiatory sacrifice (Rom. 3.25) sees the event of
salvation in the forgiveness of the accumulated *guilt* of sin, whereas
Paul himself lays his whole stress on liberation from sin's *power*. In
the ideas of reconciliation, the anthropological variant ('God
reconciles *us* with himself') and the cosmological variant ('God
reconciles *the world*') stand parallel to one another. For Paul
'world-wide reconciliation becomes the *telos* of an earthly commission, and in this commission is established the reality of the fact
that the exalted Christ has begun to exercise lordship.'[49] Paul will
have taken up these ideas in this sense in order to highlight the
justification of the godless through the concept of the reconciliation
of enemies. 'The statements about reconciliation in the New Testament are protected from extravagance by primitive Christian
eschatology and by the Pauline doctrine of justification.'[50] If this is
correct, then the 'now already' of the justification of sinners and the
reconciliation of enemies, and the 'not yet' of the redemption of the
mortal body have as their overriding aspect God's seizure of power
through his liberating and creative divine righteousness,[51] which
shows itself both here and now, and in the future, in the forsaken,
the lost and the shattered. But when what is at stake in justification
and sanctification, reconciliation and transformation, rebirth and
new creation, is the righteousness of God (as the δόξα τοῦ θεοῦ),
then the paradox of the 'already' and the 'not yet' of the soteriological topoi is also modified to a goal, a trend, a process, which in

the world of alienation takes on dialectical form: man's becoming man in the glorification of God.

(iv) *Futurum and Adventus*

This brings us to the final question: can the two approaches – 'the future of what has already come' and 'the present of what is still to come' – be meaningfully combined by the methods of eschatology?[52] The German word *Zukunft*, which is today simply used to mean 'future', in fact covers two different traditions.[53] If we take it literally, we find that *Zukunft* (which in origin means 'coming to') is the translation of the Latin *adventus*. It was given this particular significance by the Luther Bible and the hymnbook and hence – even where it is used in a transferred sense – it has inherent in it 'the advent light', so to speak, of its original usage: expectation, the anticipatory joy of coming redemption, preparation for something that is to come. It means the 'arrival' or 'coming' of something other, something new and transforming, which had not yet been present in that form and is still not present as yet. *Adventus* has its equivalent in the Greek word *parousia*, which also means the arrival of a stranger and another, but which in Greek philosophy can also mean 'the present'. Where this word is used in the New Testament, it enters the categories of expectation of the prophetic and apostolic hope for the coming of God and the coming of Christ. The word itself is Greek, but its meaning is prophetic. Parousia – advent – future – means, as it does in the Old Testament, the unique and then final coming of God and a world which is in total correspondence to him – their coming to the godless and God-forsaken. Understood in this sense, the future does not simply emerge from the present, either as a postulate or a result; the present springs from a future which one must be expectant of in transience.

As far as linguistic history is concerned ,we do not, on the other hand, find the German word *Zukunft* as a derivation of the Latin *futurum*, although today the word also simply represents the future tense. *Futurum* means that which will be, what is going to arise from the becoming of begin (γένεσις εἰς οὐσίαν).* It has a Greek

* We might perhaps compare the difference between *Zukunft* and *Futur* to the use in English of 'coming' (as in 'the coming year'), and 'future'. 'Coming' has a future but also a dynamic sense; whereas the word 'future' simply means what *is* ahead. In this interpretation, therefore, 'coming' would be the equivalent of *Zukunft*, 'future' the equivalent of *Futur*. [Translator]

equivalent in φύω which contributes to the understanding of *physis* as that which produces or brings forth. What 'will be' presupposes here the present tense of the process of becoming and begetting. That is why *physis* in the future (*futurum*) can bring forth new forms as well as mutations of forms; but everything that is capable of becoming is inherently there in the basis of the *physis*, as primal potentiality. The future in the sense of *Futur* is the temporal prolongation of being. The future in the sense of *Zukunft*, on the other hand, is 'the soul of time'. If we take over this distinction between *Zukunft* and *Futur*, then we might say: the present has no future in the sense of *Futur* unless it is the present of the *Zukunft*. But if it is the present of a larger *Zukunft* it forms the basis for a future in the sense of *Futur*.

If we apply this to the problem of the methods of Christian eschatology, we can say: the starting-point is the anticipation, the prolepsis, the sending ahead of God's future, or *Zukunft*, in the passion and resurrection of Christ.[54] If we call the destiny of Jesus 'resurrection from the dead', then we do not see his history as being separate from the divine future or *Zukunft*, which brings the Wholly Other as what-makes-wholly-other. If this future or *Zukunft* is made present in Christ, then and because of that the present determined by him becomes the germ of what is to come and gains a *Futur* which corresponds to this *Zukunft*. The presence of justification and reconciliation is the start of this transforming and changing *Zukunft* of the divine righteousness in an unrighteous and unreconciled existence. The redemption and final overcoming of enmity becomes the *Futur* of this present. Its *Zukunft* is founded on this present, because it is the present of what is to come. So it is possible for Paul to combine the two aspects. On the one hand (in I Cor. 15) he describes the lordship of Christ as a provisional one, which serves the purpose of making room for the sole lordship of God the Father; the eschatological subjugation has been under way since Easter; Christ has already been snatched from death, though we have not yet been saved from it; so that therefore the history and lordship of Christ which Paul is envisaging stands under an 'eschatological provision'. Yet on the other hand he can equally argue soteriologically, and hence conversely (Rom. 5ff.), in order to deduce the power of Christ's resurrection from the power of his passion in justification and the reconciliation of man. The soteriological 'descent' from the presence of salvation to the consummating future, however, is comprehended and enclosed by the converse theological 'descent' from the eschatological sole lordship of God to the provisional lordship of Christ. It is only out of the historical descent from the future to the present that the converse soteriological descent from the present to the future acquires its quickening power.

3. *Theological and Philosophical Eschatology*

In the nineteenth century, following Kant and Hegel, scholars frequently drew on the help of philosophical categories when they were considering Christian eschatology. In the books we have cited by Paul Althaus and Emil Brunner, large sections are devoted to a vigorous dispute over philosophies of history, revolutionary ideologies, and Kant's 'philosophical millenarianism'. The millenarian and Enthusiastic traditions of Western Christianity are similarly discussed. In more recent books and writings this sparring partner in the discussion is almost entirely missing. Writers confine themselves to pure exegetical or dogmatic eschatology, for internal professional use in the church itself, so to speak; philosophical endeavours in this field are considered to be irrelevant. Writers seek to free theology from philosophy by separating the one cleanly from the other, scenting, in everything that goes beyond biblical and dogmatic traditions, new 'interpretations of reality' which aim to 'reduce' Jesus Christ 'to a definition', and thus to bring him within our grasp. There is no question of a critical adoption of concepts and ways of thinking belonging to the philosophy of history; there are no signs even of a self-critical reflection about the concepts used by these theological writers themselves.

Jakob Taubes' *Abendländische Eschatologie* ('Western Eschatology', 1947) has remained almost unknown in theological circles, although it contains a wealth of instructive material taken from the philosophical eschatology of the nineteenth century. With the theological surmounting of neo-Kantian theology, Kant's work *Das Ende aller Dinge* (1794), with its criticism of all cosmological and salvation-history eschatologies, has apparently been consigned to oblivion. Hegel's dialectic of history now only counts as being a discouraging example of untheological panlogism. People see in the intellectual movements of the nineteenth century merely the secularization of Christian eschatology and a decline into political or economic messianism. Theological eschatology, they think, must begin with its own concern, the future of Jesus Christ, and must stick to its own material, the word of scripture. But have they not forgotten that this word has always penetrated the reality of mind and history as well? Have they not forgotten that the word seeks to penetrate reality with its transforming power? Is this really only a matter of secularization of Christian eschatology (as a peculiar theory of descent claims) and not equally eschatology's final entry into the secular world? Has eschatological belief really only 'declined' into philosophies of history and ideologies of revolution? Has it not also arrived at historical self-consciousness? 'The eschatological consciousness of crisis is coming to the historical consciousness of itself.'[55] 'If the age of interpreting the world is past, and if our aim has to be to change the world, then philosophy says farewell . . . it is time, not for the first philosophy, but for a final one.'[56] This is probably a more accurate definition of the intellectual position, historically speaking. Theological eschatology must not pass this by if its task is to help faith to the eschatological consciousness of itself. No one intends to replace faith by a philosophy of history. But the important thing is to understand what we hope for and to grasp what we have to do. This can only happen if theology 'makes a defence' of the Christian hope (I Peter 3.15) by reflecting on eschatology in the context of the problem of history, by making history the problem of the future, and by entering into critical solidarity with the seeking, questioning and suffering people of its time.

About the same time that my *Theology of Hope* was published (1964; ET 1967), Gerhard Sauter finished his professorial thesis on 'Future and Promise' (*Zukunft und Verheissung*). It appeared in 1965. 'The (unintentional) parallelism of these two books is so striking, often down to matters of detail, that the writers themselves will be more surprised than anyone.'[57] It is true that it is an unexpected pleasure to find a companion on the way so quickly. Helmut Gollwitzer has pointed to similar trends in the Catholic theology of Karl Rahner and J. B. Metz,[58] which seeks to get back to fundamentals. We could also point to the work of Harvey Cox.[59] If this basic consensus is there, then a perhaps somewhat strained and external 'united front' becomes superfluous. Differences can be stated without fear that the questions themselves will be lost sight of in the process.

In a similar way to what I attempted, Sauter describes 'eschatology as promise with a theological justification' (p. 149), thus following the investigations into the Old Testament understanding of the promise carried out by Gerhard von Rad, Walther Zimmerli and Hans Walter Wolff, as well as H. J. Iwand's distinction between apophantic Logos and creative word of promise. In the course of this he arrives at highly valuable new perceptions about the relation between creation and promise, about the promise and the future 'as the place where direct evidence of the God of the promise is to be found' (p. 152) and about 'beholding the promise', with the relationship between hoping and seeing. 'Creation is not a protological origin-myth; it is an eschatological design' (p. 174). 'Promise puts the world *in statu promissionis*' (p. 160). It is the special character of 'prophetic thinking' to witness to 'the truth *in statu promissionis*' (p. 198). Contrary to the 'suggestion of apocalyptic thinking' which he points out in Heidegger, Barth and Ernst Bloch, and in discussion with the existential and universal-history interpretation, Sauter shows revelation to be promise and Jesus Christ as the promise's 'Yea and Amen'.

The characteristic thing about Sauter's book is that every chapter and every section is full of preliminary reflections and considerations, distinctions and discussions; but that the reader continually encounters an insight which repays reflection. So we must wait until Sauter gathers together his perceptions (which in this book are initially still aphoristically formulated) into a larger study. This impression, however, is also based on the fact that Sauter (while continually making clear the boundary dividing off the philosophy of history in both its non-theological and theological manifestations) tries to work out what is specific and unique about the divine promise. He is highly successful wherever he can relate what he says to Israel's own language and intellectual world – for example in the section on prophetic thinking. But he finds it difficult when he comes to the New Testament field, and especially where he comes up against the problem of the future in philosophical discussion. Here phrases crop up which a theology of promise is only capable of circumventing by means of negations. And here there is a theology in the background which is not introduced into the discussion. Here 'God himself, God in Christ, is the future of his promise' (p. 160). 'This Logos of the future, which contradicts the prolongation of the "having been", is God's crossing of the boundary in our time and world, and leaving heuristic traces' (p. 161). Here the promise is 'proclaimed' (p. 162) and it is 'only decided in Christ what has a future . . . or is past' (p. 154). Here theology is supposed to 'echo the promise' (pp. 70, 363). Here the promise asserts that 'God's Word is indefinable, because it has not yet come to an end' (p. 151).

In this way, in 'the problem of the future' 'contacts and differences' (pp. 67ff.) arise between the theological and the philosophical discussion. That is to say, contacts arise on the level of a fundamental or, as he expresses it, 'completely polarized' difference. 'Philosophy' he says, asks – as Luther would say – about the having-become of being, about foundation and origin, about repetition (p. 41); whereas for theology the incalculable breaking-in of the eschaton indicates that for it the question of the future is re-polarized in direction and in origin (p. 42). Theology and philosophy therefore part company over the problem of the future.

On the basis, presumably, of the still unwritten parts of his theology of the promise in the concept of God and in Christology (where he still thinks in apophantic and incarnational terms), Sauter uses models to determine the relationship between theology and philosophy which have really been rendered obsolete by his own theological insights. They are models taken from early dialectical theology (transcendence/immanence, available/non-available, etc.). Yet his theological re-polarizing of the problem of the future in its whole trend is not as unphilosophical as he thinks, for the re-polarizing only applies to particular philosophers, as can be seen. Kant and Heidegger are discussed in detail; but not Hegel, Marx or Husserl, Bergson and other thinkers of the time. The book's extensive final section is taken up by a discussion of Ernst Bloch. This is excellent in its exposition, but – except for taking over the critique of immanence from W. D. Marsch and myself – it really offers no critique of Sauter's own on the basis of common ground; it merely shows contact in difference, and therefore only a line of demarcation between a theology of promise and 'the principle of hope'.

> Bloch's philosophy of hope cannot be reclaimed theologically without a considerable tribute to the revelation of being as the achieved apocalypse of a more successful world. His evocation of the eschatological conscience will make the sting of the 'not yet' felt – and hence call hope to account – but it will hardly help the call of the promise to be echoed.

... The truth of the promise, truth *in statu promissionis*, is aware of the 'not yet' because it creates reality *in statu promissionis* and is in that way the pledge of the divine future (pp.363, 368).

The question which is also philosophically relevant and which ought to be seriously discussed here is whether the 'not yet' of an ontology can be made effective in an ontology of not-yet-being, so that the dialectic of the negative is not hindered by a negative dialectic.[60] For Sauter, however, the theological and the philosophical 'votes on the problem of the future' finally divide. Divisions of this kind are certainly very useful for theology's own self-affirmation, but prove to be an impoverishment, both for its linguistic expression and its thinking. Sauter admittedly believes that 'man's destiny of promise can be shown, in the same degree as, for example, the "phenomenology" of prophetic thinking' (p. 276). The parallels indicate that this can no doubt be demonstrated in Israel's relatively independent linguistic and intellectual sphere. Ever since the exile, Judaism has had to talk and think under the conditions of the dispersion. But Christianity has to talk and think under the conditions of mission. It has no language and no theological way of thinking of its own. Consequently it has to talk in the sphere of contemporary philosophy, even though it is not under the pressure of that sphere's own particular structure. If this is not the case Christianity arrives at a kind of linguistic isolation, which cuts it off from solidarity with its companions in time and in suffering. The dispute about the future and the truth cannot be fought out by dividing the votes of philosophy and theology ideologically from one another. It can only be decided on the basis of a common ground that goes beyond concepts about the future and the truth. The real problem, in my view, is not whether, or how far, it is permissible to absorb philosophical elements into theology, but whether and how far eschatological faith can arrive at historical self-consciousness. Sauter's insight can help here:

Theological interests and the philosophical questionings encased in them have up to now showed great reserve about making a contribution towards the discussion which in its philosophical form contains plenty of theological dynamite (p.129).

At the same time, Sauter himself has not entirely broken down the mutual isolation.

4. *Interpretations of the 'Delay of the Parousia'*

Ever since the 'consistent eschatology' school showed that imminent expectation was the essence of Jesus' eschatology and that of his disciples, eschatology in general has been mainly called in question by Jesus' cross and by the non-appearance of the parousia, after Jesus' Easter appearances. Consequently systematic eschatology has sought, in continually new interpretations, for solutions to the riddle of the disappointment. For if the nature of Christian faith is supposed to lie in the eschatological hope, this question endangers its whole existence. The historical and exegetical question about the attitude of the early Christian congregations to the contradiction posed by the reality of continuing history is therefore directly linked with the present question about theology: for two thousand years we have had Christianity, for good or evil; but not the kingdom of righteousness. In view of this, can we continue to cling to the history of Christ as 'the eschatological event'?

'Consistent eschatology' claimed to be 'consistent' because in consequence of the 'absurd' history that followed Jesus' ministry it abandoned both his eschatological expectation of the kingdom, and the disciples' eschatological proclamation of Christ. 'Realized' or 'presentative' eschatology started from the same phenomenon but maintained that the presence of the eschaton (as the presence of eternity) in the moment of kerygma and faith answered every question about 'the end of world history' by cutting away the ground from under its feet. History teaches us that the Day of Judgment is not coming.

> Mythical eschatology is untenable for the simple reason that the parousia of Christ never took place as the New Testament expected. History did not come to an end, and, as every schoolboy knows, it will continue to run its course.[61]

The end of the world can never come, because it is always already present in the faith that is stripped of worldly thinking. The solution of the problem of the delayed parousia lies in the fact that, in kerygma and faith, Christ is the eschatological event constantly present at any given time. But if it is the apocalyptic, End-time horizon of expectation, that is constitutive for the Easter faith of the early church, and not the gnostic, other-worldly horizon, then theology must at every period reformulate the arch of tension which links the event that happened in the past with the end of the world that is still to come.

> The delay of the end events, which now amounts to almost two thousand years, is not a refutation of the Christian hope and of the Christian perception of revelation as long as the unity between what happened in Jesus and the eschatological future is maintained.[62]

Wolfhart Pannenberg has therefore tried to interpret this apocalyptic expectation (which is the only context in which talk about 'resurrection' makes sense) with the help of modern psychological anthropology; for it is not the temporal distance or proximity which makes the arch of tension, but simply 'the material correspondence of what happened in Jesus with the content of the eschatological expectation'.[63] In the realm of what has been thought and what is conceivable, this interpretation is undoubtedly a possible one; for it is not the ideas as such but what they are intended to express that can be made binding and can continue into new historical eras. But for all the variability of images of the world and the future, there is also something like an invariance of direction and trend.[64] Biblical texts can only be understood in the context of universal history if they point to a future horizon which gives meaning to the present.[65] This alone, however, does not solve the problem of the delay of the parousia, exegetically and systematically. Why was Jesus' resurrection not the direct prelude to the general resurrection of the dead?

The answer which an incarnational eschatology gives at this point is as follows:

> Why did He not will His commencement to be at once His goal, His self-revelation in the world at once its redemption and consummation, Easter Day at once the last day, the day of the Lord, of His conclusive return and revelation, of the last judgment and the final fulfilment? . . . The answer is quite simple, that it [i.e. His will] is His *good* will because it has as its aim the granting to and procuring for the creation reconciled to God in Him both time and space, not merely to see, but actively to share in the harvest which follows from the sowing of reconciliation.[66]

> We must not think that he has miscalculated. We must not think that the resistance of the world was unexpectedly strong, so that God can only manage it in stages! No, it is right as it is. It is God's good pleasure in Christ to be still journeying towards his coming.[67]

Ott seems to be thinking of meaningful 'stages' of this kind when he talks about the 'interruption' of the eschaton, which constitutes that interim period between Jesus' resurrection and his second parousia – the interim which is indicated and revealed through the ascension.[68] Wolfgang Trillhaas has understood the 'fulfilment of the promise' similarly 'as the crisis of eschatology' which has led to the 'splitting up of eschatology into a fulfilled promise and a still unfulfilled eschatological remainder'.[69] This view is primarily upheld when the messianic promises of the Old Testament are compared with the fulfilment which, it is asserted, has taken place in Christ. The result of this comparison is either a 'surplus', left over from the Old Testament theocratic promises (to which Christians, like Israel, cling);[70] or the fulfilment in Christ (which is supposed to be spiritual in nature) is viewed as the abrogation of the 'surplus' left over from the Old Testament promises.

> In this sense the realism of the promise points beyond the New Testament fulfilment to complete fulfilment. The tension in the New Testament awareness of salvation, as it looks towards the coming fulfilment, positively lives from the still unfulfilled Old Testament prophecy which Jesus acknowledged when he took the name of Christ.[71]

This was the way Paul Althaus took up the eschatological realism of the Old Testament in Christian terms, while attempting to discard the national realism of Israel's expectation.

> Christ is also the end of the Messiah. . . . The church is founded on Israel as the chosen people of God; but Israel also flows into, and issues in, the church . . . Israel has no longer any special position or any special 'call to salvation' in the church and for the church.[72]

We may ask, however, if this distinction is valid, in the face of Romans 9–11. The more recent history of Protestant theology always links these three elements directly with one another: (i) the discovery of the meaning of the Old Testament for future and present; (ii) the discovery of Israel as the church's partner, parallel to it (not merely its precursor); (iii) the discovery of real futuristic eschatology. Every theological decision about one of these doctrinal elements directly alters the face of the others.

How did the early Christian theologies stand up to the strains imposed on them by the delay of the parousia?[73] If at the beginning Jesus' Easter appearances were directly identified with the eschatological coming of the world-transforming kingdom of God, this kind of Easter faith very soon became aware of the contradiction presented by the still unredeemed world. The problem of the delay of the parousia is therefore basically the problem of the contradiction between faith and experience, but this is a contradiction into which faith leads and which faith poses. It is not the misery of a God-forsaken world in general; it is this particular misery, which becomes a torment for faith, because for Christ's sake it believes in God's nearness.

This experience, which faith endured, evidently threw it back on the question about Christ himself and made it realize that the risen Lord, from whose appearances and spirit faith lived, was not merely 'the first fruits of the resurrection' but the one who was crucified. The Easter enthusiasm at the beginning was therefore followed by a continually deepening perception of the meaning of the Christ who rose from the dead. 'Why was it necessary that the Christ should suffer these things?' The road to eschatological glory does not lead believers directly from the Easter appearances into the kingdom. It leads them to glory through the direct opposite: suffering. It is through the cross of the risen Christ alone that resurrection and eternal life is mediated as hope to those who sit in the shadow of the cross, under the power of sin and death. The Easter faith stamped by the theology of the cross was capable of retaining its existence as Easter faith in contradiction to an unredeemed world and – in complete uncertainty – was able to arrive at certainty. The problem of the delay of the parousia ought not, therefore, to be solved theoretically by means of interpretations based on world history, existential history, or salvation history. We ought to solve the problem through a theology of the cross. It was not faith in Jesus, it was faith in the saving significance of the cross of Jesus that modified early Christian apocalyptic; and so it is this that is the beginning and end of Christian theology.

This is not a theological answer to the Christian problem of theodicy that can completely content us (two thousand years of history without an end: was this God's good pleasure or God's impotence?). If the problem of theodicy is: *si deus est – unde malum*? then the premise *si deus* is the sting of the question that calls the present state of the world in question. The answer cannot be a theological justification of God, or a demonstration that God is self-justifying. The only answer is a real transformation and new

creation of the reality of evil and death, which is in itself contradictory to God. The theological solution or elimination of the
problem of theodicy would eliminate Christian eschatology as well.
This question of theodicy is posed by the Christian faith itself. It is
the question with which that faith, to the extent to which it is
eschatological, presses on – in prayer and through obedience in
this world – for the future of God and his kingdom. The proclamation of Christ

> creates antitheses which teach us to cry out for redemption. It is just
> those antitheses created by the proclamation of the gospel from which
> we shall be redeemed. It is as if, through the acceptance of this pro-
> clamation in our hearts, the cry for the end becomes louder, and is in
> fact born within us for the first time.[74]

For 'it is not in the theory, but only in the practice of this struggle
that we can comprehend the resurrection as *truth*; but here it is to
be comprehended indeed.'[75]

III

METHODS IN ESCHATOLOGY

1. *Eschatological Extrapolation*

In his critique of my *Theology of Hope* in 1965, Hendrik Berkhof maintained the thesis: 'The future is an extrapolation of what has already been given in Christ and the Spirit.'[1] He developed this further in *Gegronde verwachting* (1967) and followed the same train of thought in the paragraphs on eschatology in his major work *Christelijk Geloof*: 'Eschatology can only exist as an extrapolation of experiences which we have of God in our own world and history.'[2] According to Berkhof the extrapolated structure of biblical eschatology is already shown in the Old Testament: 'Because Yahweh was a historical God, his activity was necessarily that of an eschatological God.'[3] In Paul 'the eschaton is the consequence of Jesus' death and resurrection: in both instances the future is an extrapolation of the present.'

The other New Testament writings, he claims, also think along this line stretching from the present to the future. But whereas earlier Berkhof confined himself entirely to the extrapolation method, in his 'doctrine of faith' he now adds a new idea: 'In the meantime this method should not make us forget the leap that is necessary if we are to extend the christological and pneumatological line into eschatology. Extrapolation and discontinuity must be taken together'[4] in order to assert the 'leap' element in the eschatologically new thing. Berkhof's aim thereby is to pick up the element of truth in that eschatology of hope about which he says so critically: 'Extrapolation ends up in Utopia.'[5] In order, therefore, to assert continuity and discontinuity in the relationship between history and eschatology, he now narrows down his extrapolation method by introducing the element of surprise and abrupt transition, or 'leap'. In this way the extrapolation method acquires a 'hole', so to speak, through which the eschatologically new thing can enter; and God's freedom also acquires space, in hope. The Christian hope is a certain hope, founded on the remembrance of Christ and the experience of the Spirit. But because at the same time it expects the new thing of the new creation to issue from or be conferred by the divine freedom, it is open for the eschatological surprise. In this way it joins God's faithfulness with God's liberty. In view of the biblical testimony, this is undoubtedly true, and I personally welcome the fact that Berkhof has now narrowed down his extrapolation method, which earlier on he stressed in such a one-sided way. But for the stringency of theological thinking, the simple addition of two aspects ('a christological extrapolation associated with that of a leap') is of course unsatisfactory.

I should like to persuade Berkhof to drop the expression 'extrapolation' altogether and to express what he has at heart differently. I have two reasons for saying this.

(i) What is Extrapolation?

We talk about interpolation and extrapolation in the case of analytical functions. Empirical functions order the appropriate function values to a finite number of argument values. Now, in so far as, among arbitararily empirical test data, the analytical function supplies a function value to an arbitrarily chosen argument value, it *interpolates* these empirical values. These interpolations are checkable. But if one gives a meaning to the descriptive function beyond the sphere of what is measurable and checkable, one *extrapolates*. Interpolation generally presents no problems. But extrapolation becomes all the more questionable the further it is removed from the realm of direct experience. Extrapolations which exceed the realm of experience by many degrees can therefore frequently only be termed speculations.[6]

If we are clear about this scientific use of the word extrapolation, it immediately becomes clear how dangerous it is to build up theological eschatology on this method. It certainly then acquires an empirical basis, but it becomes more and more problematical the further it thrusts forward into the future. The reproach Berkhof levies against what he calls 'Utopian eschatology' then recoils heavily on himself, as long as he clings to extrapolation eschatology: the end is formalism and speculation. And when he narrows down and limits extrapolation by openess for the 'leap' of what is new, then the extrapolation really collapses altogether; for a 'leap' cannot be extrapolated. Not even the jumping-off point of the leap can be extrapolated. An 'eschatology from below' does not succeed in 'rising'.

Now one does not necessarily have to confine oneself to analytical philosophy in using the term extrapolation; it can also be borrowed from futurology, trend-analysis and computer-forecasting at elections. Then it means the prolongation of lines of development from the past and present into the future, always presuming that everything goes on acting as it has done hitherto. Thus the 1980 energy crisis can be extrapolated from present developments on the oil market, always supposing that by then there has been no 'leap' to another source of energy. In the same way election results can be forecast on the basis of representative enquiries and questionnaires, always supposing that no 'leap' of opinion takes place.

If we follow this use of the word extrapolation, then theological eschatology would have to develop from a salvation-history trend-analysis, and out of a computer-forecast based on representative experiences of God in history. Then Yahweh would be extrapolated from a historical God of Israel into an 'eschatological God'; and in the same way the historical Jesus would be computer-forecast into the coming universal judge. But the scriptures say: 'But of that day or that hour no one knows, not even the Son, but only the Father' (Mark 13.32). Consequently the extrapolation is reaching out in time into a vacuum, or into what is hidden. God's coming belongs to a different dimension of the future from the one towards which historical extrapolations are orientated.[7] Fundamentally speaking, extrapolation is not knowledge about the future at all; it is the calculated continuation of the present into the future; and this means that the present is thereby fixed and prescribed. Extrapolation sees the future as an extrapolated and extended present and it hence kills the very future character of the future. The only people who have any interest in prolonging this rule of the present over the future are those who possess and dominate the present. The have-nots, the suffering and the guilty, however, ask for a *different* future; they ask for change and liberation.

(ii) Karl Rahner's 'Transposition'
For the concept of eschatological extrapolation, Berkhof

continually appeals to Karl Rahner's 'theological principles of the hermeneutics of eschatological statements'. But Rahner never uses the word 'extrapolation' at all. He talks about a transposition of the experience of salvation from 'the mode of the beginning' into 'the mode of consummation'. He certainly starts from the present, and what he says reaches eschatologically into the future:

Biblical eschatology must always be read as an assertion based on the revealed present and pointing towards the genuine future, but not as an assertion pointing back from an anticipated future into the present.[8]

But it is the present experience of salvation which makes this necessary. Why? Because the hidden character of its consummation is already inherent in it and reveals itself as a beginning 'which strives to complete itself'.

Rahner's transposition of christological and anthropological statements out of the mode of the present into the mode of consummation, and out of the mode of experience into the mode of prospect takes place, he claims, *per analogiam fidei*. This indicates that the transposition is not a quantitative extrapolation but a transition to a new quality. Beginning and completion do not lie on the same level but are treated by Rahner as two different modes. The relation between them is therefore one of correspondence, but not one of extrapolation, prolongation or mathematical forecast.

I must express my criticism of Rahner here. He has rightly pointed to the fact that the basis of our knowledge of eschatology lies in the present experience of salvation, as this is christologically and anthropologically determined. Berkhof, better than Rahner, defines this basis of knowledge christologically and pneumatologically; for in Christian terms the experience of the Spirit precedes the person's experience of himself. The basis of our knowledge of eschatology lies here, and this is disputed neither by me nor by anyone else.

What I consider wrong, theologically and in the context of the history of religion, is Rahner's over-systematic contrasting of eschatology and apocalyptic: 'To extrapolate from the present into the future is eschatology, to interpolate from the future into the present is apocalyptic.'[9] Apocalyptic's basis in experience lies without any doubt in the Torah given to Israel, and the suffering experienced by Israel and the righteous. There is no eschatology without apocalyptic and no apocalyptic without eschatology. It is in Christology that the difference between the Jewish and the Christian hope is to be found.

But what is the *real ground* of present experience as an experience of salvation? Rahner does not go into this question explicitly. Not all experiences in the present compel us to eschatological statements, but only those experiences in which the eschatological future is really heralded. It is only if present salvation shows itself as the beginning of a consummation still to come that eschatological statements are justified. It is only if this present is the present of an eschatological future that prospective statements can be made from it. The present of salvation therefore only has a future if this future is promised, initiated and anticipated in that present. If this present is not the real beginning of this future, then the present cannot be used to assert any future still-to-come, either. In so far, therefore, as the eschatological future has entered into our historical present, the present becomes the foundation of knowledge about that future. Our statements spoken *out* of our present *into* the divine future are possible on the basis of the divine word spoken *into* our present *out* of God's future. Here Rahner has confused the basis of our knowledge and the actual basis, because he is too much concerned with warding off what he calls 'apocalyptic'. We ought to avoid following him at this point.

2. *Eschatological Anticipation*

The expression 'anticipation' or 'prolepsis' is a favourite one in recent eschatology. It seems to me to be an apter word for what Berkhof means than the word extrapolation.

Prolepsis is a term taken from Greek epistemology.[10] Epicurus uses it to mean the pre-concepts and anticipatory images with which we seek for experience and for true ideas. These prolepses are the prerequisite for an appropriate and *ad hoc* seeking and finding. Cicero translated Epicurus' prolepsis by *anticipatio*, meaning by it the *praenotio* of an *inchoatae intelligentiae*. On the one hand these are the pragmatic 'search images' for new experiences; on the other hand, however, they are based on the concept of something preceding all experiences, i.e., our innate ideas, the general concepts with which we are born.

In modern philosophy, Kant emphasized the term anticipation. Every 'advance' realization which establishes the form of objects of possible experience counts *a priori* as anticipation, provided it is legitimated by 'the critique of pure reason', which constitutes the objects of possible experience according to their form. The 'anticipations of perception' then apprehend the intensive magnitudes of what constitutes an object of sensation and of what is real in all phenomena.

Husserl used anticipation to mean the essential structure of cognition itself. For every experience of a single thing has both its own inner horizon or sphere, and also an open, infinite horizon or sphere of co-objects. Every individual experience therefore involves appreciation of that which is not yet present, but to which the manifest core of experience 'points in advance'. Consequently all cognition takes place in the mode of intentionality, which can either be fulfilled or disappointed.

Heidegger then related the hermeneutical structure of intentional anticipation ontologically to the pre-structure of existence itself, finding correspondence in the 'being ahead of oneself', in 'anticipating death' (or 'running ahead' into it), and in the possibility of existential 'anticipation of the whole of existence'.

In psychology anticipation is used to mean the presentment or expectation of future behaviour and experience. That can be an intuitive premonition or a certain expectation or the definite idea of a goal. Anticipation can be called a 'vital primary category', at least in the case of open systems, to which man belongs. It is the mode of coming to terms with the possibilities of the future.

In theology we talk about anticipations of God and about anticipations of man.

The history of Israel's relationship with God is interpreted in the historical narratives of the Old Testament as being a pattern of promise and fulfilment. To understand history as the history of promise means understanding promise as the verbal prolepsis of the promised good. Between promise and fulfilment the inchoative and partial fulfilments of history then come into being. They confirm the faithfulness of the promising God and at the same time point beyond into the wider future of the promised fulfilment. Anticipated fulfilment is then understood as the earnest and pledge of completed fulfilment. It might be called 'real prolepsis'. On the basis of the promise that has been heard and the anticipation of God that has been experienced, man's faith, for its part, then becomes anticipation, that is, tense expectation, and the historical anticipation of fulfilment according to the forces and potentialities of history. Human life acquires proleptic form in accordance with the proleptic form of the divine history. The opposite of prolepsis is *anachronism*. Just as anachronism limps after time, so prolepsis hurries ahead of it, already realizing today what is to be tomorrow.

We find this interplay of divine and human prolepsis in most of the New Testament writings as well: because the kingdom of God 'is nigh' we should repent and turn to the future it brings. Because 'the night is far spent and the day is at hand' it is time to rise, to wake and to prepare. The reason is to be found in the history of Christ: just as his proclamation is verbally proleptic, so his cross and resurrection have a real proleptic character. If he has been 'raised *from* the dead', that is a prolepsis of the general 'resurrection *of* the dead' by God. The Easter faith has therefore a correspondingly proleptic structure: it already lives from the future that has been already given in anticipatory form, and already realizes its potentialities in history to the extent in which it is no longer confined to the pattern of this world.

Pauline thinking about the ἐπαιχή embraces both Christology and pneumatology, eschatologically speaking. Anticipatory thinking strives to follow it, when it is used by modern eschatological theology not merely epistomologically but ontologically as well. The ethical consequence is: because, and in so far as, the coming God already antedates his future, giving it *in advance* in history, men and women can and should anticipate this future in knowledge and in deed. They will then understand eschatology historically and will grasp history eschatologically. They will participate in the eschatological, liberating history of God. Anticipation is the hope of those, who, through the Spirit of Christ, have become poor, who with the poor hope for the new, liberating future of God. Anticipation is not content with the present, but does not take the place of consummation either. It is the 'now already' in the midst of the 'not yet'.

A good example of the fruitfulness of this method of eschatological anticipation is given by:

1. The 1968 Assembly of the World Council of Churches in Uppsala:

> We ask you, trusting in God's renewing power, to join in these anticipations of God's Kingdom, showing now something of the newness which Christ will complete.[11]

2. The Dogmatic Constitution on the Church of the Second Vatican Council (ch. VII § 48):

> The final age of the world has already come upon us. The renovation of the world has been irrevocably decreed and in this age is already anticipated in some real way.[12]

In closing, let me quote Franz Rosenzweig; for the Christian hope cannot too carefully consider his Jewish messianism:

> The world is not yet complete. Laughter and weeping are still to be found in it. The tears have not yet been wiped away from every eye. This condition of becoming, of incompletion, can now only be grasped through a reversal of the objective temporal relationship. For whereas the past, what is already complete, lies open to us from beginning to end, and can hence be told (and all telling and all counting begins at the beginning), the future can only be grasped as that which it is – as the future – by means of anticipation. If we wanted to tell the future we should inevitably have to turn it into the fixed and rigid past. The future has to be said-in-advance, prophesied. The future is only experienced in expectation. Here the last has, in our thinking, to become the first.[13]

Summing up, we may say:

1. Eschatology cannot be a report of future history.

2. Eschatology cannot be the extrapolation of the future from history.

3. Eschatology formulates the anticipation of history's future in history's midst.

4. Historical eschatology is possible and necessary because of, and on the basis of, the eschatological history of Jesus Christ.

IV

HOPE AND DEVELOPMENT

I

The theoretical problem which this theme raises is not that the theology of hope lies on the one side, and the development and alteration of the world through science, education and technology lies on the other; the difficulty is the little word 'and'. The possible interpretations of the 'and' joining the two terms range from the radical division between Christian hope and human development, to direct identification of the two. This gives rise to the familiar questions whether we can divide the two strictly from one another, and then whether it is permissible to relate them to one another more or less as we like. The most important question, however, is: at what point does the reconciliation take place and where can it be practised in history?

The traditional patterns of thought in theology where the differences and the reconciliation of hope and development are considered are:

1. The scholastic scheme of 'nature and supernature (grace)' and
2. The Reformed doctrine of the 'two kingdoms'.

1. In the 'nature and grace' scheme, nature must not be thought of statically, as a self-contained cosmos. It can quite well be understood as history open to the future. Then grace does not hinder or destroy this nature, which is in the process of evolution, but elevates it and brings it to its supernatural consummation. It is in this sense that Vatican II's Pastoral Constitution on the Church, *Gaudium et Spes* (IV § 41), says:

> Since it has been entrusted to the Church to reveal the mystery of God, who is the ultimate goal of man, she opens up to man at the same time

the meaning of his own existence, that is, the innermost truth about himself.

The earthly process of humanization cannot therefore be identified with the growth of the kingdom of God, although it is included in the 'coming to maturity of the kingdom of God' in so far as it contributes to a better social order in human society (Schillebeeckx). Christian faith in God's grace and Christian hope for God's kingdom are therefore no hindrance to the progress and development of the nations: they absorb that progress into themselves, encouraging, rectifying and stimulating it by virtue of the infinite powers which reach beyond all finite purposes. In this way Christian hope becomes 'the hope of human hopes' (Kasper).

But the question is, where specifically does this reconciliation between eschatological grace and natural evolution take place? Does it happen in and through the church, the office of teaching and the sacraments? Is the church in the modern world at all capable of maintaining those medieval claims of supremacy over nature and society, in the face of progress and development – since after all Christianity in the world is becoming more and more of a minority creed? Does not everyone recognize the discrepancy between the church's claim and its reality? Is therefore the Christian hope, if it is related to earthly evolution in the scheme of supernature and nature, anything other than ecclesiastical ideology without any relation to reality? Is the reclamation of the humanizing process for the growth of the kingdom of God (which the church represents) practicable, either for Christians or non-Christians? Moreover, it is a question whether the Christian ideas of the incarnation and the *assumptio carnis*, which underlie the scheme of 'nature and grace', are sufficient to make the central Christian event of Christ's cross and resurrection comprehensible.

2. The other theological pattern of thought which is designed to comprehend the difference between hope and development and their reconciliation is to be found in the modern Lutheran doctrine of the 'two kingdoms'. According to this, faith has no direct effect (*potestas directa*) on human reason and the development of its world; it merely has an indirect, relieving effect. Faith frees reason from illusions and ideologies for its final reasonableness. It relieves reason and the reasonable human world from idolatries and self-justifications. It releases the world from its idolatries for its

worldliness. It makes man human and liberates him from his dreams of divinity. Correspondingly, faith frees the reason that develops and plans for true reasonableness and objectivity, by withdrawing from reason every form of belief. It withdraws from reason the categories of totality and the absolute, refusing to allow it to be the subject of history and making it thereby human, finite, historical and pragmatic. We might call this scheme the contrapuntal pattern. Faith, proclamation and the church do not influence the world by direct persuasion, by Christian ethics or Christian social doctrine or the Christian vision of the future. They influence it solely because they are different in kind.

This certainly does not mean that the doctrine of the two kingdoms has to be thought of in static terms. Properly used, it is the sword of the permanent sharp division between God and the world, and between God and man. This is undoubtedly necessary, for in reality the two kingdoms are permanently intermingled. People expect continual ultimate fulfilments from the penultimate things, such as development, technology and revolution; and they are therefore faced with one disappointment after another. On the other hand,the church's statements about the evolution of the world and the kingdom of God are often either so abstract that they have no application to the next actual steps in the development, or so concrete that they do not serve the kingdom of God at all.

There are two questions here, however. First, there is the question whether the theory that the Christian faith frees reason for itself does not merely lead to apologetic and subsequent adoptions of the modern self-liberation of reason from the infancy or immaturity to which it has condemned itself (Kant). If this is so, then the dilemma of the scheme of nature and grace is repeated here. The claim that faith is the true liberation of reason for reasonableness is the precise equivalent of the change from *potestas directa* to *potestas indirecta*. In recent decades many small nations have been occupied by great powers under the ideological cloak of being 'liberated' either from capitalism or from communism. So this theory too is no protection against false Christian claims to power. We ought to ask more precisely what interest motivates the reason liberated for reasonableness, instead of enthusing about its naked, allegedly 'sober' reasonableness.

The second question is whether here the mediation between faith and reason is not seen only in the individual who is called to faith, whereas little can be said about the collective groups of which the individual is a part.

2

I think that today we should retrace our steps from secondary schemes of mediation – through the church or faith – to the primary mediation of the rule of God and history. The pattern of 'nature and supernature' was applied specifically to the church. The scheme of the 'two kingdoms' doctrine applied specifically to believers. But the primary and, for Christianity, fundamental event that mediates between the kingdom of God and human history is the Christ event. We mean by this the event of Jesus Christ's cross and resurrection. A 'theology of hope and development' must be founded on the Christ event itself if it claims to be Christian. It must think of the mediation between God and man, the kingdom of God and human history strictly in respect of this mediator, his activity, his suffering, his dying and resurrection, and must arrive at an appropriate conclusion. The eschatological rule of God, and with it the new creation and redeemed existence, are mediated in history solely through the rule of Christ. But this rule of Christ is the reconciling and liberating rule of the crucified Jesus. How are we to think of this?

1. The central fact of the early Christian faith is the raising of the crucified Jesus and his exaltation to be the Christ of the coming God. The Christian faith in Jesus of Nazareth began with the Easter appearances. It was an eschatological faith from the beginning. For in his resurrection from the dead people saw the anticipation of the general resurrection of the dead (I Cor. 15), i.e., the anticipation of that future of history which is simply different qualitatively from future history and the historical future. In it God is God, man sees him face to face, and the whole longingly expectant creation will be filled with peace and the righteousness of a new creation. This anticipation of the eschatological future of God in the midst of history is not yet identical with the complete rule of God itself; it is only its anticipation and its representation in the conditions of history through 'the *Christ* of God'.

This title means mediation. It means roughly 'substitute', 'proxy', 'representative' or 'precursor' of the coming God. That is why, according to I Cor. 15, the inner future of the lordship of

Christ which is present here and now is the full lordship of God; and, conversely, the full redeeming rule of God is present, and is only present, in history in the helpless power of the crucified Christ who was raised. *Christ* is the anticipator of the coming God, and of the transformation and redemption of the world that will come with him, together with the humanity of the new man contained in that transformation. I believe that this understanding of Christ is increasingly crystallizing out of the ecumenical discussions on 'Faith and Order' and 'Church and Society'.

2. But the notion of anticipation, through which here the future of God and the history of the world are christologically mediated, remains vague and can lead us into illusion if we do not say clearly enough where this divine anticipation of the future has taken place and takes place. Here we shall have to turn back to a theology of the cross, away from the 'theology of hope' which understands the resurrection of Christ in its significance for world history with the help of the idea of anticipation. The anticipation of the coming kingdom of God has taken place in history in the crucified Jesus of Nazareth. That means that the coming kingdom of God is not to be found anywhere on earth, except in the cross on Golgotha. The divine future confronts us, not in dreams of the future but in the face of the crucified Jesus. In the crucified Jesus the risen Christ is present on earth – present and seeable and tellable. But if God himself is near in the risen one, then the crucified Jesus is the face and the revelation of the coming God.

What does that mean? It means, first, that the crucified Christ manifests what really is wrong with this world. The cross of Christ reveals the godlessness and the God-forsakenness of the world. We cannot therefore, in all our ideas about the world's openness to the future and the evolution of mankind, overlook the fact that the forces of history bear the names of law, sin and death, and that evolution does not mean that the world is going to get better and better in this respect. As Christians, we shall rather have to direct our glance to the victims of development. If the anticipation of God's future was found in the Christ who was condemned according to the law and crucified by the state, then the point in the social order at which the anticipation of Christian hope and Christian love ought to be found has been marked permanently: we must find it in the people whom Jesus, according to Matt. 25, called the least of his brethren, and with whom he identified himself: 'He who goes to them goes to me'. But these are not the progressive leaders of society, the spearheads of economic development; the least of the brethren are their victims – the hungry, the naked, the homeless, the unemployed, the imprisoned.

It means, secondly, that it is manifest in the crucified Christ how the future of God, and the future of freedom and righteousness, are mediated in this history of ours; namely, through the representative suffering of Jesus Christ and, following upon that, action in solidarity with those who suffer. The form which the anticipation of the resurrection has permanently worn, through the crucified Christ, is his being representative, his suffering and dying 'for others'. We do not need to go here into the different ideas about Jesus Christ's 'existence for others'. What is important is to see that the anticipation of Christian hope is living and effective only in representing those who have no future. Hope is given us for the sake of the hopeless (W. Benjamin).

3. If in Christ the future of God is mediated with this history of life and death through anticipation and representativeness, then the future paths of Christianity become clear. The gospel and the sacraments anticipate and celebrate the future glory of God by making the crucified Christ present. They are *signa prognostica* in that they are *signa commemorativa* of Christ (Thomas Aquinas).

Believers are given freedom from law, sin and death through the power of the Spirit. They are already prompted here and now by 'the earnest of the Spirit' which, according to the prophetic promise, is to be 'poured out on all flesh'. That is why they are not separated from the world, but as the first fruits of the new creation, stand as representatives for the whole longing and waiting creation. By taking the cross on themselves, they anticipate the future of redemption. By standing up for others they already live here and now from the future in which righteousness and life rule.

The community of believers lives from its acknowledgment of others. In that way it breaks through the law of human society, according to which like only draws to like. It is made up of 'Jews and Gentiles, masters and servants, the educated and the uneducated, men and women', and this is the only way in which it proves that the Spirit of Christ lives in it. Because it is made up of the unlike and 'the others', it anticipates the future of 'the human emancipation of man' (Marx).

In bodily obedience, which includes political, social and

economic obedience, believers follow Christ and thus already anticipate the resurrection of the body here and now, under the conditions
of death. Thus the present manifestations of the crucified Jesus
and the anticipations of the new world belong together.

3

After these reflections on the christological foundation of ethics,
we come back to the modern problem of Christian hope and
development, and ask about the consequences.

1. We have two possible ways of talking about the future. We
can talk about what is going to *be* and we can talk about what is
going to *come*. This makes a profound difference. What is going to
be can be calculated from the factors and trends of the present.
Developments are analysed and rates of growth calculated. The
possible future is extrapolated from past and present. This is the
method of futurology and scientific prognosis. I would call this the
calculable future. But the calculable future is not identical with the
desirable and hoped-for future. On the basis of the investigation of
possible futures, we must always decide for one particular goal, or
for several. We must fix priorities. The desirable future and the
priorities among different values by no means emerge all by
themselves from the calculable future.

We should make this distinction between calculable future and
desirable future in order to escape from the purely technocratic
prolongation of present conditions into the future and in order to
be able to conceive of a humane future in general. The history of
language has meant that there are two different groups of words
meaning future. For that which is going to be we have the Latin
word *futurum* (the English 'future'). For that which is going to
come, we have the German word *Zukunft* (the French *avenir*). The
German word *Zukunft* is not an equivalent for the Latin word
futurum; it is a translation of the Latin *adventus*, which is in its
turn an equivalent for the Greek word *parousia*. The future in the
sense of *futurum* can be extrapolated from the entrails of present
history. It corresponds to the calculable future. But *adventus*, what
is to come, can only be anticipated. Desirable future, hoped-for
future, belongs to the realm of expectation of the parousia.

Extrapolation and anticipation are different ways of making sure
of the future. But in actual practice we have constantly to link the

two together. Social policy only emerges when sociological, economic and purely scientific extrapolations are linked with ethical anticipations. It does not emerge purely from the calculable and extrapolated future, or solely from ethical maxims and desires, but only from the linking of what we know and can do with what we hope for and desire.

Modern futurology has been given scientific form in 'forecasting units' and 'lookout institutions'; but this by no means takes from us the responsibility for the desirable future. On the contrary, it sets the social imagination free. For in the expansion of possibilities and possible futures we need nothing so much as designs for desirable conditions. The reduction of planning for the future to technology and allegedly 'value-free' analyses merely provides a cloak for the existing desires of the ruling powers. It is only the person who has the power to implement his plans who can plan practically. The desirable future that is concealed in the planning mentality is the perpetuation of the present distributions of power in the world. If we therefore distinguish the calculable future from the desirable future, and stress the anticipations of the desirable future over against present planning (economic, university, or whatever it may be), which rests on pure extrapolation, we must immediately go on to ask: desirable for whom? 'Every year we seem better equipped to achieve what we want? But what do we really want?' asked Bertrand de Jouvenel.

2. We may draw two conclusions from what has been said:

(a) If the Christian faith lives from anticipations of the promised future of God in Christ and the Spirit, then its task in present-day conditions is to develop the social imagination to conceive the desirable future of a habitable earth. For today's relationship between calculable and desirable future has got out of proportion, because desires have been overrun by calculations. So much has become possible that we no longer know what we want. 'Men have become gods, but not as yet very imaginative ones' (Robert Jungk). In the May revolts in Paris in 1968, the slogan was 'L'imagination au pouvoir!' What we need, therefore, are lists of social, economic and political priorities. Anyone who fails to think of what the end is going to be, makes the future his enemy. The 'cultural lag' brought about by the one-sided investment of human imagination in the achievable and calculable future must be surmounted by new incentives provided by social, political and humane imagination.

(*b*) But as we have said, the desirable future by no means just stands there, empty and open. The reduction to technical thinking about the future conceals the obvious wish for the perpetuation of existing distributions of power. That is why the Christian faith cannot simply elevate and stimulate previous conditions which are in the process of evolution, by way of its ultimate hope. It cannot, either, simply aim to free reason for reasonableness, but is bound to ask: *cui bono?* That is to say, it must expose present interests and conflicts of interests with regard to the desirable future and must lay bare the ideological backgrounds of technocracy.

The starting point for this lies in faith's fundamental recognition that the anticipation of the divine future took place in the crucified Jesus. As a result it is not permissible for faith to develop society's future in an evolutionary way. It must develop it dialectically and in representation for those who have become, and are going to become, the victims of previous and present evolution. The future for which the Christian faith hopes does not begin 'at the top', with the spearheads of evolution and in the advanced societies but – as we can see from the crucified Jesus – 'below', among those who are without a future and without hope, the victims of world history. This reversal is brought about by the dialectic of the cross. The Christian hope must therefore develop the imagination that is prompted by love for the unloved and neglected and those who have been left behind. That always brings this hope into a certain proximity to revolutionary hopes for the future, into a connection with the rebellions of the oppressed and neglected, and into critical detachment from the 'advanced' and 'developed'. It is not the so-called underdeveloped countries that present the problem; on the contrary, it is the 'advanced' societies. On the basis of faith in the crucified Jesus, there is something like a 'messianism of the poor' from the viewpoint of the Christian hope; for in the divine future the poor will save the rich (Luke 16) and not the rich the poor. The manifesto of the Christian theology of hope is provided by the Beatitudes, in which Jesus proclaimed the future of the kingdom of God to the poor, the mourners and the hungry.

4. *Summing up*

1. The christological concept of *anticipation* of the future which we have employed makes the Christian faith conscious of its

provisional nature in all the manifestations of its life, and hence impels it to develop its imagination.

2. The christological concept of representativeness which we have employed points Christians to the place where, and the people for whom, they should exert themselves in the imagination prompted by love.

3. The knowledge, fundamental to Christianity, that the future of God has begun in the crucified Jesus, brings Christians into critical conflict with technocratic notions of development. This conflict is not waged in the name of the ultimate supernatural hope against the penultimate earthly hopes; it is carried on in the name of, and on behalf of, the people who, now and in the future, are excluded from the development process: the neglected, the oppressed and the outcasts.

4. It is essential to learn to distinguish the desired future and the planned and calculated future, first in order to expose the wishes hidden behind the future which is planned and calculated today, and to enquire into the interests and relationships of power, and, secondly, in order to formulate the true desires of all men and women and to bring them to effect.

5. The Christian hope for the ultimate future must not surrender itself to 'the higher sanctities' of hopes for what is developing now. That would be a betrayal of the cross and of those whom the crucified Jesus called his brethren. We should therefore try to think of the future for Christ's sake, without the usual scheme of 'nature and grace' and without the traditional doctrine of 'the two kingdoms'.

V

THE THEOLOGY OF THE
CROSS TODAY

1. *The Crucified Jesus as the Origin and Criterion of Christian Theology*

Only a few years ago 'the concern about God' (H. Zahrnt) was argued out in public as a dispute between the simple and indeed simple-minded theses 'God is dead' and 'God cannot die'. Since then in both Catholic[1] and Protestant[2] theology new trends of thought have grown up which are concerned to find a consistent *Christian* doctrine of God. They make Christology the cornerstone of all theology, see the heart of Christology in the cross of Christ, and understand the being of God in this death as trinitarian being. Martin Kähler's thesis – 'the cross of Christ as the foundation and the measure of Christology'[3] – thus acquires new relevance, for it now appears more radical and more comprehensive: the crucified Christ as the foundation and measure of Christian theology as a whole.

In recent years theology and the church were rightly challenged from many sides, the external criteria being their *relevance* for man, society and politics; now the inner criterion has come to the fore – the *identity* of theology and the church as Christian identity. This cannot mean a change in the centre of gravity and it must not be interpreted as a shift of interest. On the contrary, the one provokes the other: without identity there is no relevance and without relevance there is no identity.[4] Where there is relevance and topicality the identity becomes questionable and every new way of grasping the identity calls the previous relevance in question. Theology can receive its divine justification in Christian terms only when it continually and fully actualizes and makes present the death-cry of the forsaken Christ. It must not only be responsible for its talk about God in contemporary oneness with 'the sufferings of this present time'; it must at the same time always justify what it says before the face of the crucified Jesus, to whom, as Christian theology, it appeals. In this respect theology is faced with its most difficult crisis, for Jesus' God-forsaken death is for Christians either the end of every theology, or else the beginning of a theology that is specifically Christian. If 'the true criticism of dogma is its history' (D. F. Strauss), then the true criticism of Christianity and its theologies is the history of Jesus, which on earth ended in his death on the cross and eschatologically begins with that. Like Karl Barth, but in a somewhat different respect, we are bound to say: in the face of this end of his beginning, the Christian *can* no longer talk about God; in the face of this beginning in his end, the Christian *must* talk about God. He ought to endure the inability in the obligation and the obligation in the inability, and in this breaking down of all immediacy give the crucified God the glory.[5] This makes the crucified Christ the specific thing about Christian theology, both as regards its identity and as regards its relevance. He does not merely stamp its content; he also gives it its form and its *Sitz im Leben*, its situation in life. All theological statements point to him, from the doctrine of creation to eschatology, and from the doctrine of the Trinity to the doctrine of sin. As the theology of the cross, theology does not merely talk *about* the meanings of Christ's cross and interpret it; it itself becomes 'crucified theology', as Karl Rahner (rather like Luther) puts it;[6] and it also, one may add, becomes 'crucifying theology'. This makes it a critical theory of liberation. Its *Sitz im Leben* will correspondingly have to be sought among those who live 'under the cross', who suffer 'the sufferings of this present time' – the god-less and the God-forsaken, the despisers of men and those who have been forsaken by men, the oppressed and those who have become guilty of their oppression.

If the crucified Christ steps into the centre of theology and the church, then the traditional forms of mediation between the Christian faith and classical, European and Western humanism, which are to be found historically in Christianity, break down. And conversely, the rigour of the cross comes to the fore for faith in the degree to which post-Christian humanism emancipates itself from its ecclesiastical and Christian traditions. It is only the stumbling-block of the cross which. once accepted, creates justifying and liberating faith.

> There stands the cross, with roses thickly clustering.
> Who brought these clustering roses to the cross?
> The garland swells, its tender branches twining
> The stubborn wood a softer form to lend.

So wrote Goethe,[7] knowing the contradiction between the roses and the cross. Goethe, indeed, loved the healing roses more than the 'stubborn wood'; yet he plucked the roses from the Christian cross as well, as he does in *Wilhelm Meisters Wanderjahre*, where he founded the 'third religion' on 'reverence for what is below us', calling it Christian. It teaches us 'to recognize as divine even humility and poverty, scorn and contempt, shame and misery, suffering and death'.[8]

With Nietzsche, on the other hand, the 'roses' fall withered from the cross at the end of the bourgeois-Christian era:

> Modern men, with their blunted perceptions about all Christian nomenclature, no longer feel in themselves the terrible superlative which for the ancient world was inherent in the paradox of the formula 'God on the cross'. There had never been anywhere or at any time a comparable boldness in inversion, or anything so appalling, so questioning and questionable as this formula: it promised a transvaluation of all the ancient values.[9]

In this situation Christian theology can no longer present itself as the 'self-awareness' of Christianity, which is the way in which it has presented itself in world history. It would then have to depict itself as a 'white', 'rich' and 'male' theory of religion. But this would mean a softening belittlement of the God of whom the Old Testament already tells us: 'Man shall not see me and live' (Ex. 33.20) – the God whom, tradition tells us, to know is to suffer. It is not only Paul in the New Testament who links knowledge of this God with dying – 'dying to this world', or to prevailing conditions – and with being born anew and for what is new. It is only when Christian theology gives itself up unconditionally and without reserve to the primal event of faith that it will become a critical and liberating theology, and, becoming painfully conscious of the limitations of its economic, social and cultural conditioning, will go beyond these. For this it is not enough to interpret Jesus' death on the cross with a new theory of salvation, more relevant than the ones offered by tradition. We must first of all relate that death to God himself and to reality. 'The primary existent for faith, revealed only to faith and, as revelation, the very first thing that evokes faith is . . . Christ, the crucified God.'[10]

2. *What does Jesus' Death on the Cross mean for God Himself?*

From the New Testament onwards, the death of Jesus was always traditionally perceived and interpreted in the framework of soteriology. The fundamental New Testament formula ὑπὲρ ἡμῶν became, in preaching and in the Lord's Supper, the starting-point for an understanding of the saving significance of this death, and for a living remembrance and making-present of the history of his passion. Even the valuable studies of the united Evangelical churches only enquire into the meaning of Jesus' death on the cross by asking about 'the ground of salvation'.[11] This is right, but it is not a sufficiently radical approach, for we must first ask: what does Jesus' death mean for the God whom he called 'my Father'? 'Jesus died for God before he died for us', said Paul Althaus,[12] in a pregnant remark, considering it to be a serious fault in early Protestant theology not to have understood the cross first of all in the context of the relationship of the Son to the Father and of the Father to the Son, but to have at once interpreted it directly as the expiatory means of salvation for the sins of mankind. This meant that God himself remained untouched by the event through which the relationship between God and man developed from one of judgment to one of grace. But if the death of Jesus is supposed to be first a *statement about God* before it is *an assurance of salvation* addressed to men, does not that mean 'a revolution in our concept of God' (Alain)? On the other hand, is a Christian proclamation of salvation possible at all today without a new proclamation of God?

(i) *Jesus' death as the death of God*

Karl Rahner[13] has tried to understand the death of Jesus in this sense as 'the death of God': through his death our death becomes the death of the immortal God himself. Rahner was not intending to consider Jesus' death merely in its efficacy for salvation; he was considering it 'more precisely in itself'. Although this sentence is found in his 'Remarks on the Dogmatic Treatise *De Trinitate*', he only draws on the possibilities offered by the doctrine of the two natures: since we must not assume that this death 'failed to affect

God', it was a statement about him. 'The death of Jesus is one of God's declarations about himself.'[14] But how, to what extent, and in what way is God's being 'concerned in'[15] or 'affected by'[16] the fate of Jesus on the cross? Did God suffer in himself on the cross, or only through another? Does God's involvement in Jesus' death go so far that it is permissible to identify the two, symbolically or parabolically: 'Jesus' death *as* the death of God'? And if his death on the cross was a death in God-forsakenness, what assertion are we making about the dichotomy in God between the forsaking Father and the forsaken Son? Rahner evidently comes to a stop at the paradox:

> The immutable God in himself of course has no destiny and therefore no death. But he himself (and not just what is other than he) has a destiny, through the Incarnation in what is other than himself . . . And so it is just this death (like Christ's humanity) which expresses God.[17]

In these sentences the relationship between Jesus and God is thought of as being the relationship between Jesus' human nature and his divine person. Consequently the death of Jesus as the death of God is understood as being on the same level as the incarnation. Consequently it cannot mean anything new for the being of God 'in itself', but it does mean everything for God's being in the manhood of Christ for us and with us. In this way Rahner gives the doctrine of the two natures a special perspective, leading towards the death of Jesus as the death of God, but he still remains essentially within the framework of the direct soteriological interpretation of that death.

Karl Barth presented a detailed theology of the cross in his doctrine of predestination and reconciliation.[18] 'The crucified Jesus is "the image of the invisible God".'[19] According to this the divinity of Jesus reveals itself particularly in his lowering himself to death on the cross, whereas his humanity is revealed in his exaltation. Barth's linking of the doctrine of the two natures with the early Protestant doctrine of Christ's two conditions, humiliation and exaltation, leads to a new 'historical' understanding of the being of God. God's being is found in the history of the humiliation of the Son of God and in the exaltation of the Son of Man. Consequently we find in Barth many 'theopaschite' statements about God's suffering and involvement in the cross of Christ. Yet these too stand in the framework of the doctrine of election and reconciliation, i.e., in a soteriological context. Barth has really 'etched the harshness of the cross into the concept of God'[20] thereby deepening Luther's theology of the cross, not merely criticizing it. In my view Barth's limitations lie, strangely enough, in the fact that at these points he does not argue expressly enough in *trinitarian* terms.[21] Because he always stresses – and rightly so – that *God* was in Christ, *God* lowered himself, *God himself* wanted to be the loser on the cross so that man might be the gainer, he uses the simple concept of God in considering miserable and reconciled man, not yet a concept developed in trinitarian terms. That is why Barth, rather like Rahner, has to distinguish the God who in his primal decision proceeds from himself, from the God who is previously in himself 'untouched by evil and death'.[22] This certainly makes it possible for us to conceive the very being of God as being present in the death of Jesus; but the converse is difficult: how can we conceive of Jesus' death on the cross as belonging within the being of God? The death of Jesus 'for us', 'God for us' (Rom. 8.3) is the inner secret. But what does this death then mean for God himself? Here we can be faced with the simple question, *how much* is God affected by Jesus' death? For this death is supposed to touch him at his very heart, and not merely in his outward relationships. Conversely, he is supposed to meet death on the cross himself, in his own eternal life. Otherwise 'the death of God' would not be the death of death but either God would not be dead or death would be God. It is essential for the sake of the life of the one who is the victim of death, to think of the very being of God as present in the death of Jesus; but then how, conversely, is this death conceivable in the being of God himself? Barth's stress on the sovereignty of God makes 'God in Christ' conceivable to the point of the death of God in the death of Christ, but pre-eminently as the sovereign ground and pure causality of salvation for the godless person. Even then this death cannot pass God by, leaving him unscathed. So what does this death mean for God himself?

(ii) *The death of Jesus as dichotomy in God*

If we understand the death of Jesus solely on the same level as the incarnation, we remain in the framework of the doctrine of the two natures. His death remains a human one, even if it is a death accepted by God and therefore also a death affecting God himself in his turning to men. The doctrine of the *communicatio idiomatum realis* can then interpret the cross as the death of God. Incarnational statements about God *in* Christ are actually bound, logically, to lead to this assertion. Yet it makes a difference whether in this sense we talk about 'God *in* the crucified Christ' or, like Nietzsche, talk about 'God *on* the cross'. Luther was even more radical with his identification at this point: 'But of Christ faith tells us, not only that God is in Him but therefore that Christ is God Himself.'[23] If we take that seriously, we must go on to say with Luther: what happened on the cross was a happening between God and God; there God disputes with God; there God cries out to God; there God dies in God. But then God is acting here not merely through an obedient person, but in his own Son and in so far in himself. But if God is acting in himself, then he is also suffering his own action in himself. In his *Theology of the Pain of God*[24] Kazoh Kitamori has used these paradoxical phrases of Luther's against Schleiermacher and partly also against Barth.

Helmut Gollwitzer also goes beyond the doctrine of the two natures at this point and considers 'the dichotomy of God' himself:

> . . . not the doctrine of the two natures itself but its purposeful trend towards the death, towards this dying of Jesus (is) the paradox of paradoxes. The cleavage does not not only go through Jesus, it goes through God himself; God himself is forsaken by God, God himself rejects himself.[25]

For this he quotes Theodor Haecker:[26] 'My God, why hast thou forsaken me? How can God be God and remain God after these words?' His conclusion is that Golgotha requires us to overstretch the tensions of the book of Job and to conceive the inconceivable – 'God as man in God-forsakenness' – and to understand this as 'the event of love'. This is true and inescapable. But do we not first have to think of God as God in God-forsakenness and understand this event as the ground of love? If the cleavage of the death on the cross goes right through God himself, and not merely through the divine and human person of Christ, then one is reminded of Goethe's motto in *Dichtung und Wahrheit*, Book 4: 'Nemo contra Deum nisi Deus ipse.'[27] Carl Schmitt has pointed to J. M. Lenz's *Catharina von Siena* as being the source of this motto.[28] There Catharina – in a very modern, anti-authoritarian way – complains, as she flees from her father:

My father looked so threateningly at me,
Just like a loving, injured God.
Yet if he had but stretched out both his hands,
God against God (she draws a little crucifix from her breast
      and kisses it)
Save, save me
My Jesus whom I follow, from his arm! . . .
Save, save me from my father
And his love, his tyranny.

Schmitt associated with this a theological doctrine of stasis: 'Here
we come up against a real political-theological stasiology at the
centre of the doctrine of the Trinity',[29] because, as the dialectic
thinker Gregory Nazianzen recognized, 'The One is always in
rebellion against itself.' If Christian theology recognizes and reflects
on God in the happening on the cross of Christ, it too arrives at
this stasiology of contradictions in God out of the paradox: God in
God-forsakenness. But then theology can only preserve the concept
of God if it begins to think in dialectically trinitarian terms. If
Christian theology in its doctrine of God is a stasiology because
of the cross of Jesus, it still does not promote *theological
politics* in relationships between friend and enemy on earth –
contrary to Carl Schmitt's view; it becomes the *political theology*
of reconciliation in the midst of conflict and the overcoming of
conflict in God. Theology then no longer thinks only of 'God in
history' but also of 'history in God'. For in Christ's cross history is
found concentrated and integrated in God in so far as law, sin and
death constitute history in its negative aspect. If the true conflict
of history is in God himself and is fought out in God himself, then
from the point of view of this God the only conclusion could be, in
the words of the German Gloria: 'All feuds have now an end.'

   To think of God in the death of Jesus must really lead to the
reversal of thinking of the death of Jesus in the being of God. The
christological doctrine of the two natures, which formulated the
first, leads over of itself to the doctrine of the Trinity, which
comprehends the second. The doctrine of the two natures presents
God in Christ for man. The doctrine of the Trinity presents man in
Christ for God. But to consider Jesus' history and its end on the
cross for God himself means penetrating the inner divine relationship. Here simple talk about 'God' is inappropriate. From the

outside of the mystery which it is appropriate to call God, we enter that inner room that is triune. This is where the revolution in the concept of God is to be found which makes faith in the crucified God necessary. For here a God did not merely act outwards, out of his untouchable glory and his supreme sovereignty. Here the Father acted on himself, i.e., on the self of his love, his Son; and therefore the Son suffered from himself, the self of his love, his Father. Tradition has talked a lot about the *opera trinitatis ad intra et ad extra*. But where there are *opera* there are also *passiones*. What about the *passiones trinitatis ad intra et ad extra*? This question is important if the trinitarian concept of God (which is essential for the sake of the cross) is to overcome the apathetic God who cannot be touched or troubled either by the human history of suffering or by the passion of Christ.

3. *Can God Suffer?*

A fundamental point of departure for the question about God and the understanding of Christ's passion is the experience of suffering. Suffering is 'experienced' through love, through concern about life. Man always unfolds his humanity in relation to the divinity of his God: 'Whereon thy heart is set and whereon it depends – that is in truth thy God', said Luther. These 'gods' are not an arbitrary affair. In a fundamental sense they are the human situation. Men find themselves in different situations in relation to these gods, and arrive at an 'apathetic' or a 'pathetic' existence accordingly.

(i) *The apathetic theology of the ancient world*[30]
Apatheia as a metaphysical axiom and an ethical ideal was passed on to Judaism and Christianity from the ancient world with a forcefulness that was almost irresistible. In the physical sense *apatheia* means unalterability, in the psychological sense insensitivity, and in the ethical sense freedom. *Pathos*, on the other hand, means need, compulsion, urge and dependency. According to Plato God is good and cannot be the origin of evil, suffering and punishment. The stories of the gods told by the dramatic poets, which arouse pathos and emotional reactions, are therefore not appropriate to God (θεοπρεπής). As perfect being, what is divine requires nothing, knows neither anger nor love, and needs neither sacrifice nor service. Since like can only be known and loved by like, the divine is self-sufficient. From this, from Aristotle onwards,

the theological principle follows: ἀπαθὴς τὸ θεῖον.[31] As *actus purus* God is pure causality and cannot be the object of suffering. God thinks himself eternally and is hence the thought of thought. God wills himself eternally and is hence the will of willing. Thinking and willing were hence assigned to his eternal, apathetic being.

If it is the wise man's ideal to become like God and to participate in the divine sphere, he must overcome his needs and emotional reactions and lead a life free from passion and suffering in the *apatheia* of the spirit. In the thinking of thought he finds peace in God. In eternal willing he finds the eternal presence of God in which what is transitory passes away. Anyone who is free from himself and his own frail love acquires the freedom which divinity possesses by nature. Here *apatheia* does not as yet mean dullness of feeling and indifference, but is the negative, reverse side of the freedom of the spirit which is godlike and hence above the world.

In order to be fair to the theology of the ancient church, in spite of all our criticism, we must in considering the axiom of *apatheia* take note of this aspect of the freedom of God and the liberation of man. It took over the divine state of *apatheia* as a preliminary stage to the proclamation of the love of the trinitarian God. Because true love springs from freedom from egoism and dependency (loving *sine ira et studio*), *apatheia* became the premise for *agape*. People took over the concept of the θεὸς ἀπαθής, calling God's intellect the Son and calling his will the Holy Spirit. Admittedly the Trinity was written into the situation of the apathetic God, and the relationship of the Father to the Son was seen in the *generatio* and the relation to the Spirit in the *processio*. The trinitarian relationship in God was considered in terms of his eternal being, as it exists in himself before the history of Christ and the history of salvation; so there was considerable difference in understanding theologically the Father's *derelictio Christi* on the cross.[32]

As the history of dogma shows, Judaism and Christianity got entangled in insoluble theological difficulties through their acceptance of the θεὸς ἀπαθής; for the divine situations in the Old and the New Testaments look very different. The identification of the apathetic God with the pathos of Yahweh in the Old Testament, and with the passion of Christ in the New, led to the difficulties which are still facing theology today. Theologians either had to break through the religious axiom of God's *apatheia*, or had to reinterpret Christ's passion. They either had to break through the ancient world's corresponding ideal of freedom, or reinterpret the freedom of the Jewish and the Christian faith. Our difficult situation today arises from the inconsistency that neither of these two alternatives were really followed through. Yet just at the time when patristic *apatheia* theology was enjoying its heyday, there is an astonishing passage in Origen which can take us a step further today:[33]

> The Redeemer descended to earth out of sympathy for the human race. He took our sufferings upon Himself before He endured the cross – indeed before He even deigned to take our flesh upon Himself: if He had not felt these sufferings He would not have come to partake of our human life. What was this passion which He suffered for us before-hand? It was the passion of love. But the Father Himself, the God of the universe, who is full of long-suffering and plenteous in mercy and sympathy, does He not also suffer in a certain way? Or know you not that He, when He concerns Himself with human things, knows human suffering? For the Lord thy God has taken thy ways upon Him 'as a man bears his son' [cf. Deut. 1.31] . . . He suffers the sufferings of love.

(ii) *The 'pathetic' theology of the prophets*

It was Rabbi Abraham Heschel[34] who in 1936 already overcame the apathetic theology of medieval scholastic Judaism and taught us to understand the theology of the prophets as *'pathetic' theology:* the prophets understood themselves and their people in the divine situation which Heschel rightly calls *the pathos of God*. In his pathos the Almighty emerges from himself and enters into the destiny of the chosen people. In his passion he shifts his *esse* into an *inter-est* through his covenant with the people. Consequently he is himself affected by the actions and passions of his people. His pathos is here not the capricious mood of a mythical god, but his free relationship to his creation, his people and their history. He takes the people of his love seriously to the point of suffering under their actions and of being capable of being hurt by their disobedience— hurt in his interest in them. His anger over his obdurate people is simply wounded love. Prophecy, Heschel says, is not a forecast about the future; it is insight into the present pathos of God, into his suffering over Israel's disobedience and his passion for his own justice and glory in the world of the nations. As Heschel shows in a historical comparison with Greek philosophy, Buddhism, Confucianism and Islam, the Old Testament understanding of the pathos of God is unique.[35]

Yet even Jewish scholasticism adapted itself to the axiom of the apathetic God. 'He orders poverty for the one and riches for the other without any alteration in His nature, without any feeling of sympathy with the one or anger with the other. He is the just judge' (Judah Ha-Levi). 'God is free from passion. He is moved neither by feelings of joy nor by feelings of pain' (Maimonides). 'God neither loves nor hates' (Spinoza).[36]

In the sphere of the apathetic God, man becomes *homo apatheticus*. In the situation of God's pathos he becomes *homo sympatheticus*. The divine pathos is reflected in man's sympathetic participation (empathy), his pain, his hopes, and his prayers. Sympathy is a person's openness for the presence of another (M. Scheler). In the pathos of God man is therefore filled with the Spirit so that he may become a friend of God. He feels sympathy with God and his creation. He does not enter into an a-historical *unio mystica*, but into a *unio sympathetica* which opens up history. He is angry with God's anger, suffers with God's love and hopes for God's future. This sympathy is freedom too. But it is not the freedom of the spirit and the will which is above the world and repressive of the body. It is the life-quickening freedom of the heart. It is not the freedom of the apathetic ruler, but the vulnerable solidarity of brothers.

Heschel has developed his pathetic theology as dipolar theology, in a double sense:

(*a*) God is in himself free, and yet he is at the same time involved in his covenant and affected by human history.

(*b*) In the sympathy of man the spirit of God answers the pathos of God. The prophet is an *ish ha-ruach*, a 'man of the spirit'. This heralds the idea of a double personality in God. It is deepened still further in the theology of the rabbis, as Peter Kuhn has shown.[37] They interpreted Ps. 18.35 (RSV: 'Thy right hand supported me, and thy help made me great'; Luther: 'When thou dost cast me down, thou makest me great') as meaning: 'Thou showest me thy greatness through thy humiliation of thyself'; and they spoke of several stages in the self-humiliation of God: in the creation, in the calling of the patriarchs and in the history of the chosen people, God is present in a twofold way: he dwells in heaven, and with the humble and lowly; he is the God of gods, and achieves justice for widows and orphans; like a servant he carries the torch before Israel in the desert; like a slave he carries the people with their sins. So he encounters man in what is lowly and restricted and of no account. These *accommodations* of God to the limitations of human situations also contain in themselves the *anticipations* of his eschatological indwelling in a new creation. God does not only enter into the finitude of his creature, but into his guilt as well. His grief over Israel shows that God suffers over Israel and with her. Why does he suffer? He suffers from his 'indwelling' (*shekinah*) in Israel, because through this *shekinah* he goes into exile with the people and is tortured with the martyrs. But the converse is also true. It can also mean that God redeems himself when he redeems Israel. How does he redeem Israel? His suffering is the means by which he will redeem her.[38]

This rabbinic theology already heralds a practical theology of the cross and with it a doctrine of the Trinity in the understanding of God. Behind this stands a profound experience: faith in the God who suffers with Israel in exile, in the ghetto and in the pogrom preserves the people from despair and apathy, keeps its sympathy alive and sustains its hope against hope for the redeeming future of God.

4. *The Trinitarian Theology of the Cross*

The Christian faith finds itself present again in another divine situation. It is stamped once and for all by the history of the passion of the risen Christ. It is more nearly related to the Jewish divine situation than to the Greek, for the experience of the pathos of God in the Old Testament is the presupposition for the understanding of the history of his passion in the New. Moreover Christian existence in the openness of vulnerable love is more closely related to the *homo sympatheticus* than to Stoic apathy.

But whereas for Israel the direct presence of God is conferred in the covenant, the crucified Jesus, according to the New Testament, stands alone, mediating the fatherhood of God and the power of the spirit of sonship to sinners and the godless. He cannot be replaced by the milieu of a Christian society in which the soul acquires an unmediated relationship to God.[39]

Christian theology cannot therefore be dipolar theology; it has to become trinitarian.

The scriptural basis for Christian belief in the triune God is to be found, not in the scanty trinitarian formulations of the New Testament, but in the continuous . . . witness of the cross; and the most concise expression of the Trinity is the divine act of the cross, in which the Father lets the Son sacrifice himself through the Spirit.[40]

Now the event on the cross must be described in several dimensions if it is to be fully comprehended. Whereas Jesus dies as 'blasphemer' according to the judgment of the law, according to Paul the crucified Christ becomes, in the power of the resurrection, 'the end of the law . . . to every one that believeth' (Rom. 10.4, AV). Consequently the meaning of his death is described in the framework of law and gospel. Whereas, in the judgment of the Roman empire, Jesus died as a rebel, the crucified Christ becomes, in the power of the resurrection, the end of the religio-political Caesar. Consequently the meaning of his death will have to be shown in the framework of lordship and liberation. But if he died abandoned by his God and Father, his death must be understood in its meaning for God himself. The soteriological inclusions and the political dimensions can only be substantiated and developed when what happened on the cross solely between Jesus and his Father becomes clear to us. In the respect the doctrine of the two natures recedes, without losing its significance. We must start from the relationship of the whole person of Christ to the Father. The God-forsaken death stands between Jesus and his Father and reveals their relationship to each other first of all.

If we start by going back to the New Testament formulas, we can say that in Jesus' 'resurrection from the dead' God the Father *acts* in the power of the Spirit. This eschatological action of raising him shows the crucified Christ in his eschatological significance 'for others'. Enthronement and adoption formulas are therefore used to express this.[41] The christological titles depend on the eschatological action of God in the resurrection, and can be understood as titles of representation: the Christ, the Kyrios, represents the coming rule of God in a world which is not yet liberated for God.[42] But why did the Christ have to *suffer*? Paul brought out the meaning of the death on the cross of the risen one and the significance of the suffering of the exalted one when he spoke of his giving of himself (Rom. 8.32; Gal. 2.20). The word παραδιδόναι therefore belongs in the context of passion terminology. There it means 'to deliver up, to betray, to abandon'; but in Paul it becomes the expression of the incomparable love of God.

That God delivers up his Son is one of the most unheard-of statements in the New Testament; we must understand the 'delivering up'
in the fullest sense, and not soften it into 'sending' or 'giving'. Here
what Abraham did not have to do to Isaac has actually happened: Christ
was quite deliberately abandoned to the fate of death; God cast him out
to the powers of destruction . . . God made Christ sin; Christ is the
accursed of God . . . The *theologia crucis* could not possibly be expressed
more radically than this.[43]

What happens between Jesus and the Father when Jesus is
abandoned or delivered up on the cross? The Father 'forsakes' his
'own' Son and rejects him. He whose kingdom Jesus had proclaimed as being 'near' becomes the forsaking God. The Son dies
from the Father's curse. He is the forsaken God. The Son suffers
death in dereliction. But the Father suffers the death of the Son
in the pain of his love. The Son endures the being forsaken
by the Father, whose law of grace he had proclaimed. The
Father endures the being forsaken by the Son whom he chose
and loved.

Because the suffering of the Son is different from the suffering of
the Father, it is impossible to talk in 'theopaschite' terms about 'the
death of God', as the supporters of a 'God-is-dead' theology do.
But we can talk in trinitarian terms about a 'patricompassianism'. If
the Father acts in his own Son by delivering him up and forsaking
him, and if the Son suffers the forsaking delivering-up of the
Father, then the death on the cross stands between Father and Son.
It stands in the very being of God between the Father and Son and
divides the Son from the Father through the total curse. But
since – if we take Rom. 8.32 and Gal. 2.20 together – the Son also
delivers himself up and, as Gethsemane shows, accepts the cup of
forsakenness, both Father and Son act and suffer in the surrender;
and the cross brings the Son together with the Father into the
completed fellowship of that will which is called love. And when
I John 4.16 says of this love that it is the being of God himself –
'God is love' – then the community of will in the surrendering is
the expression of a community of existence in essence.[44] On the
cross Jesus and his God and Father are divided as deeply as possible
through an accursed death, and yet they are most deeply one
through their surrender. Out of this happening between the Father
and the Son the surrender itself emerges, the Spirit which accepts
the forsaken, justifies the godless and makes the dead live. The
forsaking God and the forsaken God are one in the Spirit of

surrender. The Spirit proceeds from the Father and the Son, for it has its source in the *derelictio Jesus*.

In considering the *resurrection* of the crucified Jesus, the New Testament uses a new name for God: 'God is the one who raised Jesus from the dead.'[45] That is a *nomen actionis* and corresponds to the Old Testament tradition, which talks about God as the God who works, who is efficacious, and which reflects on his acts in history. In looking at the death which the risen Jesus suffered, we have to talk about God's suffering, and understand this suffering within God himself in trinitarian terms. The crucified God is a *nomen passionis*.

If we attempt to draw conclusions from the cross about the way we should talk about God, then the traditional trinitarian theological *homousios* must first of all be understood more dialectically than the patristic theological tradition understood it, when it started with the generation of the Son through the Father and described the likeness in nature of the three persons through images like sun, light, and reflection of glory. We must then understand the one common 'being' historically, as that particular history of God which is stamped by cross and resurrection. We must do this, not merely following Schelling and Hegel, on the basis of the modern historical understanding of being, but for the sake of the cross. The nature of God then does not stand behind the appearance of history and appearance in history as eternal, ideal being; it is that history itself. The doctrine of the Trinity is not a speculation about the history of God *supra nos*, with which we would have nothing to do.[46] It is nothing other than the shortened version of the history of Christ's passion, understood as 'the history of God'. Anyone who talks about God must tell this history. Through its dialectical formulations on the conceptual level, the doctrine of the Trinity thrusts into that history which in its unique historicity can really only be told, as J. B. Metz says. That is why we can say: the material principle of the doctrine of the Trinity is the cross of Christ; the formal principle of the theology of the cross as theology is the doctrine of the Trinity.

This does not prevent us from pushing our question back from the starting-point of the history of God on the cross into the conditions of possibility for that history in God; so that the event of the *derelictio Jesu* can lead us to the eternal *generatio filii*. Nor does it exclude the possibility that we may ask another question,

pointing forward from this history of God, and think it eschatologically through to the end. But the all-important thing is that we
have our starting-point in the crucified Christ continually before
our eyes and do not replace the specific contemplation of that
history by empty theoretical concepts. We might adapt a remark of
Kant's and say that trinitarian concepts of God without the direct
intuition or contemplation of the crucified Jesus are empty, just as
the specific contemplation of the cross without these concepts about
God is blind.

What is contained in this trinitarian 'history of God'? What does
this trinitarian process grasp and comprehend? The words
'trinitarian process' do not mean a dissolution of God in world
history. They mean the being of God which is open to man and
open to history for the sake of the crucified Christ. The trinitarian
process contains in itself, in concentrated form, this world's whole
history of suffering. It also contains in itself the suffering in
suffering, that is to say the history of abandonment. It is not for
nothing that παρέδωκεν, which Paul interprets positively in
Rom. 8.32, is used in Rom. 1.18ff. as an expression for the whole
misery of the world, for the God-forsakenness of the godless,
whether Gentiles or Jews. But if this history of God contains
within itself the history of abandonment, then it contains in itself
death in death, i.e., the absolute death, the destroying nothingness
itself – as being abolished in God for the sake of abandoned man,
who is the victim of death. We can therefore term this 'history of
God' in the cross of the Son the history of history. World history –
creation's history of suffering and history of hope – is integrated in
the trinitarian process of God and is experienced and formed
theologically in the light of this presupposition. To recognize the
crucified God therefore means seeing oneself together with
suffering creation in this history of God.[47]

But does this not eternalize suffering? The 'history of God' is
opened up once and for all with the cross of Christ. But the
trinitarian process is only completed with the giving of the kingdom
through the Son to the Father, 'that God may be all in all (I Cor.
15.28, AV). As the use of the name of the Son in the context of this
passage shows, this does not mean any 'self-elimination' of the
mediator;[48] it means the consummation of his obedience on the
cross, the completion of his rule through service. If, as Paul says,
the giving of the kingdom by the Son to the Father means the

'destruction' of all earthly lordship, authority and power and the
end of the death on which they are built, then the completion of the
trinitarian process also brings the end of world history and the kingdom of glory. The passing of the divine lordship from the Father
to the Son in cross and resurrection, from the Son to the Spirit
with Pentecost, and from the Son and the Spirit to the Father
at the end, shows the historical character of God's being and
the openness of the history of God for world history. This
history does not pass God by without leaving a trace. On the
contrary, the crucified Jesus becomes God's eternal signature. This
does not eternalize his suffering, as a one-sided theology of the
cross would make us fear. Nor is his suffering finished and done
with – 'The Moor has done his duty, let him go', in Schiller's
words – as a one-sided theology of the kingdom of God would
suggest. As suffering once suffered, his suffering acquires eschatological and eternal meaning. His suffering 'for us' is transformed
into the gratitude of the liberated 'to him' and into the joy of
redeemed existence 'before him'. When the vicarious suffering of
Christ is no longer 'necessary' for need's sake, it becomes in the
kingdom of freedom suffering for which to give thanks; but it does
not disappear.[49]

If the doctrine of the Trinity is developed out of the happening
on the cross, then the distinction 'God in himself – God for us', as
well as the distinction between immanent Trinity and economic
Trinity seems to be abandoned. But then there arises the question
whether God had to be crucified of necessity, and whether in that
case evil itself is necessary. In so far as the distinction 'God in
himself – God for us' and the distinction between immanent
Trinity and economic Trinity both start from a general (metaphysical) concept of God, and make use of the difference between
idea and appearance, these distinctions must be abandoned as being
inappropriate to the crucified God. 'The Trinity of the economy of
salvation *is* the immanent Trinity' and conversely:

> God's relationship to us is threefold. And this threefold (free and un-
> merited) relationship to us is not merely an image of analogy of the
> immanent Trinity; it *is* this Trinity itself, even though communicated
> as free grace.[50]

But in so far as the questions can be distinguished from one
another – what does the death of Jesus mean for God himself?
What does the death of Jesus mean for us? These distinctions crop

up again in a different way and in a different place. The old theological dispute whether Christ's incarnation and death have their origin in God's freedom, or in his inner necessity, or in his 'inner necessity towards freedom' can be described as a dispute starting from false positions. The polarity between freedom and necessity belongs to alienated human existence, not to the being of God.[51] If the trinitarian being of God in the cross is love, then this love contains both the aspects of freedom without necessity and the inner necessity of the loving person. If, therefore, the being of God is termed love, then it is impossible to go on describing it as arbitrariness or compulsion. Ultimately the crucified figure of the incarnate God is actually determined by the evil of law, sin and death. God has taken this evil upon him in order to give man his own goodness. But we cannot conclude from this that evil is justified. As evil that has been overcome it is integrated into the being of God. 'Where sin increased, grace abounded all the more' (Rom. 5.20). This is not the effect of sin, but is inherent in grace itself. *Post festum*, out of joy over grace, even sin can no doubt be thought of as *felix culpa*; but that does not give sin any positive quality. Consequently we cannot go beyond the fact of evil, for which no reason can be given, since every reason would be tantamount to an excuse. A dialectical trinitarian doctrine of the crucified Jesus does not lead with logical cogency to the declaration that evil is necessary for the sake of good. It really only leads to the removal of evil's potency: it is no longer necessary. Its compulsion is broken. Man has been freed.

5. Can Like only be Known by Like?

Finally, knowledge of the crucified God raises epistemological questions. At a very early stage Christian tradition already took over the ancient principle *par a pari cognoscitur* – and unfortunately took it over quite uncritically. This tenet goes back to Empedocles: 'Thus sweet reached out for sweet, bitter rushed to bitter, sour to sour, the warm poured itself into the warm; thus fire pressed upwards, striving towards what was like it.' Theophrastus writes: 'For with the earth (in us) we see the earth; with the water, water; with the air, the divine air; with love, love; and we see dispute with sad dispute.'[52] From this Aristotle formulated the principle: 'The knowledge of like comes into being through like.'[53]

According to this, cognition is guided by sameness and is always a re-cognition. If likeness is understood in the strict sense, knowing is anamnesis within a closed circle: *par a pari cognoscitur*. If it extends to similarity in difference (*similis a simili cognoscitur*) knowledge becomes an open circle of learning, in which the new can be apprehended and progress can be made. Theologically, if the principle of likeness is understood in its strict sense, God is only known by God. The Trinity would then become a circle closed to man. If the principle is extended to similarity, God can be known from his operative correspondence in nature and history.

In the *Nicomachean Ethics* the corresponding ethical principle runs: 'Like draws to like.' Love (φιλία) can only exist between like and is impossible between the unlike. No free man will love a slave, no slave will love a free man. And 'no one will say that he loves Zeus'.[54]

Both principles support the *apatheia* axiom and prevent sympathy with strangers or people who are different. They hinder openness towards what is new, which is perceived painfully at first.

When the theology of the cross talks about God in the God-forsaken Christ, when it talks about his glory in his humility and consequently about the justification of the godless, it is bound to depart from this epistemological principle of analogy, and must first develop a dialectical one. A dialectical principle of this kind is derived from medicine and goes back to Hippocrates: *contraria contrariis curantur*. Or we may think of Schelling, who writes in his essay on freedom: 'Every nature can be revealed only in its opposite—love in hatred, unity in strife.'[55] But we ought to change 'can only' into 'is in actual fact'. Ernst Bloch also asks critically 'whether only like can grasp like, or whether the reverse is not true – whether the unlike would not be better adapted to do so'.[56]

If we follow up these hints, we might say that God is revealed as 'God' in his opposite – in godlessness and God-forsakenness. His righteousness is revealed as justifying righteousness among the unjust; his will is revealed as grace among the damned. Then the identity of Jesus becomes comprehensible: the people who recognized him in his truth were sinners, not the devout, the unjust not the just – indeed the demons first of all, as they were cast out. With this, finally, the Pauline doctrine of justification emerges as being *knowledge about God*: a person becomes a sinner where there is justification; he becomes godless where God is perceived.

The dialectical principle of revelation in the opposite, and of knowledge of the unlike, does not replace the analogical principle of knowledge of what is similar; but it does make knowledge of what is unlike possible for the first time. In so far as God is revealed in the contradiction of the God-forsaken Christ, he can be known by the God-forsaken, and this knowledge then brings them into correspondence with God – indeed makes them like him. The principle of analogy, exclusively applied, leads to a *theologia gloriae* in heaven. The dialectical revealing and the dialectical knowing brings heaven to earth and opens God's heaven to the godless. If the dialectical principle were to replace the principle of likeness or analogy entirely, then the *theologia crucis* would itself turn into *theologia gloriae*, because then contradiction and correspondence would have to become identical. The two principles belong together and complement one another. Knowing begins with contradiction and ends with correspondence. It begins with pain and ends with joy.

In the social and ethical dimensions, the theology of the cross must break through the cliquy principle of 'like draws to like' and 'dog doesn't eat dog' and must make fellowship possible with people who are unlike ourselves – strangers, people who are different, our enemies (Gal. 3.28). Loving people like ourselves is a matter of course (Matt. 5.43ff.). It is self-affirmation, and ultimately makes us apathetic. Love for the person who is different, for the stranger and the enemy, is the social and ethical form of justification of the other. Love for the person who is different is the opening for the sympathy which takes upon itself and endures the pain of difference and enmity, and which seeks for correspondence in contradiction.

VI

THE TRINITARIAN
HISTORY OF GOD

1. *The Foundation and the Intention of the*
Doctrine of the Trinity

What do we think of when we hear the name of the Trinity, Father,
Son and Holy Spirit? What ideas are associated with the trinitarian
concept of God?

Some people will only think of the traditional liturgical rituals
and symbols. Others may perhaps link the Trinity with cloudy
recollections of the orthodox theology of the Fathers. Many people
consider the doctrine of the Trinity to be a speculation, a kind of
theological higher mathematics for the initiated.[1] Modern Protes-
tants like to content themselves modestly with the young Melanchthon: 'We adore the mysteries of the Godhead. That is better than to
investigate them.'[2] Pragmatic in their thinking, they turn away
from pure theory towards the practice that is to change the world,
saying with Kant:

> From the doctrine of the Trinity, taken literally, nothing whatsoever
> can be gained for practical purposes, even if one believed that one com-
> prehended it – and less still if one is conscious that is surpasses all our
> concepts.[3]

But is the doctrine of the Trinity an empty liturgical symbol, a
speculation remote from experience and practice, a penetration
into the divine mystery that is above all our concepts?

What ought we to think of when we hear the name of the Trinity?
Really something very simple, very earthly and very much of this
world. Many Christians cross themselves when the Trinity is
mentioned. When the congregation is blessed in the name of the
triune God, the hand that the priest or pastor raises in blessing
usually traces the sign of the cross. In medieval pictures the Trinity

is often represented by showing the Father on the throne of glory, raising the cross beam on which the Son hangs, while from the face of the Father the Holy Spirit in the form of a dove descends on the crucified Son.

The experience that gives content to trinitarian talk about God is in fact the cross of Christ on Golgotha. The doctrine of the Trinity is the conceptual framework that is necessary if we are to understand this history of Christ as being the history of God.[4] Of course this does not mean the cross as an isolated fact; it means Christ's death on the cross as the centre and quintessence of his whole history for us, which begins with his messianic sending and which will be completed with his eschatological glorification. Because Christian theology can talk neither about an a-human God, nor about a 'Godless' man, it is bound to talk in trinitarian terms. Christian theology is hence, inescapably and of inner necessity, trinitarian theology; and only trinitarian theology is Christian theology. If Christian theology were to become monotheistic, it would be un-Christian. If it were to become humanistic, it would be atheist. The doctrine of the trinity preserves Christian thinking and living in the actual, specific community of Christ.

The trinitarian understanding of the history of Christ with God and of God with Christ is acquired by way of meditation and out of concern for knowledge. It is not directly practical; but it changes practice more fundamentally than all the possible alternatives which 'the active man' can think out. For it leads faith and practice away from the pragmatic trivializing of the concept of God, setting them both face to face with that divine reality which the young Barth rightly called 'the all-transforming fact'.[5] The man who looks upon God must die, the Old Testament tells us. Really to believe in God and to know him is therefore not a religious supplement to life. It leads to life's fundamental transformation – what Paul describes as dying and being born again. To know God means to suffer God, says an old theological maxim. But to suffer God means to experience a fundamental alteration in one's own existence. Every meditation on Christ is a submitting to this alteration, in order to experience in the pain of the new beginning the joy of fellowship with God. That is why it is this first of all that permanently changes the practice of life in the world. Meditation about the hard fact of Christian faith cannot become a flight from practice, nor can practice become a flight from this fact. In this way meditation and practice, turning to Christ and turning to the world, belong together, just as, in extreme cases, Christian mysticism and martyrdom do. We turn to the *meditatio crucis*, in order to experience the salvation of the broken world and to participate in it. Conversely, we work for the liberation of the enslaved world in order to encounter Christ and to participate in the history of God. Thus meditation and practice supplement and mutually deepen one another.

If we are bound to talk about God in trinitarian terms. in view of the history of Christ, then it is impossible for us to draw up a picture of God that objectifies him. God is not an object to be defined by a concept. God's history is not a fact that could be recognized in detachment, as something finished and complete, once and for all. For through the Holy Spirit the history of Christ with God and the history of God with Christ becomes the history of God with us and hence our history with God. Knowledge comes about because the knowing person is included in this history, because it lays hold of him and changes him.[6] In so far Christ's history with God and God's history with Christ is unfinished; in the Spirit, it is open for man and thrusts forward towards salvation. But in view of this event, which is in continual movement, how can any fixed statement be made? Can open knowledge be fixed in a particular concept? Knowledge is forced to grasp an event which is itself in continual movement, and must in addition understand itself as knowledge moved or impelled by the event. It must think of the living God in living terms, and must not desire to kill him in order to be able to define him. If, instead of talking about the Trinity, we talk about 'the trinitarian history of God', it is because this phrase means just this moving vitality of God's, and with it the knowledge that is impelled by it and is living and life-giving. If the traditional view of the Trinity has to be expanded in this way, it also brings us face to face with that insight into the dialectic of life for which we have to thank Hegel, the philosopher of the Trinity. It is then no longer possible to tie the trinitarian history of God down to a single point.

2. *The Trinity in the Sending and Origin*

The traditional doctrine of the Trinity held in the Western church can be understood as a doctrine about the *Trinity in the sending*, since for it sending is the quintessence of the relationship of the divine persons to one another and of their common relationship to the world. That is why we can read in a textbook of Catholic dogmatics:

> The Father is always only the one who sends; and he sends both the Son and the Holy Spirit. The Son can be sent, but only by the Father; whereas he for his part can also send, but only the Holy Spirit; the Holy Spirit, finally, cannot send at all but can only be sent, both by the Father and by the Son.[7]

What perception is this trinitarian concept of sending based on? Its basis is the perception of the history of Christ, seen in the light of its premise and its origin. The gospels tell the story of Jesus as the history of the Messiah sent by God into the world and anointed by his Spirit. For Mark (1.9ff.) this messianic mission of Jesus begins with the gift of the Spirit at his baptism. For Matthew (1.18ff.) and Luke (1.26ff.) it already begins with his conception through the Holy Spirit. For John (1.1ff.) the sending of Jesus begins before the foundation of the world in the eternity of the Father. That is to say, in the history of the tradition the understanding of Jesus' history and of its consequences in the light of his sending becomes more and more comprehensive. Linguistically the word πέμπειν means primarily 'sending as such', 'the fact of sending'; whereas ἐξαποστέλλειν stresses sending 'from a specific and unique standpoint'.[8] Anyone, therefore, who like John stresses the fact of the sending of the one sent by God, gives preference to πέμπειν; any one who like Paul wants to emphasize the historical *kairos* of this sending (Gal. 4.4–6), talks about ἐξαποστέλλειν. In both cases 'sending' should be taken as comprehending the whole of the appearance, the history and the goal of Jesus' history, seen in the light of God.[9]

If the messianic history of Jesus is understood in the light of his divine sending or mission, then the theological concept must enquire into the reason and origin of that mission. Is the mission of Jesus a fortuitous historical event, or does it have its foundation in God himself? And if it is founded in God himself and derives from him, does it then correspond to God, or does God appear to us in the history of Jesus in a way which perhaps does not correspond to him at all? If we push our question further back in this way, then we cannot find anything different in God that precedes this sending and in which this sending was not already inherent. As God appears in history, as the sending Father and the sent Son, so he must previously have been in himself. The relation of the one who sends to the one sent therefore includes in itself an order of origin within the Trinity, or is that order itself in its historical correspondence. The order of the history of salvation, discernible and perceivable by us in the sending of Jesus by the Father, corresponds to the order of origin within the Trinity. The *missio ad extra* reveals the *missio ad intra*. The *missio ad intra* is the foundation of the *missio ad extra*. So we move from the historical relationships of Jesus to the Father, of the Father to the Son, and their fellowship in the Holy Spirit, to the pre-existent relationships in God himself – and therefore from the Trinity in the sending to the Trinity in the origin. 'These movements or *processiones* in the Trinity are the deepest ground for the sending or *missiones* of the Son and the Holy Spirit.'[10]

What experience does this trinitarian concept of the sending rest upon? It is based on the experience with the history of Christ which men and women have in their own history. It is the experience of faith, in which the sending of Jesus to men and women becomes efficacious and through which they are united through Jesus with his Father. It is therefore the experience of liberating fellowship with Jesus and with the one who sent him – in short, the experience of the Holy Spirit. That is why Paul puts the coming of Christ and the coming of the Holy Spirit parallel to one another: 'But when the time had fully come, God sent forth his Son . . . because you are sons, God has sent the Spirit of his Son . . .'. (Gal. 4.4–6). In John we do indeed find the distinction, so important in the Eastern church, that the Spirit 'proceeds' from the Father and 'is sent' by the Son (John 15.26); but we also find the 'sending' of the Holy Spirit by the Father in the Son's name (14.26). The individual differences do not belong within the context we are discussing at present.[11] The important thing here is that the experience of the Holy Spirit, as it is found in faith, in liberation, in joy and in new powers of life, is grasped as a whole, in the light of its origin, as being sending.

If the experienced history of the Spirit is understood in the light of its divine sending, then the theological concept must in its turn enquire about the origin of this sending. By the same reasoning that led from the contemplation of the historical sending of Jesus to the pre-existent sending, within the Trinity, of the Son by the

Father, we move here too from the sending of the Holy Spirit *ad extra* to his eternal *missio ad intra* within the Trinity. In no other way could the experience of the Spirit be termed the experience of God, or fellowship with Jesus be understood as fellowship with God. But this is just what has to be asserted if experience of Jesus and the one who sent him take place in the Holy Spirit. 'In what takes place between the man Jesus and us when we may become and be Christians, God Himself lives.'[12] The one who makes us free and leads us into the messianic fellowship of Jesus is God the Holy Spirit, because he is the Spirit of the love of God the Father and the Son 'antecedently in himself'[13] and because he desires to be 'ours in advance'.'[14]

The inference to be drawn from the consideration of the messianic mission of Jesus about his eternal sending and his *generatio* through the Father, and the inference to be drawn from the experience of the having-been-sent of the Holy Spirit about his eternal sending and his *spiratio* from the Father, are theologically necessary if we are to understand the history of Jesus and our own history with Jesus as God's history. And here the inference from the Trinity in the historical sending to the Trinity in the eternal origin has two aspects.

1. On the one hand it makes clear that in the sending of the Son and the sending of the Spirit we have to do with God himself, and that God corresponds to himself in this history.

2. On the other hand, however, it presents the divine secret as being *an open secret*.

The origin is the foundation of the sending, but the Trinity in the sending at the same time reveals the Trinity in the origin as being from eternity an *open* Trinity. The Trinity is open for its own sending. It is thus open for men and women and for the whole created, non-divine world. The sending of the Son for the salvation of the world and the sending of the Spirit for the uniting of the world with the Son and the Father can therefore be summed up as the love of God issuing from itself. The Christian doctrine of the Trinity – that is to say, a doctrine of the Trinity bound to the history of Christ – therefore signifies the Trinity of sending and seeking love which has been open from the very beginning. In German the word 'Trinity' can either be translated by *Dreieinigkeit* – the three in one – or by *Dreifaltigkeit* – the threefold God. *Dreifaltigkeit* describes God as he turns to the world. In this sense the threefold God is open to man, open to the world and open to time.[15]

If in the sending of the Son and the Spirit the Trinity issues from itself, so to speak, then it not only reveals what is within it but also opens itself for history and experience. We cannot talk about God's love being open to the world and to time as we can about the creature, which is open to the world and time out of deficiency of being. God's love is open because of the divine abundance and superabundance of being. When, therefore, we talk about a 'history' of the Trinity, we do not mean the time of deficiency, imperfection, sin and death; we mean the eternity of overflowing abundance, of perfection that communicates itself, of ever-increasing grace and of life-creating life. This history of the groundless self-communicating life of God is opened up through the sending. But for that very reason the Trinity in the sending, with its transcendent background in the Trinity in the origin, cannot be the one and only trinitarian concept of God in our contemplation of Christ and our experience of the Spirit.

3. *The Dialectic of Christology and Eschatology*

Let us return to the consideration of the history of Christ. We can try to sum up and understand this history from two aspects: *protologically* and *eschatologically*, in the light of its beginning and in the light of its end.[16] Protologically we talk about the Father's sending of Christ into the world. Eschatologically we talk about his being raised from the dead to the Father. Protologically his being sent points to his origin with the Father. Eschatologically his resurrection points to his future with the Father. His messianic mission in the world corresponds to his eschatological gathering of the world. His pre-existent origin corresponds to his eschatological future. His becoming man in time corresponds to his becoming God (*theosis*) in eternity. His surrender to death on the cross corresponds to his exaltation to the right hand of God. His passion corresponds to his glorification and his descent into hell to his ascension. Historical thinking is analogous to protological thinking in being related to a given fact and in asking about its origins and grounds in order to explain it. When we relate a *historical narrative* we always begin at the beginning, and ultimately come to the end. But when we think *eschatologically* we begin with the end and from there arrive at the beginning. Historically we understand an event in the light of its origin and ask about its beginnings, its grounds and its origin. Eschatologically we understand an event in the light of its future, and ask about its goal, its end, and its meaning. The two ways of looking at things do not exclude one another; they are complementary, and belong together if we are to achieve the full understanding of a history.

For an understanding of the history of Christ this means that we have to view his death on the cross both in the light of the life he lived and his messianic sending, and in the light of his resurrection and his eschatological future – and that we have simultaneously to relate the two aspects to one another. Historically we therefore talk about Jesus of Nazareth, but eschatologically we confess Jesus the Kyrios. The historical understanding of Christ 'from the beginning' and the eschatological understanding of Christ 'from the end' will have to complement one another. So we shall have to complement our understanding of Jesus in the light of his sending by our understanding of Jesus in the light of his resurrection.

As we have seen, the classical doctrine of the Trinity was basically the idea of the Trinity in the sending, because it was built up on the contemplation of the history of Christ in the light of his sending, and on the experience of the history of the Holy Spirit in the light of his sending and outpouring. The idea of the Trinity in the origin, and the concept of the order of origin within the Trinity, developed with theological cogency from the inference that led from the history of the sendings of Son and Holy Spirit to the eternal foundation of that sending. Against the background of the Trinity in the origin, therefore, Christology pre-eminently stressed the sending of Jesus, the incarnation of the Son of God, the history of his passion and his giving of himself to death on the cross – and stressed them in that order. His sending was consummated in his self-giving and his incarnation was consummated in his death. The eschatological statements about the history of Christ, his resurrection, his exaltation, his transfiguration and his handing over of divine rule to the Father, receded into the background. The attention of incarnational Christology was concentrated in a one-sided way on the origin of Christ and asked about its basis in time and eternity.

If, on the other hand, we now enquire eschatologically about Christ's future, about the purpose of his mission and the end of his

history, then we are not criticizing or rejecting the previous
doctrine of the Trinity in the origin and in the sending, but are
simply taking them further, in accordance with the double understanding of the history of Christ 'in the light of his sending' and 'in
the light of his resurrection'. We then encounter the Trinity in the
glorification and the eschatological unity of God. From the protological origin of the history of Christ *from* God, we come to the
eschatological goal of the history of Christ *in* God.

4. *The Trinity in the Glorification and the Eschatological Unity of God*

In the framework of the Trinity in the origin, the Father was
always spoken of first, then the Son, and finally the Holy Spirit,
who proceeds from, or is sent by, the Father and the Son. The
Trinity in the sending had to be described in corresponding terms.
All activity proceeds from the Father; the Son is both passive and
active; the Holy Spirit is merely passive.

In the framework of the eschatological unity of God we must
first talk about the Holy Spirit, then about the Son, and finally
about the Father, who is united with the Son through the Spirit.
The Trinity in the glorification has to be described correspondingly:
all activity proceeds from the Holy Spirit. The Holy Spirit is the
one who glorifies; he glorifies both the Son and the Father. The
Son can be glorified, but only through the Spirit; whereas the Son
for his part can also glorify, but only the Father; the Father is
glorified both through the Spirit and through the Son.

On what perception is the trinitarian concept of the eschatological glorification based?

It is based on the perception of the history of Christ seen in the
light of its goal and its future. In the New Testament the word
doxa is the word used for the divine glory, divine splendour, divine
power and divine beauty.[17] *Doxa* is the term used both for the
godhead of the Father and for the godhead of Christ. Jesus was
raised from the dead by the glory of the Father (Rom. 6.4). He was
taken up into the glory of the Father (I Tim. 3.16). For the glory
of God the Father he was exalted after he had humbled himself,
and was made Kyrios over all things (Phil. 2.11).

Whereas for Isaiah the glory of God was the quintessence of the
divine future that was to be expected (40.5), the resurrection of

Jesus through the glory of the Father, into the glory of the Father, and for the sake of the glory of the Father, means his resurrection into this eschatological divine future. That is why, conversely, these eschatological statements about the coming glory of God can also be transferred to Christ, for in his death and resurrection eschatology becomes historical and history becomes eschatological. If he has been raised into the glory of the coming God, then in him and through his history this glory already enters the misery of this present time. That is why the 'Lord of glory' (I Cor. 2.8) now stands for the 'God of glory' (Acts 7.2). Just as the rule of God has taken on historical form in the lordship of Christ, so the glory of the Father has been anticipated in the glorification of Christ. The radiance of the divine glory is therefore reflected in the face of Christ and through him illuminates the hearts of men and women, as the light shone out of darkness on the first day of creation (II Cor. 4.6).

All statements about the glory of Christ concern his transfiguration after Easter. The application of the word to the earthly Jesus is strictly limited. Mark and Matthew only talk about his glory when they are looking towards the parousia. In Luke the visible appearance of his glory at his birth points to his divine origin (Luke 2.9), while his transfiguration on the mountain (9.28ff.) is an anticipation of his eschatology. Only John talks about the glory of the earthly Jesus, because he describes the whole life of Jesus as being the mode of being of the exalted one. Faith in the exalted one therefore already recognizes the glorification of the Father in the suffering of the Son, and the glorification of the Son in his death on the cross.

The eschatological understanding of the history of Christ 'in the light of his resurrection' will therefore recognize this history as being the history of God's glorification. This divine glorification is understood in trinitarian terms. The Son glorifies the Father through his obedience. The Son is glorified through the glory, into the glory, and for the sake of the Father's glorification.

On what *experience* is this trinitarian concept of the eschatological glorification of God based?

It is based on the experience of personal participation in the purpose and future of the history of Christ. Fellowship with Christ is not merely participation in his mission and his suffering; it is at the same time the partaking of his resurrection and his glory (Phil.

3.10). The mission of Christ is consummated in the glorifying of believers and of creation. In that glorification and with that glorification Christ arrives at his own glorification. That is why he is called 'the hope of glory' (Col. 1.27), and why we expect that he 'will glorify our lowly body to be like his glorious body' (Phil. 3.21). The power which ensures and effects this glorification of man in fellowship with Christ is the Holy Spirit. That is why the Holy Spirit is called the beginning and guarantee (AV 'earnest') of glory. The Holy Spirit glorifies Christ in believers and joins them with the new humanity of the risen Christ. In II Cor. 3.7ff. Paul makes the link between the Lord, the Spirit and the glorification of man the theme of the passage. Through knowledge of the glory of the Lord, those who know are themselves transformed, ἀπὸ δόξης εἰς δόξαν. The proclamation of Christ therefore takes place ἐν δόξῃ. But this means that through the Holy Spirit the eschatological glory of Christ is efficacious in our present life. From the hidden glory of the present fellowship of Christ, eyes turn to the future glory in perfect fellowship with God.

Here, therefore, the experience of the glorification of Christ and the Father through the workings of the Holy Spirit in us is understood in the light of his eschatological future. The meaning and purpose of fellowship with Christ is hence ultimately the glorification of man in the glorification of God the Father. The contemplation of the history of Christ 'in the light of his resurrection' and the experience of the history of the Spirit 'in the light of coming glory' is not fertile ground for protological thinking, which directs its questions back towards foundations and origin; it provides the basis for the eschatological thinking that hurries eagerly ahead towards the goal and the consummation.

As the 'theological final clauses' in the New Testament prove, the teleological principle of thought penetrates the very heart of the Christian message. Paul especially gives an expressly eschatological interpretation to the traditional confessional statements about Christ's death and resurrection; he links them together by 'final' (or intentional) clauses, introduced by ἵνα. Why did Christ come, and die, and why was he raised? For the forgiveness of sins, for righteousness, in order to be the Lord of the dead and the living, for the sake of the salvation of the world – but ultimately for the glorification of God the Father.

For finally the original purpose of creation will be achieved and all creation will realize its original destiny in the eschatological hymn of thanksgiving: 'To him be glory for ever' (Rom. 11.36; cf. Rev. 1.6, etc.)[18]

The history of the Spirit, who glorifies the Father and the Son through the liberation, the faith and the joy of man, already reveals and anticipates here and now the glorified and new creation in the coming, unhindered and uncontradicted glorification of God himself. The trinitarian history of glorification leads to the eschatological unity of God.

Just as the Trinity in the sending is, from its very origin, open to the world and to man, because it is the 'threefoldness' of seeking love, so the Trinity in the glorification is open for the gathering and uniting of men and creation in God, because it is the 'tri-unity' of gathered love. Through the sending of Christ and the Spirit, the 'history of the Trinity' is opened for the history of the gathering, uniting and glorifying of the world in God and of God in the world. In Adrienne von Speyr's words, 'The relationship of the divine persons to one another is so wide that it has room for the whole world.'[19]

The Holy Spirit glorifies Christ in us and us in Christ for the glory of God the Father. By bringing this about, he unites us and creation with the Son and the Father, as he unites the Son himself with the Father. The Spirit is the bond of fellowship and the power of unification. Together with God the Father and through God the Son, he is the unifying God. The history of the Spirit is the history of these unifications.

In protological thinking it is usual to move backwards from the sending of Christ and the Spirit to the original, threefold person of God, and behind that to arrive at the divine unity. In this inferential thinking, therefore – as the traditional doctrine of the Trinity consistently shows – the unity of God comes first, as being ontologically the basis of his threefoldness. Thus Thomas Aquinas puts the doctrine of the Trinity after the doctrine of the single divine nature. If we were to abstract from the three divine persons, what would remain would be the one, absolute divine nature.[20] In eschatological thinking, on the other hand, the unity of God is the final, eschatological goal, and this unity contains in itself the whole union of the world with God and in God. Eschatologically, therefore, the unity of God is bound up with the salvation of creation, just as glory is bound up with his glorification through everything that lives. Just as his glory is offered to him out of the world by the Holy Spirit, so his unity too is presented to him through the unification of the world with himself in the Holy Spirit. The history of the Spirit, which unites man and creation with the Son and the Father, is hence directed towards the perfect unity of the Son with the Father. In eschatological thinking, therefore, the notion of the unity in the Trinity is different from the notion of unity found in protological thinking. Here it is soteriologically imbued, whereas there it has the function of an eternal premise. So eschatologically it is also possible to talk about the 'union of God' and not merely about the 'unity of God'. Unfamiliar though this alteration sounds to Western thinking, which starts from origins, there are models for it in Old Testament thought. Franz Rosenzweig interprets the *Shema Israel* in this way: 'To acknowledge God's unity – the Jew calls it uniting God. For this unity is, in that it becomes; it is a Becoming Unity. And this Becoming is laid on the soul of man and in his hands.' Rosenzweig relates this 'divine union' to that 'cutting off of God from himself' which is described in the mystical doctrine of the *shekinah*:

> God himself cuts himself off from himself, he gives himself away to his people, he suffers with their sufferings, he goes with them into the misery of the foreign land, he wanders with their wanderings . . . God himself, in that he 'sells himself' to Israel – and what should be more natural for 'the God of our Fathers'! – and suffers its fate with it, makes himself in need of redemption. In this way, in this suffering, the relationship between God and the remnant points beyond itself.[21]

Is not what is here, in Jewish terms, entrusted to Israel, in Christian thinking the workings of the Holy Spirit, who glorifies and 'unites' God in and through believers? If the divine unity were to be described in the doctrine of the Trinity as *koinonia* of the persons, instead of as *una natura*, this idea would not seem so unusual.

5. *The Experience of God*

Between the Trinity in its origins before time and the eschatological Trinity at the end of time lies the whole history of God's dealings with man and creation. By opening himself for this history in his seeking love, and by entering into it through his sending of the Son and the Spirit, God also experiences this history in its breadth and depth.[22] In this context we must drop the old philosophical axioms about God's 'nature'. God is not unchangeable, if to be unchangeable means that he could not in the freedom of his love open himself to the changeable history with man and creation. God is not incapable of suffering, if this means that in the freedom of his love he would not be receptive to suffering over the contradiction of man and the self-destruction of his creation. God is not perfect, if this means that he did not in the freedom of his love want the humanity and creation which he loves to be necessary to his perfection. God is not invulnerable, if this means that he could not open himself to the experience of the cross. Being the history of God's seeking love, the history of the sending of the Son and the Holy Spirit is also the history of God's 'desire and thirst',[23] and is in this way the history of his pain and suffering.

The incarnation of the Son therefore brings about something 'new' even within the Trinity, for God himself. After the Son's return the relationship between the Father and the Son is no longer entirely the same. The Father has become different through his surrender of the Son, and the Son too has become different through the experience of his passion in the world. Through his love for the Son, who suffers from sin and experiences sin itself in his death on the cross, God 'experiences' something which belongs essentially to the redemption of the world: he experiences pain. In the night of his death on the cross, in the abandonment of the Son by the Father and of the Father by the Son, God himself experiences surrender in the form of death and rejection. We might add that here God has a new experience because he has resolved from eternity in favour of seeking love, and the conditions that make this experience possible are inherent in this resolve to go out of himself. God goes through the experience of the cross, but that means that he has absorbed this death into eternal life, and therefore does not want to be glorified in any other way than through the glorification of the crucified Jesus, 'the Lamb who was slain' (Rev. 5.12; 7.14ff.; 12.10ff.). Just as the crucified Christ by this means became what Käsemann calls 'the eternal signature' of the lordship of God, so he also becomes the eternal signature of God's glorification and of the eschatological unity of the Trinity.

What applies to the experience of God in the history of the Son also applies in its own way to the experience of God in the history of the Holy Spirit. God does not desire glory without his glorification through man and creation in the Spirit. God does not desire to find rest without the new creation of man and the world through the Holy Spirit. God does not desire to be united with himself without the uniting of all things with him. It is in this context that the eschatological vision in Revelation belongs – that 'salvation (*soteria*) is come to (RSV belongs to) our God . . . and to the Lamb' (7.10; 12.10; 19.1). The 'salvation' which God receives at the end is offered to him through the glorification, the thanksgiving, and the pleasure of creation in the Spirit. This world-embracing pneumatology corresponds to the no less comprehensive Christology of Paul, according to which the Son only completes his obedience to the Father when all things have been put under his feet – when all dominion, authority and power, and the last enemy, death, have been destroyed, and when he himself gives the kingdom entrusted to him to the Father (I Cor. 15.26–28), so that God 'may be all in all' (AV). The transference of the kingdom from the Son to the Father at the End-time is to be understood both as a world-embracing event which completes history, and as an event within the Trinity itself. Analogously, the glorification of God at the End-time in the Spirit and through the Spirit is to be understood as a world-embracing, world-renewing event, and at the same time as an event within the Trinity. God comes to his glory in that creation arrives at its consummation. Creation arrives at its consummation in that God comes to his glorification. For 'salvation' lies in the unity of soteriology and doxology.

If we trace the idea of the Trinity in the sending consistently through to the end, then – in view of the Son's passion, his execrated death and his descent into hell – we are bound to talk about the vulnerability, the suffering and the pain of the seeking love which is in God himself. God experiences suffering, death and hell. That is the way he experiences history. If we hope for the eschatological unity of God, then – in view of the resurrection of Christ, his exaltation and lordship, as well as remembering the history of the Spirit – we must talk about God's joy (as already in Isa. 62.4–5; Zeph. 3.17), God's happiness and felicity (I Tim. 1.11):[24] 'There will be more joy in heaven over one sinner who repents than over ninety-nine righteous persons' (Luke 15.7; cf. also Matt. 25.21: 'Enter into the joy of your master'; John 15.11; 16.20; Rom. 14.17; 15.13; etc.). This is the way God creates history.

God experiences history in order to create history. He goes out of himself in order to gather to himself. He becomes vulnerable, takes suffering and death on himself in order to heal, to liberate and to confer his eternal life. This means that there is a tendency for the resurrection to take supremacy over the cross, for the exaltation to acquire ascendency over the humiliation, and for the joy of God to have more weight than his pain. Consequently the Trinity in the glorification also has the tendency to predominate and take precedence over the Trinity in the sending. Formally it corresponds to the Trinity in the sending, but in content it goes beyond it, just as the gathering love corresponds to the seeking love of God yet goes far beyond it through the gathering and uniting of mankind and the world with God.

The history of God's passion in Christ serves the history of God's joy in the Spirit. This in its turn will only be completed in the all-comprehending and therefore eternal felicity of God. That is the final goal of the history of God's passion. But when this goal has been reached, the history of God's passion will not be superseded and a thing of the past. As suffering endured and made fruitful, it remains the ground for eternal joy in the salvation of God and of the new creation.

6. *Two Brief Methodological Comments*

1. If we think theologically in the movement of the sending, then we have God as background, so to speak, and the world in front of us, as the object of messianic activity. This theological orientation is necessary. It has led ecumenically to the relationship that is called the 'action-reflection method'. This is theology in messianic action. Practice precedes theory and theory reflects practice in the light of the sending.

If we think theologically in the movement of the glorification, then the movement is reversed: we have God in front of us, as it were, and the world with us and round about us. That is theology in doxological joy. Protestant theology especially has lost this orientation, for it has moralized the rule of God and made Christian obedience a matter of the law. But the lordship of God is not revealed without the beauty of his grace, and there is no free obedience either without astonishment, gratitude and pleasure. Without this aesthetic side of faith, its moral side becomes joyless and constrained. Without the love of God, love of our neighbour loses the character of spontaneous love.

2. Were these ideas about 'the history of the Trinity' speculative and abstract? They really aimed to comprehend the individual event, the special experience and the particular practice in the context of the movement of the whole in the history of God. That cannot be called abstract. To be abstract rather means isolating the individual event from its history, isolating the individual experience from the context of its life, and isolating particular actions from their time. We isolate objects by removing them from their surroundings, by subjecting them to one particular point of view, and by blotting out all other aspects. Some people think that by doing this they are being 'quite concrete'. But really they are thinking highly abstractly. Speculative thinking is not abstract thinking. It has nothing whatsoever to do with remoteness from experience and practice. It tries to understand the single event *within the context* of its history, the individual experience *within* the whole of life, and the action *within* the context of meaning of its future. Without the (in this sense) 'speculative' understanding of the history of Christ and the history of the Spirit in the supervening movement of the trinitarian history of God, perception, experience and action are blind, meaningless, abstract and – isolated. Integrating trinitarian thinking, however, sees itself as element of unification in the history of God, and as being to this extent doxology.

VII

THE HOPE OF RESURRECTION AND
THE PRACTICE OF LIBERATION

1. *The Cry for Freedom*[1]

Today the cry for freedom can be heard all over the world. Everywhere we find the signs of a 'revolution of mounting expectations' and at the same time an ever-deeper sensibility towards suffering. When freedom is near the chains begin to gall. Where others have freed themselves from century-long oppression, people see that the limitations and failures which they had previously silently accepted and borne are unnecessary and can be overcome. What had been thought impossible has become possible after all. Wherever people and nations recognize their potentialities, they glimpse the dawn of their future and hunger for liberty. Yet this hunger for liberation is shown first of all by the change from dumb suffering to conscious pain. Quiet apathy is transformed into noisy protest.

People are suffering from the economic exploitation of man by man and are crying out for social justice. People are suffering from the political oppression of man by man and are fighting for the political recognition of their human dignity and human rights. People are suffering from the cultural alienation of man from man through racism and sexual discrimination, and are seeking for the fullness of a truly human life in solidarity with one another. People are suffering from the emptiness of their personal life, which disappears so meaninglessly among the structures of a technocratic and bureaucratic society, and are seeking for personal identity. Finally, in, with and under capitalism, dictatorship, racism, sexual discrimination and nihilism, people are suffering under the deeply ingrained primal fear which makes them so aggressive and inhumane towards other people. 'Man' is the

original name for the messianic mystery or secret; but in the reality
we live in it is often an expression for 'the mystery of evil'. That is
why we are suffering not so much from 'the death of God' as from
'the death of man'.[2]

But the cry for freedom is not only the cry of exploited, oppressed,
alienated, divided and frightened humanity. It is also the cry of the
creation which man is destroying. *Nature* and *our own bodies* have
become alien to us. We have turned the natural environment into
material for our exploiting domination. We have debased the body
we *are* into the body we *have*, and thus have condemned them both
to death. That is why 'the creation itself will be set free from its
bondage to decay' and 'waits with eager longing for the revealing
of the sons of God' (Rom. 8.19ff.). Nature waits for her 'true
resurrection' into the human kingdom of man, said Marx. The
body waits for its liberation from the sublimation of the spirit and
the repressions of morality, said Freud. Matter in us and round
about us is hungering for the power of the new creation.

The cry for liberty therefore unites humanity and nature in a
single hope. They will either be destroyed by their division and
enmity, or they will survive as partners in a new community.[3]

But the cry for liberty does not only run through mankind and
nature. It is *God's own cry* as well. The spirit of God himself
hungers and sighs in the groans of the hungry, in the torment of
prisoners and in nature's silent death pangs. The messianic
traditions of Judaism and Christianity do not talk about an
apathetic God, enthroned in heaven in untouched bliss. They
show us the God who suffers with his forsaken creation because he
loves it.[4] He suffers with his people in exile, he suffers with his
humanity which has become inhuman, he suffers with his creation
which is enslaved and under sentence of death. He suffers with
them, he suffers because of them, and he suffers for them. His
suffering is his messianic secret. For he has created man for liberty
– to be the image of himself. He created nature for joy – as the play
of his good pleasure. That is why God is affected by the world's
history of suffering through his creative Spirit, and is involved in it
through his own pain. His Spirit hungers, sighs and cries out for
liberty. His Spirit intercedes for those who have fallen dumb,
intercedes 'with sighs too deep for words' (Rom. 8.26), and not
with a glorious shout of victory. It is only in this way that he keeps
the hope of creation alive.

The cry for freedom is therefore *universal*. It is the hunger of men and women. It is the desire of nature. It is the passion of God, as it was revealed in the crucified Christ. So as long as all men are not free, the people who now believe themselves to be free are not truly free either. As long as man fails to be reconciled to nature, and nature to man, there is no complete happiness. As long as God himself is still enduring his passion and has not yet come to rest in a new creation that corresponds to him, everything only lives from hope, not yet in fulfilled joy. Struggle is still the order of the day; victory has not yet been won.

A *theology of liberation* sees all individual sufferings and failures in the world against the background of God's patient suffering. It therefore sees all partial movements towards liberation against the horizon of God's own perfect and final history of liberation. In this way it introduces the testimony of God's suffering and God's freedom into each individual liberation movement.[5] That can be of immense importance for these liberation movements in at least three ways:

(*i*) When we have to do with freedom, we must not think trivially. We must free ourselves from egoism and begin to think about other people, and even about the enemies of our own freedom. It is understandable that every political or cultural liberation movement takes the stamp of its opponents in its daily struggles. In doing so it conforms to the law of reciprocity and often enough to the law of revenge. But this corrupts the freedom and humanity which we have to fight for. The alienations which inevitably come about in the course of the struggle must be overcome again if we want to show that there is 'a better justice' without losing our credibility. 'Will this inevitable revolutionary degradation of people to the status of things come to an end in the course of the struggle itself, or is it in fact something that is only to be ended after the revolution?' Herbert Marcuse answered this question, which was put to him by a Berlin student in 1967, with a sure instinct for the disquiet that Jesus causes: 'In a world in which hate has been everywhere institutionalized, nothing is more frightful than the preaching of love, "Do not hate your enemy".'[6] Marcuse called the hatred of exploitation and oppression a humane and humanistic element in itself. But if justifiable hatred of exploitation does not go hand in hand with hope for the birth of true man in the exploiter, revolution will become more and more like the oppression itself. So the 'revolutionary degradation of people to things' must already be eliminated during the struggle itself. Liberated humanity cannot be postponed eschatologically to some date 'after the revolution'. A Christian theology of revolution lives from the anticipation of humanity in the midst of inhumanity, and from the goad of present reconciliation in the midst of the struggle for the redemption of this still unredeemed world.[7]

(*ii*) When we have to do with liberation, we must not think in particularist terms but must overcome our ideological fixation, or concentration on our own interests. It is unfortunate that a dispute has broken out between the different liberation movements about 'the root of all evil'. Socialists maintain that capitalism is the source of everything that is bad, and call racialism and sexual discrimination merely capitalistic epiphenomena. Others believe that racial humiliation is the chief calamity. Supporters of women's liberation view the sexual oppression of the woman as being the beginning of all oppressions. Ecologists, finally, find the pattern of all exploitation in the material exploitation of nature. This dispute is reminiscent of the dispute of the pre-Socratic philosophers about primal matter, and whether this was to be found in water, aether or fire. It is a kind of negative metaphysics of evil, to which ideological fixation has led. Only seldom does anyone ask the question, why and through what have people arrived at capitalistic, racialist and sexist aggression? But in most situations the one thing causes the other: everywhere we find oppressed oppressors, who aggressively pass on to others the suffering which they themselves experience. It is like a chain without an end and without a beginning. A Christian theology of liberation sees a primal fear of cosmic breadth and trans-personal depth at work in, together with and beneath the repressions in the different sectors of life – a fear which is always and everywhere turning into aggression. This insight does not mean that Christian theology will call the very real movements for liberation unimportant; on the contrary. But it will break down the ideological fixation and press for co-operation with other liberation movements. The struggle for liberation is always a self-critical struggle too. There are few people who are able to say: I am quite simply oppressed, and am not, in some other respect, myself the oppressor. The anti-capitalist struggle does not lead to new humanity unless it becomes at the same time a fight against dictatorship and racialism, and unless it issues out of actually experienced liberation from that primal fear and aggression. The chains that form the vicious circles of oppression have many links. Without an alliance between the liberating forces, these vicious circles will not be broken.

(*iii*) Freedom is a rare blessing, but a dangerous one as well. We cry out for liberation, but at the same time we are frightened by freedom. The risk of freedom in an unfree world is a big one. In order to take that risk we need an unshakable hope, which would rather be disappointed than disappoint others, and a firm trust, which would rather be wounded than hurt others. 'Anyone who helps the lost is lost himself', said Berthold Brecht,[8] in order to show how high the price of freedom is. And it is true that anyone who is prepared for freedom must be prepared for the cross. The messianic secret 'man' is seldom revealed in any other way than 'as dying and behold we live'. Freedom on the cross: that is the gospel. For Christ is not the one who brings order into the world but what Reinhold Schneider called our 'deadly freedom'.

Many enthusiastic liberation movements have perished because of their superficial optimism. Without that 'hope against hope' which is born out of readiness for suffering and the cross, resistance and assurance can find no firm ground. Franz Kafka expressed this very soberly and yet hopefully in his description of a 'world without people'.

> It is not a contradiction of the premonition of some final liberation, when on the following day the captivity remains unchanged or is even stricter, or even if it is expressly declared that the captivity is never to end. On the contrary, all this can be the necessary presupposition for ultimate liberation.

The Job-like figure of Israel, the people of the Exodus, suffering for a thousand long years, remains a point of orientation for all liberation movements which in the depths of their hope encounter the messianic kingdom of 'man'.[9] And the fact that the liberty of the resurrection became manifest through the forsaken, oppressed and crucified Son of man remains the sign of hope for the hopeless.

2. *Freedom in the Light of Hope*

Christian faith understands itself as being initially the beginning of a freedom such as the world has not yet seen. The Christian does not merely believe *in* freedom. His faith *is* his liberation – from fear for hope, from self-seeking for love, and from the enslavement of evil for resistance to evil. 'For freedom Christ has set us free', says Paul in Gal. 5.1, 'therefore do not submit again to a yoke of slavery.'[10] Wherever man believes, he experiences his resurrection into the liberty of eternal life in the midst of this life, which leads to death.

Freedom in Christian terms does not only mean 'insight into necessity', as it did for the Greeks. Nor does it any longer mean the autonomous power over themselves of individuals or of political bodies. Christian freedom is born out of the resurrection of Christ and is alive in resistance to the vicious circle of law, sin and death. Christian faith participates in the inexhaustible potentialities of God. 'With God all things are possible' and 'all things are possible to him who believes'. This inexhaustible fullness of divine potentiality reveals itself in the creative act of the raising of the crucified Christ. Faith therefore means participation in the creative act and participation in the process of the new creation of the world out of God. Resurrection is the revelation of this new, creative liberty of God, which was unknown to the ancient world of the Greeks and Romans. Faith means being raised into this creative liberty of God and acting out of its potentialities.

God is no longer the Roman emperor; he is no longer man in his beauty and strength, as he was for the Greeks. He is not the promise of power. He is the assurance that we can only create a qualitatively new future if we identify ourselves with those who are the poorest and most wretched in the world – if we throw in our lot with them to the point that we can conceive of no true victory but theirs alone.[11]

A faith like this is the power 'to move mountains', as the Bible puts it. The Bible also talks about the mountains being made low and the valleys being exalted, so that all people may see the glory of the Lord *together*. In other words, Christian faith is the resurrection faith of prisoners, the blind, the guilty, the oppressed and the ill-treated; and it leads to creative life in places where death rules.

Christian freedom is therefore not a purely religious freedom, or a freedom of the mind, cut off and separate from the universal cry for freedom in the world. Nor does it exhaust itself in 'the free practice of religion' in 'the church of your choice'. Christian freedom understands itself rather as the beginning and foretaste of that all-embracing freedom for which all men and all things yearn. That is why Christian faith does not separate men and women from the world but makes them one with unredeemed creation. 'Their very faith makes them one with unredeemed creation, in so far as faith is in its very nature hope and therefore a looking for the redemption of the body.'[12] Hegel, Heine, Weitling and others were therefore right when, during the nineteenth-century revolutions in Europe, they called Christianity the religion of freedom. If that were not the centre of Christianity, liberation from that religion would bring more freedom than life in it does. Wherever the church does not liberate people for this creative faith, but instead spreads religious, moral and political oppression, it must be resisted for Christ's sake. In our existing churches too, the freedom of faith and the religion of fear are at odds with one another.

Liberty can be interpreted as the free choice of the will (*liberum arbitrium*). In this case one imputes an absolute sovereignty to man and provides him with divine attributes. Ever since Kant, German Idealism has considered the problem of autonomy. In its analysis and reflections it has never encountered the 'I' itself as an autonomous court of appeal; it has always only arrived at the 'process of autonomy', so that Fichte said, 'it should never have been asserted that "man is free", but only that "man inevitably strives, hopes, assumes that he is free".'[13] For man, liberty of choice only arises out of the fundamental and overriding process of liberation. Without free scope there is no freedom. Without liberation there is no liberty of life. And even in the free choices that are open, freedom must choose freedom and not lack of freedom. It can only be freedom for life, not freedom for death.

Freedom in the light of messianic hope is something different from freedom of choice: it is passion for the possible. It comes into being when the fetters binding people to the past and to the transitory are broken, and when, in the free scope open to us, the future of God is laid hold of in anticipation. Liberation takes place where the new creation of all things, which Christ will complete in his day, is already anticipated. 'A man experiences this condition of *being* free only as a perpetual *becoming* free.'[14] Freedom as the completed process of liberation is for Christian hope the eschatological goal of God's new creation. But in Christ and in the activity of the Spirit this future casts its light ahead of it into the darkness of history. The reality of freedom is the eschatologically new and free world. The effects of this freedom are present in the experiences and actions of liberation. Freedom therefore only comes about when we pass through the doors of prisons in hope for the space of eschatological freedom which opens up behind them. Or, to put it another way: we do not only achieve freedom for the first time in 'the promised land'; we have it first of all in the 'exodus' and in the 'long march' through the desert. This means theoretically that we should no longer reason deductively from a promised subject of freedom to freedom's effects, but should think inductively from the specifically experienced effects of freedom in liberation to the freedom that is to come. With this reversal eschatological theology becomes concrete and leaves behind it idealism's illusions about freedom.

Liberation in the light of hope for freedom has two sides. It lives in the category of 'nevertheless' and in the category of 'how much more'.[15] Its right is the right to resistance and the right to a future.

What does its 'nevertheless' stand in opposition to? Because resurrection is a resurrection from the dead, the liberating hope is in opposition to death. It loves life, not death. Only 'life as the good, the wholly living life, wholly snatched from death, is *peace*.'[16]

In this context death is not merely the physical end of a human life. Death is a personal and political power in the midst of life. Many people have given themselves up to the death instinct (Freud's term) while they were still alive. Others make 'a pact with death' and the threat of death, out of despair or cynicism. Whole cultures can become necrophile, Erich Fromm tells us, when the possessing of dead things spreads its tentacles over living human relationships and suffocates them. Wherever fear of freedom spreads, dying already begins. Conversely, liberation begins when we are delivered from fear and are set in a free space. All liberation movements begin when a few people are fearless and act differently from what their oppressors or their environment demands of them. Every oppression uses the threat of death. That is why one can say that everywhere the rule of force is built up on death and has associated itself with death.

Liberation in the light of hope resists fear, the death instinct and the threat of death. It resists the noisy death of bombs and the creeping death of souls. This resistance is the first aspect of liberation. A person experiences liberation where he experiences resistance of this kind. The future of liberation is the other side, and its hope is greater. '*How much more*', Paul often says, when he has stopped talking about 'liberation from' and is talking about 'liberation for' (e.g., Rom. 5.15-20). How much more is God's grace than man's sin. How much more is his future than the misery of the present. How much more is his freedom than merely the liberation of what is not free. With Paul Ricoeur, we can call this 'the economy of undeserved abundance'. If we wanted to put it in theological terms we might say: the liberating God is himself on the move and open for the future that lies ahead of him.[17] The liberating God is on the way to his kingdom, in which he will be all in all. This 'surplus' of hope for freedom is really inherent in all liberation movements. The oppressed peoples in Africa and Asia began with the national struggle for liberation from colonial rule. In a second phase, the people in these nations must now free themselves from the rule of class and caste. First of all they need liberation as independence; then liberation as social justice; then liberation for a society that respects human dignity; then liberation for the full development of the human person. Liberation in the light of hope is like a train that is travelling through history into an ever-wider future. It cannot be stopped. We cannot be content with any success, because of the surplus of hope in the process of liberation. Consequently what freedom itself is cannot be very well defined. For in this world all definitions are a form of domination. They establish and fix something that is still fluid. Definitions bind but do not free. We experience what freedom is in real, inward and outward liberations. A corresponding liberating way of thinking and talking must therefore treat freedom in a way that frees, not one that binds, 'in-fining', not defining, pulling frontiers down, not building them up. Otherwise it cannot become thinking about something living but remains the thinking that kills.[18]

The 'nevertheless' with which liberation resists oppression is only the dark, reverse side of the assured 'how much more' of its hope. The necessary resistance must be founded on this hope if it is not to degenerate into mere reaction and end in disappointment. But the free hope for freedom must lead to resistance if it is not to become illusory.

3. *The Church in the Liberating Process of God*

Today it is not easy to talk about the role of the church in the divine liberating process. Many people who are working for liberation in one way or another no longer expect anything from the church. Many others, who are living in the church, have become so blind that they no longer see that the need to free the oppressed has a Christian justification. They do not see because they do not want to see. Unless the churches are rescued from their imprisonment in the ruling classes, races and nations, there will hardly ever be a rescuing church. Without the liberation of the churches from the ties binding them to particular levels of society, there will hardly ever be a liberating church for the poor. Today criticism of the church from outside can really be summed up under a single point: the church, with its religious symbols, its morality, its public institutions and its money is in many countries linked with a social system which spreads discord and injustice in the world. That is why the social criticism voiced by the victims of oppression will always become criticism of the religion of that particular society as well. This affects the church, wherever, and in so far as, this bourgeois religion is represented by the church. There is a growing feeling that the church is no longer free.

Who can liberate the church from its new Babylonian captivity? I do not believe that the church can be renewed by means of social and political criticism from outside, important though this is. There is no real need for the church to adapt itself to the modern world and new social and political tendencies. What it needs is renewal from within outwards, so that it becomes Christ's church. The nerve centre of the church is Jesus himself, for every church calls itself by his name and appeals to him. We must take the church radically at its word. *Jesus is the criterion within the church.* He is the one who shows up its lack of truth and its enslavement, for he alone is the origin of its truth and its freedom. Whether a church or a Christian community in a divided, oppressive and alienated society gives the impression of being itself divided, alienated and oppressive is determined first and last by a single criterion: has Jesus become a stranger, or is he the Lord who determines the church's existence? The social crisis of the church in the contemporary world is its crisis of identity. But its crisis of faith creates the crisis of its credibility. The church will be renewed and will become the representative of the liberty of Christ to the extent to which it remembers Christ and listens to his voice and to no other, following him alone and no other power.[19] How does this happen?

According to the testimony of scripture, Christ encounters the church as the crucified liberator. He came into this world, as Luke says 'to preach good news to the poor, to proclaim release to the captives and recovering of sight to the blind, to set at liberty those who are oppressed, to proclaim the acceptable year of the Lord' (Luke 4.18). Because of this unheard-of messianic mission he was finally crucified on Golgotha. A church which follows him, without any sidelong glances either to right or to left, will participate in his messianic work with all its powers and all the possibilities open to it. His mission is the church's mission too. But the more it brings the gospel to the poor, liberation to captives, and perception to the blind, the more it will also be drawn into Jesus' destiny and become a 'church under the cross'. It will come up against misunderstanding and resistance and ultimately persecution. Anyone who helps the lost must reckon with being lost himself. But the true church of Christ will be recognized by the powers of liberation which quicken it and radiate from it; and often enough also by the signs of the cross which it has to bear because of its resistance. It was right that the Reformation – and not only the Reformation – originally counted suffering as being among the notes of the church, after word and sacrament.

According to the testimony of scripture, Christ encounters the church as the risen liberator, who was raised from the death of humiliation into the glorious liberty of God. In him God has already broken the power of death and the spell of fear and the fetters of oppression. In him, the crucified Jesus, the world of death has already been overcome and unvanquishable life has already appeared. A church possessed by this risen liberator has been born again to a living hope. In the light of Easter it has been sent with a great hope into the dying world. It will strengthen all the little, limited, interim hopes with its assurance, freeing them both from arrogance and from resignation. In the resurrection of Christ, in this one person, the last limitation of freedom, the frontier of death, has been broken through. A church which lives from this breakthrough can therefore no longer take account of the little boundaries of death's rule in economic, political and cultural life; it will try to overcome the deadly forces of the negative in these sectors of life. And how should anyone who is filled with a great hope, in the light of Easter, be able to despair over life's many little disappointments? 'The risen Christ makes life a continual feast', said Athanasius. He makes life the feast of freedom.[20] By humbling

himself to death on the cross, this risen Christ has experienced all
the dimensions of suffering and forsakenness; and consequently
failures, suffering and finally death are also part of this feast of
freedom.[21] The spirit of the resurrection can only make life 'a
continual feast' in fellowship with the crucified Christ. The church
of the risen Christ can be called the community of the exodus. It is
the community of those who depart from slavery in Egypt and take
the long march through the wilderness to the promised land.
Israel's march through the desert was geographically a journey
from one country to another. The 'long march' of Christians does
not take them from one country to another but, in all countries,
from the past into the future. It must be understood historically,
not geographically. It is the long march through the institutions of
society out of oppression towards the goal of new, liberated forms
of life, in the expectation of that life which swallows up death
(I Cor. 15.55ff.).

According to the testimony of scripture, Christ encounters the
church in the Spirit.[22] This is the divine Spirit which, according to
Joel and Luke, 'is to be poured out on all flesh', in order to make it
live eternally. According to Paul, the Spirit is the power of the
resurrection, which gives mortal bodies life. This Spirit must not
be understood idealistically as some form of intellectual capacity,
or romantically as something emotional. The Spirit is the creative
power of God that makes the impossible possible and calls into
existence the things that do not exist (Rom. 4.17). A church which
is filled with the Spirit becomes a charismatic community. It
becomes the place of 'the manifestation of the Spirit' in the fullness
of the Spirit's gifts (I Cor. 12.7). Every charisma is both gift and
charge. The relation between the two is suggested by the German
words we would use here. *Gabe* – the gift – leads to *Aufgabe* – the
task: we are given something *for* some purpose. Every charisma is
a power of the new creation. The Spirit descends upon the talents
and potentialities which an individual possesses and activates them
for the kingdom of God, for the liberation of the world. According
to Paul this applies equally to the preacher and to the widow; it is
as true of the bishop as of one who exercises mercy. Through the
Spirit the whole of life, a person's profession, his political responsibilities, his relationships in the family, even his being Jew or
Gentile (circumcised and uncircumcised, I Cor. 7.18ff.) is taken
possession of by Christ and quickened for the liberation of the

world. That is why there are as many and varying charismata as there are many and varying people; but only the one Spirit and the one common future goal. The multiplicity of the charismata is as protean as creation itself. And this variety is not repressed or oppressed by the Spirit – life is freed from oppression and repression. For the Spirit descends upon all flesh in order to make it alive. In a charismatic community, therefore, there is no fundamental difference between the clergy and the laity; the only difference is a practical and charismatic one. Charismatically the whole people of God is involved religiously, politically and socially in the all-embracing liberation movement of God.

The more the church has its mind set on Christ alone and testifies only to his messianic mission in the world, the less it is a religious reflection of society. It then becomes a church under the cross, an exodus community, and a charismatic fellowship, showing in this way the powers of the new creation and the liberating fore-tokens of the free world that is to come. It is only when the church has grasped its own role in God's process of liberation that it can 'test the spirits' without fear and without being conformed to this world, and can so enter into an open and critical relationship with today's liberation movments.[23]

4. *Liberation in Five Dimensions*

Man is not a one-dimensional being. He always lives and suffers in many different dimensions at once. Consequently the process of liberation cannot proceed in a single dimension either. It has to work in different ways simultaneously, and must co-ordinate its efforts in life's different sectors. The process of liberation must be 'catholic' in the original sense of the word, for what is at stake is the freedom of the whole, and not the liberation of certain individuals at the cost of others. This orientation towards the whole must take account of every partial liberation movement. We cannot strive to liberate in one sphere by setting up a dictatorship in another. So we seek the traces of man's liberation in a whole series of dimensions. Only those are mentioned here which have separate validity, and cannot be reduced to other headings. At the same time, in every particular situation these dimensions combine, making up the fullness of life, in all its negative and positive aspects. But to distinguish between them can give us guiding lines for specific action. We begin with liberation in the economic dimension and end with liberation in the religious one. This is intended to indicate that liberation from hunger is the first thing, but not the most important. 'Man does not live from bread alone.' It is also intended to show, further, that religious liberation is the most important, inasmuch as without the liberation of men and women from apathy, fear and aggressiveness there can be no liberation in other spheres. Only people who have been liberated can liberate others. The mission of Jesus embraces all areas of life, from daily bread to the forgiveness of sins, because it means the messianic liberation of the whole; and 'the revelation of the Spirit' reaches all the areas of oppressed life in the charismata. So in the same way liberating activity must be present today in all sectors of life.

Liberation takes place today:

(*i*) In the struggle for economic justice against the exploitation of man.

(*ii*) In the struggle for human dignity and human rights against the political oppression of man.

(*iii*) In the struggle for human solidarity against the alienation of man from man.

(*iv*) In the struggle for peace with nature against the industrial destruction of the environment.

(*v*) In the struggle of hope against apathy in asserting the significance of the whole in personal life.

Today exploitation, oppression, alienation, the destruction of nature, and inner despair make up the vicious circle in which we are killing ourselves and our world. The cne involves the other to such an extent that many people are no longer able to see any way out. In this vicious circle what is individually good also makes for evil, because we often only achieve liberation in one sphere by building up repression in another. But by doing this we merely shift the mass of suffering and, instead of overcoming it, increase it, It is impossible to drive out one devil by another. That is why everything depends on the open co-operation of liberation movements and on co-ordinated strategies. I should like to illustrate this by a few examples:

(*i*) There is no liberation from economic need without political freedom. There is no political freedom without economic justice. If, and to the extent to which, 'socialism' means economic justice, and if, and to the extent to which, 'democracy' means political freedom on the basis of human rights, we shall be able to say, with Rosa Luxemburg, 'No socialism without democracy – no democracy without socialism'.[24] To try to achieve the conquest of economic need with the help of a political dictatorship would be to drive out one devil by another, and we should not be one bit nearer to freedom in the widest sense. On the other hand, to set up a political democracy without, or at the cost of, social justice would leave us in the same vicious circle. In actual fact we find 'socialism' in many countries today without democracy but with party dictatorship. We find countries in which swift industrial development is bought at the cost of political oppression, the suspension of constitutional rule, and martial law. We know other countries in which economic imperialism is allied with political democracy. These incongruities do not promote freedom. So in political democracies people must press for social justice and economic freedom, and in socialist dictatorships, or in the dictatorships of the developing countries, the goal must be political freedom and the establishment of fundamental human rights. There is no other way of achieving liberation in the context of these two dimensions of life.[25]

(*ii*) If we add the third dimension of the alienation of man from man through racialism, nationalism and sexual discrimination, the reciprocal effect of conditions on one another expands even more.[26] As long as the alienation of man from man is not overcome, it will be impossible to achieve either economic liberation from hunger or political liberation from oppression; for one group of people will always look on the other groups solely as enemies in 'the struggle for existence'. On the other hand, racialism, nationalism and sexual discrimination will remain active until we establish the economic and political conditions under which they can be overcome. We have called the conquest of the racialist, nationalist and sexist alienation of people from people 'solidarity'. We do not mean by this the repression of differences between races, peoples and sexes; we mean identity in recognition by others and the recognition of others in their own identity. The person who is different is not a rival in the struggle for existence. Fullness of humanity is shown in the motley variety of human temperaments and gifts. People can only become 'human' with one another – not without one another, and not against one another. The liberation from social roles which were fixed in the course of the ancient struggle for power does not arise automatically out of economic or political liberation; it is a complement to that liberation, but with its own rank and difficulties. Socialism cannot take possession of Black Power, and the democratic movement cannot take possession of women's liberation.[27] Anyone who reduces these things to a common denominator is betraying freedom.

(*iii*) Further, a human society deserving of the name cannot be built without peace with nature. We cannot overcome famine through forced industrial development, if at the same time we drive the world into ecological death. The values of the ecological crisis are neutral towards capitalistic and socialistic industrialization. This shows that here again there is a separate dimension which cannot be reduced to a common denominator together with others. In which way 'the limits of growth' are infringed is a matter of indifference to them. Exploited nature expresses her protest through her silent death. The dispute between socialism and capitalism is of only relative importance where these limits are concerned. Today a new phase must succeed the long phase of man's liberation from nature: the phase when nature is liberated from exploitation. The change of values which is necessary here – the values of progress, profits and the increase of power – will have a repercussion on the other dimensions of life and the movements for liberation there. At all events, in overcoming exploitation, oppression and alienation, we must not lose sight of suffering nature. Otherwise all our efforts will be, in the last resort, vain.

(*iv*) Unless we are prepared to fall victim to a materialistic illusion, we must recognize that the improvement of living conditions on the economic, political, cultural and natural levels does not automatically produce better people. Unless a person is liberated inwardly from the primal fear which makes him aggressive, or drives him into apathy, living conditions cannot be improved by anyone. In many countries today a growing helplessness, uncertainty and despondency is spreading below the surface of personal and public consciousness. People certainly see how they can contribute to liberation and what they must do, but there is no one who does it. This inward poisoning of interest in life is spreading, not merely in poverty-stricken societies, but in the prosperous ones as well. Fear and apathy will not be overcome simply through the conquest of economic need, political repression and cultural alienation. They represent a human misery of their own which cannot be reduced to any other dimension. Exploited, oppressed and alienated people are often 'a product of their bad conditions'. Aeschylus once said, 'Man loses half his virtue when he is enslaved.' Liberated man, on the other hand, is not a product of his own free conditions. Aeschylus did not say, 'Man acquires half his virtue when he is free'. Bad conditions drive men to evil. But good ones do not drive them to good. Here it depends on man himself whether and how he realizes his free potentialities. That is why the personal dimension, and with it the religious one, is of the greatest importance for life's emptiness or fullness of meaning. There will be neither economic nor political liberation, nor the liberation of nature, without man's conversion from fear and despondency to the faith which Paul Tillich called 'the courage to be', in defiance of non-being. In the situation of general discouragement, with all its well-known forms of escapism, Christian faith becomes the justification for hope.

This is shown by liberation from panic and apathy, the fear of death and the death instinct. It is shown practically through hope expressed in actions of liberation from the universal vicious circle in which the world has become involved. Without faith's hope for the divine messianic future there is no hope in action which can stand its ground. Without hope in action faith's hope becomes ineffective and irresponsible.

When we recognize the extent of the interdependencies of oppression in that vicious circle, we shall recognize the need for co-operation between the different forms of liberation. Not everyone can do everything all at once all the time. There are different gifts and different tasks, but the freedom we seek is one and therefore indivisible. Here we may remember once more the Pauline picture of the charismatic community, with which (in Rom. 12 and I Cor. 12) he tried to overcome the narrow-minded divisions in his congregations. The picture seems to me helpful, both for the church's position in the different situations in the world, and also for the forces which are working for the world's liberation. We find churches which only live in liturgy and prayer, because they have no other possibilities open to them. We find preaching communities, sacramental congregations, action groups, shalom groups, and many others. They do what they can with their charismata, according to the possibilities at their disposal. If they were mutually to recognize their different ways of approach they could complement one another and learn from one another. This mutual recognition could show them the latent potentialities which they had hitherto failed to activate in their particular situations. If one compares the action reports of groups working for the liberation of people in their particular sectors, one is faced again and again with the five dimensions we have mentioned. The 'points of entry' differ, and are bound to differ, according to the context. Not everyone can do everything all at once. Historically there are different paths to liberation, but only one goal of freedom. Without openminded co-operation between the different forces of liberation and their ability to learn from one another, we shall not get to see the kingdom of freedom. We only hear the divine cry of freedom when we listen to the universal cry for freedom and make it our own, wholly and not partially. For the hope of resurrection fills everything with the new life of love.

VIII

CREATION AS AN OPEN SYSTEM

1. Two Problems

(*i*) We all know that since the beginning of modern times there has been a crisis in the relationship between science and belief in creation. Science emancipated itself from the religious culture of the middle ages and founded the secular culture of modern times. Theology became apologetic, fighting a mere rearguard battle against the triumphal progress of science – either by limiting belief in creation *deistically* to the original contingency of the universe;[1] or by limiting it *existentially* to the personal contingency of human existence;[2] or by cutting off *church dogmatics* so completely from the sciences that the two neither interfere with one another nor have anything to say to one another.[3] In its intention to co-exist with the sciences, theology itself deepened the cleavage which it wanted to overcome. If today we are striving for a convergence between science and belief in creation, this presupposes a revision both of theology's traditional concept of creation, and of classical science's concept of nature. The ecological crisis caused by the progressive destruction of nature was brought about by Christianity and science together; and if man and nature want to win a chance to survive, then Christianity and science must together revise both the picture of man found in the traditional belief in creation ('subdue the earth', Gen. 1.28) and the picture of man reflected in Cartesian science ('Maître et possesseur de la nature').

(*ii*) Since the development of Christian dogmatics within the sphere of Greek thinking, theological method has always begun with the description of the creation of the world, and has finally arrived at the idea of the world's redemption. By thinking in this way, it always related redemption to creation and understood redemption in its light. The creation of the world was really the foundation of everything. In the beginning was God, the Creator, and his creation was very good and perfect. At the end it will be again as it was at the beginning: τὰ ἔσχατα ὡς τὰ πρῶτα. Redemption is then nothing other than the restoration of original creation with all its goodness: *restitutio in integrum*. If we understand redemption in this way, in the light of creation and for the sake of creation, then we have *a protological understanding of eschatology*. History between creation and redemption is then primarily the history of the Fall. It cannot bring anything new, except the increasing deterioration and ageing of the earth. Only redemption will restore creation. The revision of the doctrine of creation which is, in my view, necessary today (both for exegetical reasons, and for reasons of experience and our dealings with nature) is a changeover to *an eschatological understanding of creation*. If we make this changeover, not only will eschatology continue to be understood in the light of creation, but creation will also be understood in the light of eschatology.[4]

2. *Is Creation a Closed System or an Open One?*

The final syllable of *Schöpfung* – the German word for creation – indicates the completed process of creative activity and its result. Consequently when we talk about creation, we instinctively think, theologically, about the original state of the world and the beginning of all things, imagining them as a condition that was once finished, complete in itself and perfect. Belief in creation repeats the judgment of the Creator over his creation: 'Behold, it was very good.'

Unfortunately man cannot, like his Creator, rest at this point. For experience tells him, 'Behold, it is unfortunately not very good.' This difference between the judgment of faith and the judgment of experience has led people to put the 'very good' creation before history and to describe it in terms of an image of religious memory, by means of religious symbols of origin. Dogma called Adam's status in paradise the *status integritatis*. As the man whose creation was 'very good', Adam possessed *justitia et sanctitas originalis*. The first man and woman were driven out of this perfect state because of their sin. To this perfect state redemption will lead them back.

What, then, is history? It is first of all paradise lost, then the road to exile. What is redemption? It is the way back and, as the final

outcome, paradise regained. Sin perverts the good creation. Grace
restores it. What emerges from the history of sin and grace is the
good creation as it was originally. In the history of religion this
pattern corresponds to 'the myth of eternal return', described by
Mircea Eliade.[5] Did Thomas Aquinas mean anything different
when he said: 'Finis rerum respondet principio, Deus enim
principium et finis rerum. Ergo et exitus rerum a principio
respondet reductioni rerum in finem'? At all events for Thomas
time has a symmetrical, circular structure:

> In exitu creaturarum a primo principio attenditur quaedam circulatio
> vel regiratio, eo quod omnia revertuntur sicut in finem in id, a quo sicut
> principio prodierunt. Et ideo oportet ut per eadem quibus est exitus in
> principio et reditus in finem attendatur.[6]

Does not Rudolf Bultmann have the same thing in mind when he
writes:

> No light shone in Jesus other than the light that always shone in crea-
> tion. In the light of the revelation of redemption, man does not have to
> understand himself any differently from the way he was always sup-
> posed to understand himself in the face of revelation in creation and
> law: as God's creation.

At all events, time has a symmetrical, circular structure for Bultmann
too:

> So what meaning has the divine righteousness or the forgiveness of
> sins? . . . Its meaning is that the original relationship of creation will be
> restored.[7]

According to what its wording would seem to suggest, as well as
traditional interpretations of it, original creation is non-historical.
History only begins with the Fall of man and ends with the
restoration of creation in redemption. Creation itself has neither
time nor history. The picture of creation which is painted in this
way is the picture of a closed system, perfect in itself and totally
self-sufficient.

Modern exegesis of the Old and New Testaments will not allow
us to maintain this notion of creation. Biblically, faith in salvation
as a historical process determines belief in creation; and in so far as
redemption determines faith in salvation as a historical process,
eschatology also determines the experience of history and belief in
creation. We may mention the following as being systematically
important findings of Old Testament exegesis:

(*i*) The Israelite belief in creation developed out of Israel's historical experience of God – the exodus, the covenant, the occupation of the promised land – and is moulded by this experience. Israel had a 'soteriological understanding of creation'.[8]

(*ii*) In both the Yahwist and the Priestly Document, creation in the beginning does not mean an unscathed primal condition; it means the history that precedes salvation history. That is why creation, with its various orders, is itself understood as the work of Yahweh's grace and is narrated in the form of the *toledoth*. Creation in the beginning opens up 'the historical prospect'.[9] God's historical relationship with the world does not merely begin after the Fall; it begins with creation. Creation is aligned towards the future, so that we can say: 'In Old Testament theology creation is an eschatological concept.'[10]

(*iii*) The information 'in the beginning God created' establishes time together with creation. But if time begins simultaneously with 'creation in the beginning', then creation must be subject to change from the beginning, for time is only perceived from alteration. But if creation is subject to change and is open to time from the beginning, then it cannot be a closed system; it must be an open one. Consequently the time that begins with creation does not have a symmetrical structure either, in which future and past, goal and origin correspond to one another, like the two halves of a circle. Time's structure is a-symmetrical. It is open for a future which does not have to be the return of what was at the beginning, in the form of *restitutio in integrum*. Some scholars have thought that 'creation in the beginning' already envisages the consummation of creation 'at the end', because the idea of *acharith* and the idea of *reshith* belongs together.[11] Even if this does not follow directly from the concept 'in the beginning', according to the Priestly Document creation at the beginning does point forward towards 'God's resting', and, according to the Yahwist, towards the universal fulfilment of the blessing to Abraham. This determination of a goal may be termed eschatological. 'To the beginning there corresponds an end, to creation there corresponds a consummation; to the "very good" here a "perfectly glorious" there.'[12]

It follows from this that theology must talk about creation not only at the beginning, but also in history and at the end. That is to say, we must have in view the total process of divine creative activity. 'Creation' as the quintessence of God's creative activity comprehends creation at the beginning, the creation of history, and the creation of the End-time. It embraces the initial creative activity, creative activity in history, and the eschatological consummation. The reduction of the concept of creation to creation in the beginning has led traditionally either to the cleavage between 'creation and redemption' and between 'nature and super-nature', or to a division between 'the first and the second creation'. But this calls in question the continuity and unity of the divine creative activity itself. The concept of the unity of God in the unity of meaning of his creative activity can, in my view, only be preserved through the concept of the coherent, eschatologically orientated process of creation. If this is correct, then the position of man with regard to creation changes as well. He no longer merely confronts God's non-human creation as its lord, the creature who was made in the image of God; together with all other things, he also stands in the Becoming of the still open, uncompleted process of creation. Creation is then not a *factum* but a *fieri*. This leads to a new interpretation of man's destiny in creation; and 'subdue the earth' cannot be this destiny's final word.

If theology wants to sum up God's creative activity, then it must view creation as the still open, creative process of reality. In traditional terms, we mean by this the unity of the *regnum naturae*, the *regnum gratiae* and the *regnum gloriae*, each viewed eschatologically, in respect of its particular time. The initial creation points towards salvation history, and both point beyond themselves to the kingdom of glory. It is not the covenant of grace which already provides the 'inner ground' for creation in the beginning; the inner ground is only given with the kingdom of glory. For the kingdom of glory is the inner motivation of the divine history of the covenant. At the same time, in the process of creation which is totally aligned towards glory, we can distinguish between the following, according to their different conditions:

(*a*) creation in the beginning;
(*b*) creative acts in history;
(*c*) the creation of the End-time.

3. *Creation in the Beginning*

According to the texts, creation in the beginning is evidently creation without any presuppositions. The expression *creatio ex nihilo* (οὐκ ὄν being meant, and not μὴ ὄν, to use Platonic language) is intended to convey the liberty of the Creator and the contingency of all being – both its initial contingency and its permanent, fundamental contingency. The question: why is there something rather than nothing? cannot be answered by pointing to any necessity. But it cannot be answered by pointing to pure chance either. *Creatio ex nihilo* defines in a negative way the positive ground of creation in God's good pleasure. Out of 'the inner necessity of his love', to use Barth's phrase, the Creator makes something that corresponds to him and gives him pleasure. That is why creation has a meaning in its contingency. This is the reason why it is pleasurable and lovable beyond 'chance and necessity', as Monod puts it.[13]

Creation in the beginning is also the creation of time. It must therefore be understood as *creatio mutabilis*. It is perfectible, not perfect, for it is open for the history of both disaster and salvation, for both destruction and consummation. If we understand creation individually and as a whole as *an open system*, then its beginning is at the same time the condition for its history and its completion.[14] Creation at the beginning is the creation of conditions for the potentialities of creation's history. It pegs out the experimental field of constructive and destructive possibilities. It is open for time and for its own alteration in time. We cannot see in initial creation the invariant nature of history, but we can see the beginning of nature's history.

The creation accounts tell us that the initial creation out of chaos is also a creation of order in chaos. In the symbolic language of the Bible, the forces of chaos – night and the sea – thrust themselves into creation, even though they are excluded and confined by God. *Creatio ex nihilo* is therefore *creatio in nihilo* as well and is consequently creation that is threatened, and only protected to a limited degree against that threat. In the apocalyptic visions of the creation of the End-time, on the other hand, the encroaching forces of chaos are absent (Rev. 21.1; 22.5). The creation of glory is to be a creation that is no longer threatened and no longer vulnerable. In it God will be 'all in all' (I Cor. 15.28, AV), for then his glory is apparently to interpenetrate everything and overcome not only destruction but even the possibility of destruction, not only death but even the possibility of death. The Augustinian doctrine of freedom says the same thing: the initial *posse non peccare* is to be overcome by the *non posse peccare* of the End-time, and the initial *posse non mori* by the End-time's *non posse mori*. The inference is that man was created as 'potentiality *for*'. He is certainly destined for righteousness and not for sin, and for glory, not death. But he can still fall short of what his potentiality is destined for. This cannot be said to be what Barth calls an 'impossible possibility' in the ontological sense; but it can in the ethical sense be called a potentiality which ought not to be realized.

4. *Creative Acts in History*

In ascribing to Israel a soteriological understanding of creation in the beginning, we must also, on the other hand, recognize that Israel had an understanding of salvation in history which was based on creation. The prophets use the word *bara* more frequently for the divine creation of new, unexpected and unmerited salvation in history than for creation in the beginning. Like the Psalms, the prophets saw the exodus and the creation of the world, the creation of the world and the universal exodus of the End-time as belonging to a single perspective. Consequently belief in creation also serves faith in salvation, because for that faith, salvation proceeds from God's new creations. That is why creation in the beginning can be praised as an act of salvation, and the redemption can be expected in terms of a new creation.

The *bara* events of history are God's free acts and hence contingent. But they are not without premises, as was creation in the beginning. They are depicted as the creation of something new out of something old – of salvation out of wretchedness and life from dead bones. The divine creative activity at the beginning is conceived of as being an effortless creating through the Word; but the divine creative activity of redemption is understood as God's weariness and labour (Isa. 43.24; Isa. 55). The creating of salvation for those who are without it proceeds from the suffering of God's love for his people. Because Israel understood itself as being exemplary for the nations and for the whole of creation, we can view its experience of history as exemplary for the understanding of history in general. Here the hidden actions of God in history are manifest in an exemplary way.

What are God's creative acts in history related to? Theological language related salvation to sin, and redemption to slavery. But what are sin and slavery? Having called creation in the beginning a system open for time and potentiality, we can understand sin and slavery as the self-closing of open systems against their own time and their own potentialities.[15] If a person closes himself against his potentialities, then he is fixing himself on his present reality and trying to uphold what is present, and to maintain the present against possible changes. By doing this he turns into *homo incurvatus in se*. If a human society settles down as a closed system, seeking to be self-sufficient, then something similar happens: a society of this kind will project its own present into the future and will merely repeat the form it has already acquired. For this society the future ceases to offer scope for possible change; and in this way the society also surrenders its freedom. A society of this kind becomes *societas incurvata in se*. Natural history demonstrates from other living things as well that closing up against the future, self-immunization against change, and the breaking off of communication with other living things leads to self-destruction and death. Although isolation in man and human society can hardly be compared with other phenomena (in so far as man and human societies have particular destinies) analogous phenomena can be shown in other living things too. Whereas the word 'sin' only means human misdemeanour, the concept of deadly self-isolation can lead to a fuller understanding of the 'subjection of creation to futility' which Paul talks about in Rom. 8.19ff.

If in history God creates salvation for the people that lacks it, then he liberates that people from slavery, whether it is self-imposed or imposed from outside. If he creates grace for the sinner, then he frees him from his self-isolation. We can therefore call salvation in history the divine opening of 'closed systems'. The closed or isolated person is freed for liberty and for his own future. A closed society is brought to life so that it can look upon the future as being the transformation of itself. Non-human life systems enter into communication with one another once more. But because closed or isolated systems can only be opened again by means of renewed communications with others (if they are not to be destroyed), the opening to God takes place through God's suffering over their isolation. Because God himself suffers over man's closedness towards him, he keeps his communication with man alive in spite of opposition, creating the domain where isolated man can open up and transform himself.[16] Thus man's openness to God is brought about by grace, and grace springs from the suffering of God in his faithfulness to isolated man. The opening of man's closed society for openness towards man's neighbour and towards the world can be conceived analogously. Closed systems bar themselves against suffering and self-transformation. They grow rigid and condemn themselves to death. The opening of closed systems and the breaking down of their isolation and immunization will have to come about through the acceptance of suffering. But the only living beings that are capable of doing this are the ones which display a high degree of vulnerability and capacity for change. They are not merely alive; they can make other things live as well.

Anyone who looks for statements about creation in the New Testament often finds the results disappointing. Apart from the beautiful 'lilies of the field', creation does not seem to be a new theme. But we only get this impression if we are looking for statements about creation at the beginning. The New Testament testimony to creation is embedded in the kerygma about the resurrection, and in pneumatology. In these God's creative activity is understood eschatologically as καλεῖν (to call to life), as ἐγείρειν (to raise) and as ζωοποιοῦν (to make alive), for they are related to the creation of the End-time or 'the new creation.'[17]

For Paul the creation of the End-time begins with the raising from the dead of the Christ who had been surrendered to death. He describes creation as a process which has begun with the raising of Christ, which continues to be efficacious in the revelation of the Spirit, and which will end with the quickening of mortal bodies – that is to say, the resurrection of the dead. For Paul the perfect tense of the resurrection of Christ always points to the future tense of our own resurrection. When in certain passages he talks about a *taxis* in this process (I Cor. 15 . 20ff.), he does not mean that different parts are divided from one another. He makes the unified character of the new process of creation clear through the concept of *aparche*.[18]

When quickening and resurrection are described in the categories of divine creative activity, it is because this event is supposed to correspond to creation in the beginning (Rom. 4 . 17; II Cor. 4 . 6). In so far as they have as their premise the surrender, the suffering and the death of Christ in our stead and for our sakes, the historical weariness and labour of the Creator is completed in them. Because God in Christ has suffered our isolation – that is to say our death – he opens the fullness of his eternal life to us through Christ's resurrection. Eternal life is no longer a life which is merely preserved from death; it is life that has overcome death. Consequently this opening up of eternal life through Christ's death and resurrection must be understood as the completion of the process of creation. According to Paul, the crucified Christ has been raised to be the Kyrios and transformed into the 'life-giving Spirit'. Consequently the quickening powers of the Spirit proceed from him to the church. In the Pauline doctrine of the charismata, the Spirit is the power of the new creation, as well as the power of the resurrection. The powers of the new creation are to descend on 'flesh' in the community of Christ and through it, in order to quicken that flesh for eternal life.

If we want to interpret salvation in this perspective, then we shall have to see it as the ultimate and, in trend, universal opening of closed and isolated men and women and this closed world for the fullness of divine life. God's openness for the world becomes manifest in Christ's suffering and death. That is why Christ's resurrection brings about, in faith, limited openness to God on the part of men and women. The 'revelation of the Spirit' in the charismata of the community of Christ makes this mutual opening of God and man specific in the opening of the frontiers which men and women set up in order to cut themselves off from others: Jews and Gentiles, Greeks and barabarians, bond and free, male and female (Gal. 3.28). The liberation created through Christ's passion and glorification works in a liberating way through the charismatic quickening of the world. Openness to God, openness to our world are established wherever possible; and community in freedom is conferred.

5. *The Consummation of Creation*

Statements about the future of creation and of history in the kingdom of glory can only be made along the guiding lines of historical experience and hope. Ideas which we form in the midst of history about its end take the form of anticipation. In the prophetic and apocalyptic visions we find two formal principles: first, the negation of the negative and, secondly, the fulfilment of anticipations. In this double form the visions remain both realistic and futuristic. The negation of what is negative – 'death shall be no more, neither shall there be mourning nor crying nor pain any more' (Rev. 21.4) – defines the space that is open for the positive reality that is to come. The vision of 'the classless society' also follows this method of describing the future by means of a negation of the negative. But the mere negation of what is negative does not necessarily lead to a definition of the positive. Consequently eschatology too cannot be developed merely as negative theology.[19] The negation of the negative must itself be founded on an anticipation of the positive, latent though this anticipation may be. If this were not the case, the negative could not be experienced as negative and judged accordingly. For biblical eschatology, the negation of what is negative is rooted in experiences of the divine promissory history, which lets us seek for fulfilment. The pattern of promise and fulfilment and the negation-of-the-negative scheme together mould the pattern of the eschatological visions.

The completion of the creative process in the kingdom of glory is presented as God's indwelling in the new creation. 'Behold, the dwelling of God is with men. He will dwell with them, and they shall be his people' (Rev. 21.3). It is no longer merely heaven that is named as the place where God dwells; heaven and earth are now newly created, so that God himself may dwell in them: *finitum capax infiniti*. In the consummation, the hidden, anticipatory indwelling of God in temple and people are to be universally fulfilled. At the creation in the beginning there was as yet no talk of such an indwelling. But creation was to be open for that, and for that it was designed. I Cor. 15 links this fulfilment of creation and promissory history with the negation of the negative: '[He will destroy] every rule and every authority and power . . . The last enemy to be destroyed is death' (vv. 24–26). The Son is to fulfil his liberating rule by giving over the kingdom to the Father 'so that God may be all in all' (v. 28, AV). Moreover, according to Paul the Creator does not remain confronting his creation but enters into it with his glory, so permeating everything. This includes the destruction of all destructive forces and therefore the new creation of all things out of the divine glory. Man is not merely restored as the image of God; he is 'glorified' (Rom. 3.23; 8.30). That is to say, he acquires a part in the life and glory of God. Together with man, the whole creation will be free from the enslavement of futility and so participate in the all-permeating glory of God. Glorified man and glorified creation are consequently finite but no longer mortal; temporal but no longer transitory. The patristic doctrine of *theosis* tried to think this through against the background of the life of the risen and transfigured Christ. If we understand finitude as a qualitative and not a quantitative term (as we must do, if infinity is to be anything different from endlessness) – if we perceive time from change and not merely from transience, so that a change from 'glory into glory' becomes conceivable, then these ideas do not seem so unusual.

We have now termed creation at the beginning an open system, and have understood the history of God as being the opening up in time of closed systems. This gives rise to the further question, whether the completion of the process of creation is to be conceived of as the final end of the open and opened systems. Is the kingdom of glory the universal system which has finally come to a close? The new creation would then be the end of time and in itself timeless. The open system 'man' would then only be an unfinished system, and the open systems of nature would be only systems that are not yet closed. History would be the condition of a cosmos that was not yet thoroughly determined. And in this case the consummation would be the end of human liberty and the end of God's potentialities. Time would be abolished in eternity, and possibility in reality. But completion cannot be thought of in this way theologically. If the process of creation is to be completed through God's indwelling, then the unlimited fullness of divine potentiality dwells in the new creation; and through his participation in the unbounded liberty of God, glorified man is free. The indwelling of the limitless fullness of God's potentialities therefore means the openness of all systems of life *par excellence*, and hence that they will be eternally living systems and not fossilized ones. It will therefore be permissible for us to assume that there will be time and history, future and possibility in the kingdom of glory as well, and that they will be present in unimpeded measure and in a way that is no longer ambivalent. Instead of timeless eternity we would therefore do better to talk about eternal time, and instead of the end of history to speak of the end of pre-history and the beginning of the eternal history of God, man and nature. We must then, however, think of change without transience, time without the past, and life without death. But it is difficult to do this in the history of life and death, growth and decay, because all our concepts are stamped by these experiences.

Yet both the structure of the natural system and human experience of history point in this direction. The material structures already show a margin of undetermined behaviour. When we pass from atomic structures to more complex systems, we discover greater openness to time and a growing wealth of potentiality. With the evolution of more complex systems the indefinability of behaviour grows, because the possibilities increase. The human person and man's social systems are the most complex systems that we know. They show the highest degree of indeterminate behaviour and the widest measure of openness to time and the future. Every realization of potentiality through open systems creates new openness for potentiality; it is by no means the case that potentiality is merely realized and that the future is transformed into the past. Consequently it is impossible to imagine the kingdom of glory (which perfects the process of creation through the indwelling of God) as a system that has finally been brought to a close, i.e., a closed system. We must conceive of it as the openness of all finite life systems for infinity. This of course means among other things that the being of God must no longer be thought of as the highest reality for all realized potentialities, but as the transcendant making-possible of all possible realities.

6. *Associations of Man and Nature that are Capable of Survival*

The misunderstanding of creation as a primal, finished and in-itself-perfect condition has meant traditionally that the designation of Gen. 1.28, 'Be fruitful and multiply, and fill the earth and subdue it', has been seen as man's true and essential destiny. People did not read this designation in the Priestly Document in the light of the history of tradition, seeing it in the context of earlier texts such as the Yahwist (who interpreted this 'having dominion' as 'tilling and keeping'), or in the light of later Old and New Testament passages. Instead they related all the later texts to this single 'creation text'. What followed was a one-sided stress on man's special position in the cosmos. Man is the subject who rules; all other creatures are subject to him and are his objects. His rule over the world was understood as the proof that he was made in the image of God.

In modern times there followed from this the division of reality into subject and object, the *res cogitans* and the *res extensa*. Through science man was to become, according to Descartes, 'maître et possesseur de la nature' – i.e., was to fulfil the destiny for which he had been created. Because he understood redemption from the Fall as being the restoration of original creation, Francis Bacon declared that the goal of the scientific knowledge of nature was 'the restitution and reinvesting (in great part) of man to the sovereignty and power . . . which he had in his first state of creation'. The restoration of man's universal rule through science and technology was to make man again God's image on earth. In Bacon and Descartes we can see the fatal reversal of biblical thinking which, with the rise of technology, has led today to the world-wide ecological crisis. According to the Bible, man's lordship over the world is justified because he is made in the image of God. According to Bacon and Descartes, it is man's rule over the world that substantiates his divinity.[20]

The triumphal progress of classical science and modern technology dates from the time when Bacon and Descartes described the relationship between man and the world as the relation between a subject and an object, and this pattern came to be generally accepted. It is a pattern of domination and exploitation. Quantum physics has not made this pattern totally outdated, but it has relativized it:

> The old division of the world into objective processes in space and time and the mind in which these processes are mirrored – in other words, the Cartesian difference between *res cogitans* and *res extensa* – is no longer a suitable starting point for our understanding of modern science. Science, we find, is now focussed on the network of relationships between man and nature, on the framework which makes us as living beings dependent parts of nature, and which we as human beings have simultaneously made the object of our thoughts and actions. Science no longer confronts nature as an objective observer, but sees itself as an actor in this interplay between man and nature.[21]

It is precisely this reciprocal play which is not comprehended in the pattern of rule and subjection. So it is necessary for us to develop a new scheme. According to the model of communication and co-operation, nature is no longer the subjugated object of man, but a cohesion of open life systems with its own subjectivity. The Cartesian phase, in which nature was objectified, has been fundamentally exhausted, scientifically speaking, and offers no new insights. The recognition of complex open systems in the environment demands a model based on a theory of communication. Two subjects with, of course, different subjectivity enter into a mutual relationship with one another. Wherever we come across undetermined behaviour in natural systems, we can talk about a certain subjectivity or 'freedom of choice'. The more science advances towards a recognition of more complex systems, the more it will cease to provide merely technically applicable results, but will also offer findings showing that, out of consideration for our partner 'environment', we must not do what we would be able to do. Investigations into the ecology of survival on the sub-human level have shown that in 'the struggle for existence' symbioses between competing organisms have a far greater chance of survival than conflicts of competing organisms. The subject-object relationship of man to nature, and the pattern of domination and exploitation, do not lead to any symbiosis between human and non-human systems that would be capable of survival; they lead to the silencing of nature and to the ecological death of both nature and man.

Because, now, all processes which change our natural environment have their roots in economic and social processes in human societies, and because these in their turn are based on man's interpretation of himself, it would seem a task for Christian theology to work for the revaluation of previously accepted values. Man will not again become God's image here on earth by subjecting nature to himself, demolishing the natural systems and exploiting them for his own purposes.

For Christian faith, Christ is 'true man' and 'the image of God' on earth. That is why 'all authority in heaven and on earth' has been given to him (Matt. 28.18). But he came 'not to be served' – not to rule – 'but to serve'. And he served in order to make us free for fellowship with God and for openness for one another. In the light of Christ's mission, Gen. 1.28 will have to be interpreted in an entirely new way: not 'subdue the earth' but 'free the earth through fellowship with it'. For according to Romans 8, the whole enslaved creation waits for the revelation of 'the glorious liberty of the children of God', so that it itself may thereby be free. Karl Marx called this 'the true resurrection of nature' and hoped that it would come from 'a naturalization of man' and from the 'humanization of nature'.[22]

The conclusion to be drawn from this for the ethics of human society is that we need a new orientation, away from the will to power towards solidarity, away from the struggle for existence towards peace in existence, and away from the pursuit of happiness towards fellowship. The most important element in the further development of civilization is social justice, not the growth of economic power. We shall not be able to achieve social justice without justice for the natural environment, and we shall not be able to achieve justice for nature without social justice. For the pattern of exploitation has dominated both human labour and the resources or 'wealth' of nature. If today the 'limits of growth' are becoming visible, and if we are entering a situation where there is going to be a general shortage of foodstuffs, 'doing without' will be unavoidable. Solidarity and fellowship are the values which make unavoidable suffering and necessary sacrifices endurable. Justice is the form of authentic interdependence between people, and between society and the environment. It comes into being in the symbioses between different systems of life, and is the basis for common survival. Its presupposition is the recognition of the independence and subjectivity of the other life-system.

> Independence, in the sense of liberation from oppression of others, is a requirement of justice. But independence in the sense of isolation from the human community is neither possible nor just. We – human persons – need each other within communities. We – human communities – need each other within the community of mankind. We – the creation – need God, our Creator and Recreator. Mankind faces the urgent task of devising social mechanisms and political structures that encourage genuine interdependence, in order to replace mechanisms and structures that sustain domination and subservience.[23]

This outline of an eschatological doctrine of creation with the help of a theory of open systems and their mutual communication, is designed to serve this task. For if the task is not fulfilled, man and nature have no chance of survival.

IX

ETHICS AND BIOMEDICAL PROGRESS

1. *Science and Interest*

If science and ethics are separated, ethics always appears too late on the scene. It is only after science has taught us the methods of power that ethics is supposed to teach us power's responsibility. After the facts and the data have been listed, ethics is supposed to interpret them for people. Once the apparatus is at hand, ethics is supposed to enquire into its proper use, so that its misuse may be prevented.

This pattern of discussion leads into a cul-de-sac. From year to year we are better equipped technically to achieve what we want, yet ethically we ask helplessly, with Bertrand de Jouvenel: what do we really want? The greater the number of *possible* futures open to us, the less people seem to be able to agree about a common *desirable* future. The pressure towards progress in the sciences seems to make the humanities, culturally speaking, increasingly a matter of arbitrary choice. The mistake in this pattern of thought is that it starts from the assumption that science is something detached from society, and only then goes on to enquire about the ethical and socio-political integration of scientific and technical power in the humane goals of society. But because no values can be deduced from a science that is 'free of values' and separated from them, the values according to which scientific results are judged stray into the arbitrary regions of already existing social, economic and political interests, or of personal taste. On this level of discussion a great many ethical postulates can be set up and discussed, but they all remain without any relevance to actual practice and are generally only part of the window-dressing that accompanies public symposia. But I believe that this pattern of discussion has grown up out of an optical illusion.

I am therefore going to try to take the reverse method. We shall begin with an analysis of the present ethic of biomedical progress and then enquire about the repercussions of that progress on this ethic. We shall begin with the human and social motivations for biomedical science and technology (which have not been very thoroughly investigated up to now) and shall ask how they have been changed by the results of that science. In this way we shall reverse the theme of this session, and ask first of all about 'the influence of man and society on biomedical progress', and then go on to ask about 'the influence of biomedical progress on man and society'. It is only when we have come to know the interests that direct this science's investigations and perceive the interests that underlie the the application of these humane techniques that we have the well-founded justification for enquiring into the reciprocal effects of interest and knowledge under today's conditions.

The segregation of science from society, of science from the humanities and of technology from ethics was and is necessary in order to free science in its research and its application from the limits set by the existing religious and moral systems, as well as by the ideologies, of society. Remembrance of the conflicts between the church and science in the cases of Galileo and Darwin is still alive. The conflict between state Marxism and science in the Soviet Union show that that liberation is necessary under other circumstances as well.

Today, however, the *integration* of science and society is just as necessary if the sciences are to be freed from the new, quasi-religious roles into which they have strayed through their self-styled segregation from social interests and value systems – a segregation which gave them a quasi-sacred position. Whereas once the priests guarded the knowledge required for power from the laity, today the experts have taken over this function – and the layman is in the same situation as before. This division of roles is a check on progress. It overwhelms scientists with responsibility, while the fascination and horror exerted by science makes the layman play a less than adult role. The task of science can only be to lay open the possibilities for decision and the consequences of decision which would not otherwise be perceptible. Science is thus itself dependent on the dialogue between science and politics, and science and ethics; for it is in this dialogue alone that a consensus can be arrived at about guiding interests, values and value priorities.

Here the integration of science in society cannot proceed without the integration of society in science. We should otherwise arrive at conditions in which the planners and the planned, the makers and the made are no longer both 'man'; and when the objects no longer recognize themselves as being the subjects of science, and the subjects no longer recognize themselves science's objects.

2. *On the Ethics of Biochemical Progress*

In both its research and its application, science is a task taken up for a purpose. Human interests precede it, are bound up with it, and are incorporated in its progress. As long as these interests are 'self-evident', there is no need to discuss them. But in many sectors today the morality of what is 'self-evident' has become a problem. In the name of which human interests is this progress being pursued?

The invitation to this symposium said: 'The position of the firm (Hoffmann–La Roche) in the medical world has been strengthened in recent years because it views the fight against sickness and disease as an indivisible whole.' So our primary human interest is the fight against sickness and the fight for health, the struggle against death and for the prolongation of life.

That sounds like a matter of course, as long as man is dominated by his natural deficiencies, which he has to counterbalance by cultural achievements in order to survive. But this becomes a problem when life's immediate needs have been met and no longer provide the negative yardstick for his efforts. What comes after the struggle for existence?

'The struggle for existence' is linked with the elementary interest of man in his self-liberation from dependence on nature, in the environment and in his own body. It is the reverse side of his will to power over nature and himself. Man has become man – i.e., a person capable of action – since he has emerged from his dependence on nature, and in the degree to which he has mastery over nature. Today it is increasingly possible for him to determine not only his mental and private life but his physical and social existence as well. But liberation and power are only of interest as long as one does not have them. The more a person acquires them, the more the *humanum* that has to be projected and lived is called in question. 'What are people there for?'[1] Julian Huxley talked about the fact that after the struggle for existence, what was now increasingly coming to the fore was the 'striving for fulfilment' – that is to say fulfilment of human potentialities.[2] But which potentialities ought to be fulfilled and which ought not? He added that for men the control of the evolution of nature – or at least his own evolution – was now going to become the inner determination of his power and liberty.

For three thousand years the biblical religions have seen the vocation to rule over nature as the fulfilment of human destiny; but they have linked it with man's vocation to be the image of the creative God. He was not to be the image of nature and nature's forces. He was not to be an image of the destructive negation of being, and destroy nature and himself. At the time when these insights developed, the possibilities open to man were few and his dependence on impenetrable nature, on the other hand, great. In the wake of scientific and technical progress, man then (if we see the matter positively) entered into a hitherto undreamed-of realization of these destinies of his – given that he is 'man'. Out of elemental interests in liberation and power, a series of hopes sprang up in the history of civilization which were invested in biomedical progress. These hopes were directed towards the improvement of the human condition, the expansion of the world's understanding, the increase of its capacity for happiness, and the raising of its morality. Out of these hopes, specific visions are being developed today, as for example at the Ciba symposium in 1962.

(*i*) The conquest of illnesses due to viral or bacterial infection gives rise to the vision of a germ-free world.

(*ii*) The development of psychopharmacological drugs is linked with the utopia of a life free of pain.

(*iii*) The first techniques of organ transplantation lead to the notion of parts of the body being replaceable and of an endless life.

(*iv*) Modern eugenics make the control and acceleration of human evolution seem possible. This is linked with the vision that 'in the future people will create better generations of men and women' (Müller).

On the foundation of these human interests, hopes and visions, biochemical progress itself is a splendid ethical undertaking on mankind's part. But it only remains alive as long as these interests and hopes of mankind are accepted as being a matter of course.

3. *The Repercussions of Progress on Ethical Interests*

Every human action does not merely solve existing problems; it also produces new ones. Things usually turn out differently from what one had expected. These new problems can be divided into three groups:

(*i*) Everything that can be used can also be misused. Consequently biomedical progress is ambivalent as long as man is an unreliable being.

(*ii*) Hopes can be disappointed if they are not fulfilled. But they can also be disappointed through their very fulfilment. The problem about the biomedical utopias we have mentioned – the problem, that is, for the ethics underlying them – is not that they are probably incapable of fulfilment. The difficulty is that they probably *can* be fulfilled.

(*iii*) Every step forward in any sphere of life brings the life-system of the whole out of balance, Consequently when any individual piece of progress is made, the balance has to be restored again. Linguistic symbols, legal codes, the morals on which we have depended, and the conditions of production must all be ordered anew.

(*i*) As long as the increase of power serves to overcome elemental needs, it is obviously useful. But if it goes beyond what is necessary, it can be used in a way that is detrimental to life and can produce new misery.

Apart from the positive utopias we have mentioned, there is an equal number of negative utopias in the field of biomedical progress today. With the help of biomedical progress a public health service can be organized; but biochemical warfare is possible too, and so is the domination of a genetically highly bred *élite* over masses that have been reduced to idiocy by biochemical methods. Even without speculations of this kind, it is possible to become more successful in the struggle against disease on the one hand and yet ask, on the other, whether everything that is good for the growth of the pharmaceutical industry is necessarily good for the rest of the world as well.

(*ii*) Hopes are generally disappointed when something different emerges from what one wanted. The liberation of man from dependence on nature has not only overcome natural deficiencies on man's part, but has also broken through a series of natural, self-regulating systems. These have to be replaced by social systems regulated by men and women.

Biology and medicine have reduced the death rate, but have let loose the population explosion instead. They have overcome a certain natural selection; but have acquired in exchange a deterioration in human inheritances. They have fought bacteria and insect pests; but have created instead the 'silent spring' through DDT. They have fought pain; and created a world-wide drug problem. This liberation of man from nature forces us to undertake the social organization of that liberty, and this produces a wealth of new forms of social dependencies. The visions of a pain-free, endless, and improvable life in a germ-free world are abstract, because they do not take the social, political and ethical costs of such a world into account. No guarantee of happiness is bound up with biomedical progress. Human progress is always unequal, non-simultaneous and uncoordinated. It disturbs the traditional natural and social order and upsets its equilibrium, so that tensions and conflicts are forced on people.

In terms of space, biomedical progress has led to new social conflicts between rich and poor, men and women, the family and society. In terms of time, as Margaret Mead already stressed, it has destroyed the natural succession of generations through a rise in the ratio of the old to the young, on the one hand, and premature maturity on the other. In personal life, it has destroyed the balance between the self and the body, and produced new identification conflicts. A new social policy must bring about justice with regard to participation in health services. A generation policy must seek for an adjustment between the ageing of the population and its growth, so that the present is not sacrificed to the future and the future is not sacrificed to the present – that is to say, that neither are the old sacrificed to the young, nor the young to the old. We can no longer push responsibility on to 'nature', or on to the so-called free play of natural forces. What 'nature' once regulated through disease, early death and selection has now been taken over by social organization: by birth control, eugenics, and – at some time probably – through passive euthanasia as well. Interference with natural systems has to be compensated for by achievements. This ecological law also probably sets certain tolerance limits to man's experience with himself and his future self-creation, if the costs of progress are bigger than the returns.

(*iii*) But hopes can also be disappointed through their very fulfilment. If a pain-free, endless and improvable life in a germ-free world is to be possible, then a human hope will be fulfilled; and at the same time a dream will come to an end. For it is questionable what meaning a life of this kind can have, or what people of this kind are there for.

Is a life without pain not also a life without love? Is a life without opposition and struggle not also a life without the experience of living? Will an endless life not be a boring life, without the character of uniqueness? Monotony, boredom and poverty of experience are already human problems today in industrial society, and have to be laboriously suppressed by means of new psycho-pharmacological drugs and psycho-technology. The more human interests and hopes are fulfilled through biomedical progress, the more the ethical motivations that spur on progress dissolve. People no longer know what they mean when they talk about 'I', or 'my body', or 'life', or 'death'. The consequence is that general interest in this progress can also ultimately flag or die out. Why should medical progress make people more efficient and productive, when most human achievements in this society can be formalized and taken over by machines? How can this progress make people more capable of happiness, when happiness can no longer be defined? It is not satisfactory to construct things which acoustically ejaculate the formula, 'I am happy'. The more the humanity we have hitherto sought for becomes possible, the more humanity has apparently to be newly interpreted and formulated, so that we can also do something meaningful with the possibilities open to us. This is the question about the new balance in the life-system, which faces us as a result of the outstanding progress achieved in the sphere of biomedicine. But first of all we must consider the question about the changes brought about by that progress itself in the interests guiding scientific discovery and practice.

4. *Changes in Human Interests*

(*i*) *From the struggle for existence to the struggle for fulfilment*

In psychosocial evolution the struggle for existence has been replaced by what might be termed the striving for fulfilment. The main operative agency in this phase of evolution is psychosocial pressure.

Let us take up this fruitful idea of Julian Huxley's and so characterize the changes in human interests brought about by biomedical progress. As a vision of evolutionary humanism, he calls the goal

> fulfilment: greater fulfilment for more individuals and fuller achievement by more societies, through greater realization of human possibilities and fuller enjoyment of human capacities.[3]

If the struggle for existence is replaced by the striving for fulfilment, then people's interests and moral systems change fundamentally. The struggle for existence was a struggle for survival. In it people were ruled by the negative things that threatened them – lack of food, sickness, a hostile environment, and competing groups. The meaning of their life was determined by self-preservation. But the more people acquire power over hostile nature and their own frail bodies, the less self-preservation and naked survival can be the meaning of their lives. The more they overcome natural deficiencies and produce an artificial wealth of possibilities, the more life in this wealth of possibilities becomes a problem. What was once self-evident, as being necessary for life, loses its power as stimulus when the necessities of existence have been overcome or no longer stand in the foreground. Consequently the evolution of man goes beyond the negation of the negative in the struggle for existence, out into the projected design of the positive, which is to be won from the superfluity of possibilities. This makes human life for the first time *de facto* a moral task. Once life itself has been secured, it is a question of the good and happy life in harmonious existence. This by no means makes life easier, for now it lacks the clear standpoints and tasks that belonged to the struggle for existence. The hostile environment and hostile competitors no longer provide the negative yardsticks for the decisions of existence. The goal of life's fulfilment and man's joy in the play of his capabilities still point back to the life that was unfulfilled and restricted in the struggle for existence, and draw on the hopes developed then. But today these hopes are losing their power, as the spiritual helplessness of youth in the industrial countries already show. The 'man of potentiality' is becoming what Robert Musil called 'the man without qualities'.

The more power man acquires, the greater his responsibility. His interest in self-fulfilment is therefore inevitably bound up with responsibility for the sectors of nature which can be ruled. And it is of the essence of its inner structure that 'responsibility for something' is always linked with 'responsibility to somebody'. The authority to which rule has to answer therefore goes beyond the sphere of the thing *for which* one is responsible and so can only be experienced as something transcendent. I believe that at this point for many people today – and especially for scientists – the 'pain of transcendence' is appearing, a transcendence which demands responsibility and at the same time eludes previous images and symbols. This pain of transcendence can be an even more important incentive than psycho-social pressure. The Jewish-Christian symbol of man as the image in the visible world of the invisible God must also be newly interpreted today, in view of man's wealth of power and potentiality, if it is to be an effective symbol of his responsibility for the control of evolution in nature and his genetic experiments on himself.

(ii) *From social Darwinism to 'harmonious existence'*

If the struggle for existence is being replaced by new destinies for human life, then the moral systems that have stylized the struggle for existence must be surmounted too. Forms of life can be developed which make creativity and love possible in rational world conditions.

The ethics of the struggle for existence must be changed into the ethics of harmonious existence.

The principle of self-preservation against others can be transformed into the principle of self-fulfilment in others and with others, i.e., the principle of solidarity.

The systems of fear and aggression which were necessary for self-preservation can be demolished in favour of systems of hope and co-operation.

The group egoism which arises from self-preservation and leads to the struggles of competition and power is today threatening mankind with collective suicide. Even if this can be prevented, that egoism is already leading to societies of segregation. Wherever tensions and conflicts arise today, peace is established, not through reconciliation, but through division, expulsion, separation, apartheid and ghettos. Even without race and class conflicts, we are producing social divisions: the elderly in old people's homes, the sick in hospitals, the mentally ill in institutions, etc. Then the competent and the people who have got on in the world have things to themselves and can divide the spoil of the gross national product. According to doctors' estimates, about 50 per cent of the mentally ill would not have to be in hospital if their families would take them. But the social structure of the towns and cities is intolerant. The same applies to the elderly in old people's homes. If in our society the struggle for existence is continued in this hardly civilized way, even the competent will only be able to survive for a limited time – as long, that is, as they are neither ill nor old.

'Like draws to like' was what Aristotle called the natural principle of association. Today this principle is acting in our society in a way that is hostile to life, because it is a principle that divides. Consequently the principle of recognition of the other belongs to man's new self-experience and self-fulfilment, so that people who are not similar may live together and consider their differences and divisions as being fruitful. There is no other way of winning harmonious existence.

Finally, part of the ethics of the struggle for existence is the ideal of health, in which health is identified with the capacity for achievement and enjoyment (Freud). With this, health ultimately amounts to the unhindered participation in production and an undiminished sharing in the gross national product. Sickness and age are then merely evils which have to be suppressed. The incurably ill and the old are treated accordingly, not to speak of the way (and the place) in which people actually die in our hospitals. A new view of sickness, age and death belongs to an ethics of harmonious existence. Illness can be just as important an educative and formative process for the sick person as healthy, active life. Activist society elevated youth into an ideal to a positively comic degree; now it is time to rediscover the dignity of age. Death has been viewed merely as a tiresome nuisance; now there are reasons for learning the *ars moriendi* again, so as to die with dignity. The struggle against illness and for health is a good thing if it makes people ready to expose themselves to the human pains of love and the productive conflicts of life and death, so as to assimilate them in a truly human way. The ethics of the struggle for existence would otherwise lead to a sick society. Where today this struggle is successful to a certain degree, it often leads to a life of stagnation, to a passive 'consumer' attitude, without any passion for living. Where it is continued it leads to societies of superfluity set down on earth like islands in an ocean of impoverished societies. Only when an ethic of 'harmonious existence' overcomes every ethic of struggle can the state be reached when the healthy learn from the sick, the young from the old, and the living from the dying; and when rich nations learn from poor ones, showing interest in them and feeling solidarity with them because of that interest.

5. *The Right to Live and the Right to Die*

Biochemical progress has broken through a series of natural systems, making them accessible for man's intervention. These systems must be replaced by social systems regulated by people. That is why we talk about population policy, health policy, and will one day have to link the new genetics with the word policy as well. Disturbed natural balances must be replaced by social regulations. This will make life more conscious and deliberate. Birth and death, both the content and the form of life, are no longer self-evident; they have to become evident to man, if they are to be dealt with appropriately; and this must issue in his linguistic symbols, his legal agreements and a new morality.[4]

(*i*) *The self and the body*

Man's self-consciousness is shown in his capacity for saying 'I' and meaning himself. 'I am so-and-so', he says, identifying himself physically. How is this possible, in the face of developments in physical medicine and organ transplantation?

> Since we have achieved success in isolating the disease theoretically from the sick person, and since we have gained control over the whole chain of cause and effect, from the bacillus to all the important conditions in the process of the disease, a selective and purposeful therapy has become possible.[5]

But this presupposes the detachment of the self from its *physical nature*, in the form of *the body it possesses*. The spontaneous physical identity of the person is replaced by the person's detached attitude to his body – the attitude of someone to a piece of property. If, now, organs belonging to this body can be replaced – like the mechanical parts of his car – then a diffusion of the self arises.[6] What does the symbol 'I' represent? Physical existence, or my body, or a replaceable set of parts belonging to a physical system? One aspect of organ transplantation is the domestication of the parts that have been introduced, as in the case of artificial limbs, etc. This does not only apply to the body which has to accept and integrate what is at first an alien part. It also applies to the self, as the body's organizing centre. The difficult medical process of the objectification of 'my body' into a 'physical organism' then involves, conversely, the no less difficult and protracted process during which the physical organism is subjectified into the body of the self. The isolation of the disease from the sick person is, in its turn, dependent on the integration of sickness and recovery by that person. Medical changes in the body, and even more every conceivable genetic change in the human condition, live from the truth that, as W. Korff said, 'the object over which [medicine] exercises control is a subject and must remain so' – or must become so.

This sets the goal of the particular operation, and sets certain limits to it as well. If the person involved can no longer assimilate medical treatments and operations as a person – if they can no longer be 'fed back' into his personality, then they are senseless, from the human point of view. The interests of the patient, the interests of the health of a people in general, and the interests of scientific progress must therefore 'be orientated towards a total view of the human person in a community of persons'.[7] Progress in physical medicine must consequently be balanced by the development of an expanded sensibility of the self, if it is to be assimilated by the person as such. Today finding the appropriate balance between 'being a body' and 'possessing a physical organism' is already an ethical problem for many people. If the self can no longer physically incorporate itself, but has to keep its body in the permanent detachment implicit in the interchangeability of physical parts, then indifference towards one's own physical life and the physical life of others is the result. This can be seen from 'body-counting' in Vietnam to the attitude expressed in the phrase 'play it cool'. To experience the self as a thing makes a person invulnerable in a certain way, but it also makes him incapable of loving, and unproductive. The more invulnerability and painlessness is possible medically speaking, the more we should remind ourselves of vulnerability through the meaningful, human pains of love. The application and use of medication finds its limitation in the emotional coldness that is threatening men and women. This means that the consciousness of the self, which has hitherto been given by man's physical nature, is becoming a personal task. We must consciously seek our bodily incarnation, and deliberately accept the risk of our vulnerability. Capacity for suffering is part of health.

(ii) Life and experienced life

A second linguistic symbol important in our context is 'life'. In the struggle for existence, life means surviving. Today survival can be greatly extended and death can be delayed. People can be kept alive, although they no longer feel life in any way. Consequently when we talk about 'life', the meaning of the word is questionable. For medicine, however, which is in duty bound to preserve life, it is very important to know what can be called human life, at least broadly speaking. It is no longer possible to rely on life's being something that is self-evident, something that has to be accepted and given up without any human effort. The more it is possible for people to determine the destiny of others, the more they need a human definition of life. This is particularly precarious in controlling birth and death, but it is just as' much of a problem in the middle of life. Without losing sight of the perilous practical questions and legal problems, I should like to propose a provisional definition, for the purposes of discussion: *Human life is life that is accepted, loved and experienced.*[8]

Where life is not accepted, loved and experienced, we are not dealing with human life. If a child does not feel that he is accepted, he falls ill. If a person does not accept himself, he loses his living character. If a life can no longer be experienced, it is dead. We can go on to say that human existence or being (*esse*) is being interested (*inter-esse*). Being is alive as long as it can sympathize with other life and experience sympathy from other life. We therefore call apathy and desolation 'death in life'. In industrial society, and in societies which are well looked after medically, poverty of experience, apathy and lack of interest in life are spreading to a frightening degree.

> There has arisen a world of qualities without a man to them, of experiences without anyone to experience them, and it almost looks as though under ideal conditions man would no longer experience anything at all privately and the comforting weight of personal responsibility would dissolve into a system of formulae for potential meanings.[9]

The monotony of apathetic life is a sickness which is no longer curable medically. It can only be healed through the overcoming of

the unified cultures which we have produced, by cultural multiplicity, by living together with people different from ourselves, and
by the conscious acceptance of the pain which differences and
conflicts bring with them. Experienced life is a life which contains
contradiction within itself and which finds the strength to grasp
contradictions within itself and to endure them. Johannes Hersch
has spoken of man as a being who has the duty of preserving
the meaning of life – his own life – in sickness and in the face of
death, by the way in which he endures these things. This
meaning, he says, is not just health; health simply serves the
meaning.[10]

(iii) Family planning and birth control

As a result of modern medical knowledge and methods, the birth
of a child is no longer merely a matter of nature; it is also a matter
of the liberty and responsibility of men and women. By means of
'the pill', acts of sexual intercourse can be distinguished from acts
of conception. This means that the conception and birth of a child
has become a moral and social question. It is true that hitherto
parenthood was part of the fulfilment of human life as much as
childhood. But the responsibility for a child has shifted from the
period after birth to the time before conception. In this way
responsibility has become very much greater. Conscious will and
accepted responsibilities for the child therefore belong to a child's
birth. If the parents are living as citizens in a community they have
also taken over a responsibility for the community together with
the responsibility for their children; just as, on the other hand, the
community participates in the parents' responsibility for their
children. Consequently the acceptance by parents and the community belongs just as essentially to the human life of a child as the
biological process of conception and birth. *The right to life* is
therefore no longer a natural phenomenon; it is a task for the
parents and community which have to confer that right. The
result is, first of all, the rights of birth-control by parents and
community. Certain eugenic rights could result as well later,
although this would presuppose a 'humane' society, whose criteria
of choice would refute hitherto well-founded suspicions about the
misuse of power.

Children must be accepted. That is, in my view, the truly human side of a birth. The act of acceptance precedes the conscious conception of a child on the part of the parents. But it also follows the child's birth, and must be continually repeated in the conditions of his growing up. If rights also have to be conceded to society by birth control, so we must expect the conscious acceptance of children by society too. It will then no longer be possible to build towns and cities hostile to children. People in society who are themselves childless would then have to receive this right to accept children, and the right of access to them. That would mean a cautious removal of families from the purely private sphere, although the essential personal relationship between parents and children must not be dissolved. If we start from the assumption that human life is *accepted life*, then these questions are more important than questions about the point of time at which human life begins – questions which are still important in the context of abortion, but will become superfluous through progress in family planning.

(iv) *The death of the body – the death of the person*

It is difficult today to determine the definitive end of life, for a person can be 'survived' by some of his bodily organs. The differentiation between the death of different organs has blurred the frontier between life and death. Biologically speaking, dying is a negative 'feed-back' process which extends in several phases over a considerable time. There are people whose brain finally ceased to function after the heart had long ceased to beat, but whose heart and breathing then resumed their functions. Their bodies go on living an unconscious life, but they are no longer alive in the sense of life that is conscious of existence. It is a no-longer-experienceable life. Because, according to the present state of our knowledge, the complete cessation of the brain functions is irreversible, the death of the brain can be viewed empirically as 'true symbol for the end of human life'.[11] With the death of the brain the human person as a legal entity ceases to be, even if certain organs can continue to be kept alive.

If biologically speaking the frontier between life and death is becoming blurred, and death is losing its clear definition (depending on the state of medical knowledge and skill), then it is all the more important to understand death in a human way as being the death of the whole person, and to integrate it in life as we experience it, by means of a conscious attitude towards death. Death can indeed be established as having taken place by the dying of vital organic parts; but it is experienced by the person in the love which gives the soul corporeal form and gives a soul to the body. The more we incarnate ourselves in love, the more vulnerable we shall be through death – through the death of the people we love and through our own deaths. The more, on the other hand, interest in life is quenched within us, the less we notice grief and pain, because we have already anticipated death spiritually.[12] Many people today have with the help of drugs developed techniques – techniques of indifference and apathy – so that when it actually comes to the point of death, they do not have to experience life any more. Consequently an ethic of accepted, loved and experienced life must for its part practise attitudes towards death and must liberate dying from its suppression or the euphemisms with which we gloss over it. Life and love are an art, and being able to die is an art as well. We know how 'to take life' (in both senses of the phrase); but we know very little about how to leave it, as human beings and with dignity. Man has a right to his own death, just as he has a right to his own life. The medical possibilities of shifting the frontier between life and death and making people unaware of it will be applied humanely if a person prepares himself for death and yields up his life, when the time comes, with more awareness than is the case today.

This other attitude to death demands a process of education which abolishes the barriers of suppression which are raised against death and grief, so that life becomes again worthy of our love. Just because biomedical progress is not linked with any guarantee of happiness, a human ethic which is a match for that progress must have both things in mind; the medical alleviation of suffering and the abolition of certain diseases on the one hand; and on the other the human acceptance and conscious coming to terms with suffering, periods of illness, and dying. Just as the order of the body has to be integrated into the order of the human person, so bio-medical progress too must be integrated into the order of humanity.

6. *Summing-up*

(*i*) Scientific progress and human interests are involved in a process of mutual conditioning and alteration. The ethical question is the question about motivations and about the forms and alterations of the human interests invested in the scientific and technical progress of biochemistry. This ethical question therefore includes not only the reactions of man and society to the results of biomedical progress, but also, at a still earlier stage, the actual actions of people and society in biomedical progress.

(*ii*) The previous ethic of biochemical progress is to be found in human interests in the struggle against disease and for health, as well as in the self-liberation of nature, and in power over nature. Arising out of these interests, certain hopes grew up for the improvment of the human condition, the expansion of the world's understanding, the increase of its capacity for happiness and the raising of its morality. From these hopes specific visions developed : the vision of a germ-free world, the vision of a world free of pain, the vision of an endless life and an acceleration of human evolution.

(*iii*) Biomedical progress changes the fundamental ethical interests of man and society. Progress is ambivalent as long as man is an unreliable being. He disappoints his own hopes because their fulfilment is bound up with surrogate achievements in the social field (designed to compensate for shattered natural systems), whose cost is greater than the gain can be. He disappoints his own hopes through their very fulfilment, inasmuch as the meaning of life must be newly formulated if the struggle for existence no longer makes its meaning self-evident.

(*iv*) The change in human interests evoked by biomedical progress can be described as a transition from the struggle for existence to striving for fulfilment. Definitions of the meaning of human life which transcend the struggle for existence therefore become of immediate relevance. The change from the ethics of the struggle for existence to the ethics of harmonious existence becomes our present task. The principle of self-preservation against others can be transformed into the principle of self-fulfilment in the other. Systems of aggression can be overcome by systems of co-operation. Group egoism ('like draws to like'), which turns our societies into societies of segregation, must be overcome through a new interest in a life with others characterized by tension and inner conflict ('recognition of the other'). A new evaluation of illness, age and death belongs here too. Illness is just as important a learning process for the sick person as healthy, active life. Growing old has its own dignity, which cannot be measured by standards of 'achievement'.

Dying is just as important a process, humanly speaking, as birth and life.

(*v*) The right to live and the right to die are no longer a matter of course but must be consciously formulated; and consequently we have to find a new symbolism for life's meaning. In the face of the medical possibilities, man must find a new balance between being a body and possessing a physical organism. Medical intervention finds its goal and its limit in the patient's power of assimilation of that intervention on the human level, and in the power of assimilation of society. The healing of human wounds has meaning if it makes people capable of opening themselves for the pains of love and for the vulnerability of creativity. If life is no longer mere survival, then we can see human life as being life that is accepted, loved and experienced. Life that is not accepted and life that can no longer be experienced is no longer life that is worthy of men and women. This means that in considering the question about the point when a human life begins, its acceptance by parents and society is of paramount importance. It means that in considering the definition of a person's death, his capacity for experiencing life and his conscious acceptance of dying is of immediate relevance.

X

JUSTIFICATION AND NEW CREATION

According to Protestant understanding, the doctrine of justification formulates the heart,[1] the 'centre and the limits'[2] of Christian theology. That is to say, it does not aim to be one article of faith among others, or to communicate one interpretation of Christ among other possible ones; it claims to formulate the *articulus stantis et cadentis ecclesiae* and the essence of the gospel, the gospel that is in accordance with Christ.[3]

Is this a justifiable claim? Is the conclusion that, by God's grace and for Christ's sake, the sinner becomes righteous through faith,[4] the only possible and only true perception of what has taken place for us through God in Christ, and what still takes place in us through Christ? Is it solely this message about the forgiveness of sins that is the legitimate proclamation of Christ, which meets man as he is in all his real and utter wretchedness? In asking this question, we are not merely asking about the correct doctrine of the church, in the context of a discussion about other church doctrines, or the doctrines of other churches; we are enquiring first of all about the essential form of the proclamation of Christ to the godless. We are enquiring, that is to say, not only about the *articulus stantis et cadentis ecclesiae*, but about the *articulus stantis et cadentis hominis*.[5] That ought really to be the same thing. But unfortunately the doctrine of justification became almost exclusively a mere point of controversy within the church and between the churches. In Paul it was the foundation of his universal mission to Jews and Gentiles, i.e., the point on which the truth of Christ for Jews and Christians, for Christians and pagans, takes its stand. And today too the doctrine of justification must be the point on which the Christian faith takes its stand in its conflict with secular ideologies of legitimation and doctrines of salvation.

1. *Some Dubious Points about the Doctrine of Justification Today*

(*i*) Have *the external presuppositions* for an understanding of the justifying gospel become hazy?

When the context surrounding a living thing disappears, the thing loses its living quality. When the exigency that showed something to be necessary ceases to be known, the necessary thing loses its reasonableness. If the presuppositions collapse, then what was built on them is left in the air. Consequently the proclamation of justification becomes questionable if man's question about righteousness ceases to be applicable.[6]

But what is this question that is cast up by the proclamation of justification? Against what background does this event become necessary, understandable and convincing?

Is it the crisis about God and the question about God, cast up by the fear of judgment, which Luther uttered when he was a monk: 'O when wilt thou finally become godly and do enough so that thou mayst get a gracious God?'[7]

Is it God's law, about which Paul said: 'I do not do the good I want, but the evil I do not want is what I do' (Rom. 7.19)?[8]

Is it fear of the Last Judgment, before which no man shall stand?

Is it man's inner crisis of conscience, in his self-disintegration and his alienation from his true being, as Kierkegaard said: 'The principle of Protestantism [has] a particular premise: a man who sits in mortal terror, in fear and trembling and much temptation'?[9]

Is it the general transitoriness of all finite beings, who – delivered over to futility, chaos and death – ask questions that go beyond themselves and are dependent on something greater to give them a foundation and continuance? Where is the hermeneutical point at which what is said about the justifying God can convince us and prove to be necessary? Is it in the crisis of our need of God, the crisis of conscience, fear of judgment, the crisis of being of everything that is and yet does not abide? Luther said: 'Temptation teaches us to pay heed to the word.' But are the crises we have named really that temptation, accusation and affliction in which and against which the Christ event manifests and proves itself as being the saving righteousness of God?

(*ii*) Have the *inner presuppositions* become hazy or obscure? In the nineteenth century, liberal theologians such as Wrede, Wernle and Schweitzer declared that the Pauline thesis about the revelation of the saving divine righteousness, without the works of the law, was only comprehensible in the light of its antithesis in the Jewish righteousness of the law. It was therefore a 'fighting doctrine' on Paul's part – anti-Jewish apologetic – and hence, both for the Gentiles of his own time and for people of the enlightened nineteenth century, incomprehensible, non-binding, and of merely historic interest.[10]

The deeper question is: has Paul's doctrine of justification any foundation and sustainability at all in Jesus himself and his message about the kingdom of God and the God who is our Father? Is it the only possible and true interpretation and continuation of Jesus' proclamation, or is it a theologoumenon of Paul, the former Pharisee, which can only be understood subjectively? The question crops up today in a different form, when people ask about the continuity between Paul's doctrine of justification and Jesus' preaching about the kingdom. It is quite true that the doctrine of justification cannot maintain its ground as Christian unless it finds its foundation in Jesus, and in what was revealed in him and through him about God. Wilhelm Dilthey, accordingly, postulated the thesis (in connection with the Reformation): 'The doctrine of justification itself exists only as long as its dogmatic premises (Christ as God and man and his sacrificial death) are valid.' He absolutely denied that 'the heart of Reformed piety is contained in the renewal of the Pauline doctrine of justification by faith'.[11] We may maintain, like Iwand and Wolf, that the Reformed doctrine of justification is the proclamation of Christ and finds its inner substantiation in the history of Christ, as the confessional writings of the Reformation say (Confession of Augsburg IV, Schmalkaledic Article II); yet the question still remains whether the statements about Christ simply serve to substantiate and form the theological background for the present event of justification in word and faith, or whether the doctrine of justification serves as the present-day interpretation of our knowledge of Christ with respect to lost man. That is to say, does the doctrine of justification interpret the

Christ event? Does Christology substantiate the event of justification and that alone?

(*iii*) Finally, *the goal* served by the justification of the sinner is
obscure and disputed. Does justification restore a lost state of
salvation or is it the beginning of something fundamentally new for
lost and perished man? Does justification mean the restoration of
the original creation which was pronounced good, the restoration
of broken fellowship with God, the restoration of man's dis-
integrated identity with himself, the restoration of the peace of
creation: *restitutio ad integrum, reconciliatio, remissio, renovatio*?
Is faith in justification therefore bound up with recollection of the
beginning, anamnesis?[12] Or is this the beginning of the new
creation? Or has something new, something there has never been
before, been called into life with justification: *incipit vita nova*,
namely 'life from the dead' (Rom. 11.15)? In short, is faith in
justification bound up with unconditional hope, *elpis*?

The question of what the justificatory event amounts to touches,
first, on the question of the external presuppositions: is whatever
causes the crisis that makes justification necessary (i.e., law and
conscience) at the same time also the framework and the pattern of
the thing that becomes good once more in justification? But,
secondly, this question also touches on the substantiation of
justification in the Christ event. If this Christ event is really in
itself greater than that which the gospel of justification at present
reveals to lost man, then its meaning and its future also reaches
beyond the present of word and faith, opening to man the future
of salvation and the lordship of Jesus Christ by securing for him,
in his transitory existence, the hope of a new life, thereby setting
him in eschatological liberty.

2. *Christology and the Doctrine of Justification*

*Jesus' preaching of the kingdom and the Pauline doctrine of
justification*

It is no longer possible to ensure the christological substantiation
of the doctrine of justification by means of mere dogmatic statements, or by pointing to the credal formulations of the church. If
we come across the doctrine of justification as a central theme for
the first time in the Pauline epistles, then the question about its
christological substantiation must be directed towards the conti-

nuity between Paul's doctrine of justification and Jesus himself. Consequently we must ask first of all whether the Pauline doctrine of justification is a legitimate extension of Jesus' preaching of the kingdom – that is, whether it corresponds to what the earthly Jesus said and did.

(*i*) Looking at the matter *from the aspect of the history of religion*, Johannes Weiss and Albert Schweitzer were the first to recognize the analogical 'eschatological character of Jesus' preaching and Paul's doctrine'. An eschatological explanation of this kind 'establishes the complete solidarity between Paul's doctrine and the doctrine of Jesus', as Schweitzer put it. For him, the difference lies in the fact that 'Paul connects the expectation of the kingdom and the redemption effected in it with Jesus' appearance and death in such a way that faith in redemption and faith in the coming of the kingdom are dependent on whether the kingdom will come soon or will fail to appear. Without giving up eschatology, he already stands above it.'[13] Here, therefore, the origin and character of certain ideas are investigated first of all, and are identified as being apocalyptic concepts of hope. Next – and now from the standpoint of religious psychology – the pure, imminent expectation of the kingdom in Jesus is compared with Paul's expectation on the basis of the redemption which had already appeared in Jesus. This way of approach, however, remains a superficial one. On the one hand it does not enquire whether these possibly similar ideas are also 'employed' in the same way. On the other, it only finds analogies, and no genealogy; only comparable features, no fundamental connection between them. Like Rudolf Bultmann, we are bound to establish that Paul is not directly determined by the earthly Jesus in forming his ideas. He was neither Jesus' disciple nor his opponent, and only came to know the gospel through the Hellenistic and Jewish Christian church, which he persecuted. His doctrine of justification cannot therefore be accounted for as being a direct continuation of Jesus' preaching, on the analogy of a philosophical or theological 'school'.

(*ii*) Bultmann[14] looked at the matter in a way that was substantially more profound. He saw the continuity and difference between the eschatological preaching of the two in the kerygmatic presence of the heralded eschaton. Jesus proclaimed the nearness of the kingdom of God in the call to decision and to repentance:

What he says, he does not say as something new, as something not heard before. But *that* he says it, that he is saying it *now*, is the decisive event; and the saying changes the situation for all who hear him into a new and decisive situation. . . . Such a call to decision in the light of his person *implies a Christology.*[15]

It is not the *what*, the content, of his proclamation that is put in question by his death on the cross. What is put in question is his legitimacy as the proclaimer, the *that*, the fact that it is really he who is the messenger of God bringing the final decisive word.[16]

Because the primitive church believes in the crucified Jesus as the one who is risen, the 'scandal' of the cross is overcome. This finds expression in the fact that now Jesus is preached as the Christ in the sense of Jesus' eschatological message. '*That* this word is said, the fact of the *saying*, makes the new age present.' This new age is only visible in faith. 'But just here the *second* reality appears: *there can be and there is faith.*'[17] According to this, the factual continuity between Paul and Jesus lies in the 'that' and the 'now' of the eschatological announcement of the time. The difference is that for Jesus this eschaton is the swiftly approaching present, whereas for Paul the eschaton has already taken place in Jesus.[18] Jesus looks into the future, but Paul looks back: the turn of the age has already come. What for Jesus is the already present future is for Paul the present that has dawned in the past of Jesus. A continuity lies in the eschatological announcement of the time. The difference is to be found in the change in the time fixed for the eschaton, which has already been brought about by Jesus' crucifixion and resurrection.

In a corresponding and complementary way Gerhard Ebeling has seen the continuity and the difference in the event of *faith*: it is noticeable and without precedent that (according to the miracle stories transmitted to us) Jesus grants faith, expects faith and demands faith: 'Your faith has saved you.' This is not faith in Jesus, nor is it belief in new ideas about God either; moreover faith is talked about here with singular absoluteness: 'All things are possible to him who believes' (Mark 9.23) and 'all things are possible with God' (Mark 10.27). According to this, faith lies in the power of God himself; it is 'participation in the omnipotence of God'.[19] This entirely corresponds to Jesus' preaching: he proclaims the kingdom of God as being near. His call to decision presents the direct and radical claim of God to the whole man and his simple, undivided obedience – presents it in the presence of what is to come.

But in the Christian proclamation the proclaimer, Jesus of Nazareth, becomes the proclaimed Christ. The one who calls to faith becomes the one who is believed. Is this change-over a sharp break? Does it mean that something different and new has been put in place of Jesus' proclamation and faith – or does it only mean that 'the cause of Jesus goes on' and that the proclaimer is risen to become the proclamation, the awakener of faith to become our own faith? Is this faith, as power from the almighty power of the God who draws near, the continuum, the permanent element in which changes occur? Does something new enter the history of Jesus with Easter? Or is Easter an interpreting event in which the disciples express and hold fast to the faith they won while they were together with Jesus?

(*iii*) Both grounds for the Christian preaching of justification – the word or the faith of the earthly Jesus – become paradoxical when they are faced with the cross. For in Jesus' death on the cross nothing remains of his claim, his proclamation or his miracles, and nothing of the faith which people may have found in him. The cross was not only a stumbling block to the Jews and foolishness to the Gentiles. It is a permanent mystery for Christians. Because of his death, Jesus is no longer totally one and the same as the word of his proclamation. Here we do not only have to do with 'pure word' (Ebeling). Here his word enters into his suffering. We have to do with his silence and with a speechless, incontrovertible fact. The passion texts tell of the flight of the disciples with curious narrative harshness. If we can talk at all about faith in Jesus before his death, we must at least assume that this faith collapsed completely when he was executed. We must take this 'death of God' among the disciples as seriously as the sacrifice of Isaac or the suffering of Job, for it is harder to look on at the extermination of the person on whom one has set one's hope, one's faith and one's love, than to be exterminated oneself.

Neither the remembered words of Jesus nor our own faith over-comes the pain of the cross. That is why it is only the Easter appearances of the crucified Jesus which provide the foundation for the Christian proclamation and the Christian faith. 'The Easter event is the bridge between Jesus and the whole of the later kerygma; it both divides and unites them.'[20] Equally paradoxically, it is the Easter event which first 'sets aside'* this death, making his end a true beginning, and also 'keeps'* (in the sense of preserving and actualizing) the earthly Jesus, with his proclamation and faith. In the face of the cross the continuity between the Christian proclamation and Jesus himself cannot be understood either in the continuation of his proclamation or in the continuation of the faith which he arouses; it springs, in all its depth, from the presence of the crucified Jesus, by virtue of his resurrection from the dead through God. It is only on this foundation that the proclamation of Jesus can be preserved and carried further; and the proclamation must be such that no proclaimer of the gospel can disregard the fact that these are the words of the one who was called from death on the cross into the life of God. It is only on the foundation of the creative proof of the power of God, who calls the crucified Jesus into life, as he calls into being the things that are not, that faith can be life in the presence of the one who is to come, and be participation in the creative power of God, and that it can hence become a victorious certainty in the dispute with the powers of the negative. Faith will therefore also preserve the stories of Jesus' miracles and proclaim the faith which Jesus confers; but it will never be able to disregard the fact that this divine power and nearness is only shown in radical power – i.e., in its power to raise from the dead – in the helplessness of the crucified Jesus. The problem of how the proclaimer became the one proclaimed, of how the one who calls to faith became the one believed in, is only a problem of linguistic history or anthropology to a secondary degree. It is primarily a christological problem, which finds its solution in the resurrection of the Jesus who was crucified.

In the context of our question this means that the message of justification, and faith in justification, find their foundation in the raising of the crucified Jesus and draw their strength from the cross of the risen Christ. They must therefore prove themselves to be the interpretation, 'deduction', manifestation and meaning of this particular event. The justification of the godless through word and faith puts the liberating will of God in history into effect, and this will is revealed in his actions in Jesus – in his surrender to death on the cross and his resurrection from that death into new life.

* The German word 'aufheben' which is used here means both 'to rescind' and 'to preserve'. [Translator]

3. *The Knowledge of Christ and the Understanding of the Divine Righteousness in the Early Church*

Jesus was delivered up to death on the cross in the name of Israel's divine law. What that meant for the righteousness of God (which was put into force in him and manifested in the gospel) was not so much discerned through the remembrance of Jesus' position with regard to the law before Easter, but rather discovered from the position of the risen Christ with regard to the law of Israel. Jesus' death on the cross in the name of the law is not a problem as long as the cross is irradiated by the splendour of his messianic appearances, and as long as the splendour of his appearances in glory are perceived from the Israelite point of view, in the sense of late Jewish apocalyptic. The very early church, which after Easter lived in imminent expectation of Jesus as the coming Son of man, hardly made the cross the subject of theological thought. The Easter appearances, understood as the beginning of the general resurrection of the dead, let the cross first of all recede into the background of a superseded past. The hymnal fragments of the Hellenistic Jewish church do not talk about the cross either, or if they do, they mention it merely as a transitional stage on the path of redemption – 'from cross to crown'.

In this historical tradition there is evidence for the following interpretations:

(*i*) If God raised from the dead and exalted the Jesus whom the Jews killed, then by so doing he put the Jews in the wrong.[21] If this God is the God of the Torah, then the Jews obviously condemned him wrongly and acted in ἀνομία and contrary to the manifest will of God (Acts 2.23f.; I Thess. 2.15). He was not crucified in the name of the Torah; he was crucified contrary to the will of God, to which the Torah witnesses. It follows from this that the Jewish Christians are the true 'God-fearers' in Israel, the holy remnant, the beginning of the people of the twelve tribes in their messianically renewed form. By observing the will of God in Jesus, and by expecting him as Messiah and Son of man, they are also trying to fulfil the true will of God in the law, in that they keep the commandment of love.

(*ii*) If the crucified Jesus is expected as the coming Son of man on the basis of his appearances, then the messianic hope is directed first of all towards Israel – towards the renewal of the people of God and the true fulfilment of the law – and only then and afterwards towards the salvation of the Gentiles. The death of Christ is made comprehensible, not by the antithesis of the law, but by the evidence of scripture. But this only counts as 'proof' for the Jews, who live according to the scriptures. The divine 'must' is revealed in Jesus' death in the framework of God's historical dealings with Israel. The testimony of scripture was necessary for the interpretation of the crucifixion, as the passion narratives show. But this was not true of the resurrection. That was directly clear to faith, without mediation. But the resurrection of Christ made the cross of Christ a mystery. 'Why was it necessary that the Christ should suffer these things?' That is why all statements about the meaning and significance of his death are based on the perception of the eschatological person of Jesus; and this perception is in its turn based on the recognition of his appearance in glory. The understanding of the risen Christ, however, had to be verified against his cross. The criterion for the interpretation of Easter is the full perception of Jesus' cross. Here it is evident that scriptural proof was not yet able to overcome the scandal of the cross with the divine δεῖ. The cross remained a more difficult paradox and a more resistant riddle.

(*iii*) Another interpretation of Jesus' death is evident in the early Aramaic-speaking church. Here the cross was understood as atoning death, as the fragment of tradition taken over by Paul shows (I Cor. 15.3b–5): 'Christ died for our sins in accordance with the scriptures.'[22] Late Israelite ideas and Isaiah 53 as it was used describe the saving meaning of Jesus' death as atonement. It is historically probable that in I Cor 15. 3b–5 we have the 'oldest kerygma of the atoning death of Jesus Christ'.[23] The reason for his suffering is our sin, the goal of his suffering is our atonement, the grounds for his suffering are to be found in the gracious will of God. The entry of Greek-speaking Jews from the diaspora into the community of Christ may have led to this interpretation of Jesus' death. Yet even these ideas of expiation do not lead to the development of the gospel of justification apart from the law, for they presuppose the unbroken validity of Israel's covenant and law, and interpret Jesus' death as being the inner restitution of this covenant.

(*iv*) The attitude to the law becomes a problem, however, at the moment when the messianic expectation changes because of knowledge of Christ – when, in the present experience of the Spirit, in some circles of the primitive church (the group round Stephen) the apocalyptic temple prophecies seem to be fulfilled – the destruction of the earthly temple and its replacement by a new, more perfect temple, according to Tob. 13.15ff.; 14.5; Jub. 1.17; Sib. 3.290; Enoch 90.28; and where, through the coming of faith among the Gentiles, the Israelite order of hope – 'first the Jews – then the Gentiles' – is thrown into confusion.[24] Apocalyptic enthusiasm caused conflict with the temple and the law and led to persecution both by the Jews and by Jewish Christians. If the cross of Jesus was not as yet a subject for discussion in this conflict between Jewish and Hellenistic Christians, the messianic disciple-ship of the exalted Christ leads all the same to conflict with the law and its guardians. The coming of faith to the Gentiles was bound to be interpreted by the messianic hope in such a way that that future, which was only suppposed to dawn after the restitution of Israel, had now dawned already, and had even passed Israel by. A congregation made up of Jews and Gentiles can no longer see itself as a messianic movement of renewal for Israel, but only as 'the new people of God'; it is no longer the synagogue, but 'the eschatological temple', the ἐκκλησία. This made the law of Israel and the way to the divine righteousness in the law a problem for Christians for the first time. In reaction, the Jewish Christian community became more strongly nomistic than before. On the other hand, the apocalyptic experience of the Spirit in a congre-gation of 'Jews and Gentiles' leads to antinomianism. Whereas in the one group the righteousness of God was measured against the law (so that people wanted to make this a condition for Gentile Christians as well), in the other group the righteousness of God was found in the Spirit: 'God manifested in the flesh, vindicated in the Spirit' (I Tim. 3.16). Between incarnation and enthronement in the Spirit of God there is no room for the law and the cross.

(v) Finally, in Hellenistic enthusiasm we meet the beginning of Gnosticism, a radical gospel free from the law. If the new 'divine covenant' exists in 'the Spirit and liberty', then it no longer knows any difference between Jews and Gentiles: they are 'all one in Christ'.[25] Here apparently the law, in contrast to the Spirit, moves into the sphere of the transitoriness of flesh and death. 'The Lord is the Spirit' and makes the already existing transcending of flesh, law and death, possible everywhere. The resurrection has already

taken place in the Spirit. In the Spirit there is already liberty
(II Cor. 3.17). He who has the Spirit lives in the heavenly sphere
of righteousness beyond the earthly law. Transitory man becomes
just when he becomes spiritualized in the immortal Spirit.

We can therefore see how, in the conflicts of the first congregations, different experiences of the exalted Lord correspond to
different attitudes to the law and to the divine righteousness. The
attitude to the law is justified by differing perceptions of the risen
Christ and of what is present through him. Among Jewish
Christians the righteousness of God is evidently understood as the
messianic renewal of Israel, as the permeation of the law by the
Spirit and as the expiatory restitution of a covenant. In Hellenistic
Enthusiasm it is interpreted as spiritualization. On the one hand
the righteousness of God is bound to Israel's priority in salvation
history. On the other hand, in a way of thinking which is dualistic
and Greek, it is opposed to the world and the history of transitoriness.

If we ask how the event of the resurrection of the crucified Jesus
can be appropriately expressed, we are bound to realize that on the
one hand the cross of the exalted Jesus does burst asunder the
known categories of Jewish messianism. Yet on the other hand, it can
hardly be made clear that the Lord who is present in the Spirit and
as the Spirit is the Jesus who was crucified. On the one hand the
gospel is not universal and presuppositionless; it is conceived under
the presupposition of Israel's law and in the framework of Israel's
messianic expectations. On the other hand it is conceived so
completely without presuppositions that it can hardly still be the
gospel of the crucified Jesus of Nazareth. The identity of the crucified and risen Christ cannot be expressed either by the addition of law
and messianic hope, or in the dualistic antithesis of law and Spirit.
Jewish Christian apocalyptic and Hellenistic spiritualization both
run aground on the Christ event; they strand, that is, on the *cross*
of the risen Christ.

4. *The Knowledge of Christ and the Pauline Doctrine of Justification*

Paul was the first to reflect theologically about the problem of a
gospel free of the law. He solved it through his Christology of the
crucified Jesus, by interpreting Christ's accursed death on the

cross as redemption from the curse of the law (Gal. 3.13) and by proclaiming Christ as the 'end of the law' (Rom. 10.4).[26] If the gospel of Christ is the power of God for salvation because it brings the divine righteousness without any presuppositions and reveals it χωρὶς νόμου, then this gospel is 'the word of the cross', as the parallel between Rom. 1.16f. and I Cor. 1.18 ('the word of the cross is to us who are being saved the power of God') shows. Paul therefore gives serious weight to the fact that Jesus was condemned in the name of the law. Paul does not see divine activity for the first time in the resurrection; he already finds it in the crucifixion: the Son has been 'given up' by the Father (Rom. 8.32). His Christology is therefore theocentric. It is an interpretation of the working formula that 'God has raised him from the dead'. For Paul, Jesus' death on the cross is not accounted for by the error or the lawlessness of the Jews, or by the mortal nature of all men. He understands it as God-forsakenness, as the curse, as the divine judgment itself: 'For our sake God made him to be sin who knew no sin' (II Cor. 5.21). Jesus therefore dies in the name of the law as one condemned and cursed by God (Gal. 3.13).

If God raised this condemned, forsaken, crucified Jesus, then everything is changed: if the earthly Jesus, with his claim, dies because of the law, then the law with its claim dies because of the exalted Jesus. If judgment is passed on him in his crucifixion, then the judgment ends with his resurrection and is turned into grace. If death is the end of him, then the risen Christ becomes the end of death. The raising of the crucified Jesus (who in this sense is as if 'given up' by God) cannot therefore mean only a messianic hope in addition to, or within, Israel's law. Nor can it mean the spiritualization of everything mortal. It must rather be understood as new creation. If the one who is annihilated through the judgment is called into the life of God, then God's righteousness χωρὶς νόμου emerges in the raising of the crucified Jesus. Just as the resurrection of the dead and creation out of nothing are without any presuppositions (since they come solely from God's free good pleasure and free grace), so the divine righteousness becomes manifest to all wretched men and women, without the presupposition of the fulfilment of the law. God's action in Christ is the self-revealing, self-asserting and all-conquering divine righteousness.

For men and women this means that obedience to the law is no longer the presupposition for the winning of righteousness and life.

The law becomes God's accusation and challenge to sinful man, for it makes his misery obvious to him (Rom. 7.8ff.). The cross of Christ turns the law from a human path to salvation into God's prosecuting witness against inhuman man. 'The just shall live', we are told in the law. The law itself was the condition of righteousness. If Christ becomes 'the end of the law' through his crucifixion and resurrection, then he also becomes the end of this condition. That is why we now read 'The just shall live by faith' (Rom. 1.17, AV). The promise of life is not achieved by the works of the law. Christ's resurrection means that God has fulfilled the promise of life and made it effective in the one who was cursed in the name of the law. That is why the law does not have the power to make alive. But if it does not have that power, then it thrusts the person who seeks life in the law even deeper into his own death. The power to make alive is inherent in the gospel of the resurrection of the crucified Jesus, for it is in this that the victory of life over death appears. It communicates the life-giving Spirit to the dying (Rom. 8.11). 'Christ was put to death (AV 'delivered') for our trespasses and raised for our justification' (Rom. 4.25). 'For our sake he made him to be sin, so that in him we might become the righteousness of God' (II Cor. 5.21). If this perception of Christ is in line with the event of the cross and resurrection, then the gospel of the justification of the sinner becomes the true interpretation of that event.

Let us sum up our most important findings:

1. If in what God has done in Christ the righteousness of God is manifest χωρὶς νόμου, i.e., without any presuppositions, then the universal meaning of Christ for all sinners, whether Jews or Gentiles, is manifest here too. The presuppositionlessness of God's grace is the inner foundation of the gospel's universality.

2. The external reason for this universality of the gospel then lies in the fact that it is the sinner who is justified (Rom. 3.23). The gospel declares sinful, captive dying men to be just and free, and in this way it is addresssed to man in his real wretchedness, whether he be Jew or Gentile, master or slave, man or woman, Greek or barbarian.

3. That is why this gospel is heard at the time when God's wrath and his judgment over the godlessness of man becomes manifest, and all men arrive at solidarity in their wretchedness, because of the pressure of their afflictions (Rom. 1.18; 8.18).

The two things are directly connected with one another: on the one hand the basing of justification on the raising of the crucified Jesus; and on the other the apocalyptic horizon of the miseries of the present time, the general misery of all men and of the whole creation, into which the gospel is sent and in which it is necessary.

If the raising of the crucified Jesus is no longer understood Hellenistically as his spiritualization, and is no longer interpreted in Jewish terms as his enthronement as Son of man, but if we see it as God's new creation – then in this case the resurrection manifests something new for the whole creation which has been reduced to misery. Here the *ex nihilo* is not simply to be understood ontologically and as a theology of creation. What is here called 'nothing' and 'annihilation' becomes manifest in the cross of Christ. It does not mean, that is to say, the finitude of existence or merely the transitoriness of all things. It means an *annihilatio* such as descends on all being in the end of all things. It is not transitoriness within the world but the passing of the world itself; not merely the mutability of timeless being, but its ultimate inability to endure. It is 'absolute suffering', the 'infinite pain of the negative', as Hegel put it. That is why the cross of Jesus has universal meaning for the whole wretched creation, assailed as it is by the intruding Nothingness. The wrath of God and the misery of creation, its inability to endure and its sinking into nothingness hangs over everything; but it is manifest and comes into effect in the one 'who was made sin for us'. In the cross of Christ the relentless pressure of creation is laid bare and is enforced on him in creation's stead. God 'gave up' his Son (Rom. 8.2) for those who were 'given up' to the power of their godlessness (Rom. 1.24). The 'giving up' formula is universal: all men are given up to the power of sin and the wrath of God; and the formula is to be understood christologically: Christ is given up 'for all', so that they may live in him. That is why his cross can no longer be interpreted merely as being a prophet's destiny, or as an expiatory offering under the old covenant. Its historical Good Friday reveals and puts into force the 'speculative Good Friday . . . in all the truth and stringency of its godlessness'.[27] What is revealed in the raising of this one person is hence *nova creatio* for everyone. If we want to be precise we must say: the raising of the crucified Jesus is a *nova creatio per annihilationem nihili*: out of the annihilation of nothingness the Being emerges that has overcome death – this 'absolute death' – and is hence life and eternal bliss. The new creation does not emerge out of the restoration of the old creation; it follows from creation's end. Out of 'the negation of the negative' a Being arises that has overcome the conflict between being and non-being and is hence absolutely new.

If this is true, then sin cannot be merely understood in anthropological terms as transgression of the law, guilt, and distress of conscience on man's part. Law and conscience reveal the oppression of 'the power of sin', which is at once godlessness and God-forsakenness. That is why behind sin is death – absolute death and the total end. Sin is not merely the anthropological problem of man's self-division and self-alienation, nor is it merely the theological problem of remoteness from God. It is an apocalyptic pressure of affliction for everything that wants to live and has to die. 'The power of sin' is not merely a religious or moral power. It does not merely comprehend the question of human guilt. It is also the divine lament of all senseless suffering in the world, the suffering and injustice 'that cries out to high heaven'.

We have to see the justification of the sinner through word and faith as nothing less than the beginning of new creation and the transformation of the creation that is sinking into negation of being. It is salvation as *soteria* and *shalom*, salvation as life from the dead and the annihilation of death, and the extermination of the godless powers of futility. It is the new creation of the world on the foundation of God's righteousness – as glory. The forgiveness of sins does not make 'the wiping away of tears from every eye' superfluous or unimportant; on the contrary, it makes it necessary and the possible object of hope. These are not merely the tears of one's own repentance, but tears over 'this world, in which children suffer and die'.[28] The gospel of the self-revealing divine righteousness cannot be unfolded merely against the existential question of guilt. It must also be developed in the light of the general divine lament of suffering. Faith does not secularize man, in the context of this second question. It makes him one with the sighs of the whole afflicted creation, because it makes him one with the divine complaint of the Christ dying in forsakenness.

The gospel answers the question of guilt with the assurance of the borrowed righteousness of Christ; it responds to the sighs of oppressed creation with the avowal of confidence. We shall now be free from the damning power of our past, because the generative power for a new future will be embedded in our present.[29]

5. *The Resurrection of Christ and the Justification of the Sinner*

We must now come back to the three sets of questions from which we started and subject them to a systematic examination. We shall begin with the second question, which had to do with the foundation of justification in the Christ event.

The credal documents of the Reformation (Confession of Augsburg IV and Schmalkaldic Articles II) offer '*propter Christum*' as the basis for the present event of justification. For this they always quote Rom. 4.25. If Christ 'was raised for our justification', then the goal and divine intention of the Christ event seems to lie in the present event of justification of sinful man. As Augustine said long ago, the present justification of man through word and faith appears to be the true *usus resurrectionis Christi*: '. . . in illo vera resurrectio, ita in nobis vera justificatio.'[30] This can lead to Christology's becoming the metaphysical background for the present anthropological event of the justification of man in faith. Then the present event of justification and faith becomes the 'centre and limit' of Christian theology, in the sense that all theological statements are made for its sake, and find their *Sitz im Leben* there. What goes beyond is then *error et venenum in theologia*.[31] Contrary to this, Barth maintained that 'The *articulus stantis et cadentis ecclesiae* is not the doctrine of justification as such, but its basis and culmination: the confession of Jesus Christ . . .'.[32] Barth says this so that in his doctrine of reconciliaton he can treat justification, together with sanctification and vocation, as an aspect of reconciliation. H. J. Iwand talked in a similar way about 'the primacy of Christology'.[33]

(*i*) *Justificatio impii* is in fact the present *usus resurrectionis* for godless and God-forsaken man. But it must be noticed that in Reformation theology *usus* does not mean the use which man makes of the gospel when he believes. It always means the *usus Dei*, the use which God makes of the gospel for man. *Justificatio impii* is the present *usus resurrectionis Christi* employed by God in the sinner; but it does not therefore itself already have to be *finis resurrectionis Christi*. The meaning of Christ and the meaning of God's act in the Christ event are not exhausted in what they now mean to me, sinful man. If I ask about the meaning of an event, I do not only ask what it says to me, and says to me now; I ask what its own purpose is, what it indicates and presents. The 'meaning' of an event means initially its own future – the sense, the promise, the goal and the intention of this particular event. That certainly includes the meaning of the event for me, but it is not totally engrossed by that.

If we ask about the goal of the Christ event according to Paul's interpretation, as he expounds, discloses and preaches it in his 'final clauses', we do not merely arrive at 'for our justification'; through that and beyond that we come to his lordship 'both of the dead and the living' (Rom. 14.9), and to the brotherhood of the new people of God with the Son of God (Rom. 8.29). The end is not only 'our reconciliation' but also 'the reconciliation of the world' and the coming of the creative power of the Spirit (Gal. 3.13). It is not only 'reconciliation' but also 'life from the dead' (Rom. 11.15), the resurrection from the dead and the sole lordship of God as well (I Cor. 15.25). In the pre-Pauline hymns the goal is the world lordship of the humiliated one, in the deutero-Pauline ones the ἀνακεφαλαίωσις τῶν πάντων. God did not therefore deliver Christ up merely 'for our sins'. Christ is not only the author of faith but, through and beyond faith, the author of life from the dead as well. He was, in general, not merely raised 'for our sakes'; he was raised for the sake of the new creation of the world and the universal lordship of God. That is why he will ultimately give the kingdom over to the Father, so that God may be all in all (I Cor. 15.28, AV). God's actions in Christ's crucifixion and resurrection lead ultimately, through the justification of the sinner, to God's own glorification in the new creation.

(*ii*) The present event of man's justification is therefore orientated towards Christ and his future. Because it reveals the divine righteousness in man effected in Christ, the revelation of it belongs to the rule of Christ's parousia and its preparation. This event is consequently both determinative of the present and revealing of the future: the righteousness of God is believed (Rom. 1.17) and hoped for (Gal. 5.5). The righteousness of God which reveals itself in the gospel to the godless is therefore both gift and power, assurance and promise, obedience and liberty. It does not as yet set man down at his goal, but only puts him on the road to it. It makes him part of the process through which God establishes his divinity, his justice and his glory, and brings the whole creation into his own liberty. It is therefore received in faith and reached out for in hope and love. It is possessed in the rejoicing of the divine sonship and in sighs shared with the whole suffering creation – the one is not without the other.

In the existing event of justification, the future for which Christ died and rose again is already present with the poor, the oppressed and the dying. The God who creates life from nothing shows his divinity in the new liberty of the godless and forsaken. The Father of the crucified Jesus shows the power of the resurrection in the Spirit of hope in those heavy laden with guilt and those who sigh over the suffering of the world. So this present event is God's way to the godless; it opens up a way of access for the God-forsaken into the liberty of his kingdom.

(*iii*) In the event of the justification of the godless and the promise of liberty for the oppressed, Christ exercises his rule; and through this God proves his divinity. It is only when we note this 'theocentric character' of the event of justification that we catch sight of the cosmic breadth and become aware of the human depth with which Paul proclaims the righteousness of God as being the future of the whole of creation. In the Christ event the revelation of God's divinity and of the liberty of the children of God begins. In the liberating event of the justification of the miserable there is a 'reference forward to the resurrection of the dead'.[34] The righteousness of God is therefore not exhausted in the forgiveness of sins but aims, through the forgiveness of sins, at the new creation of all things on the foundation of righteousness.[35] The goal of the *historia Christi* lies beyond the *fides justificans* in the overcoming of the whole misery of the longing and waiting creation. That is why it is above all the justified who hunger for the divine righteousness. That is why it is above all the children of God who sigh for liberty, in solidarity with the whole creation. That is why it is love that makes the suffering of others unendurable for the first time. That is why it is the idea of this God that is the driving incentive behind the problem of theodicy. For the absurdity of injustice and of suffering in the world only acquires meaning in the degree to which we declare ourselves opposed to these things. Trust and hope in this God are the incentives to declare ourselves opposed to that injustice and suffering, to call evil and death in question, and as far as possible to combat them.

6. *The Justification of the Godless and the Transformation of the World*

The third set of questions with which we began was connected with the goal of the justification of the sinner: does justification restore a lost condition, or is it the beginning of something creatively new?

As long as man's misery, poverty, sin and death is measured against a remembered primal condition when there was fellowship with God, when man was in identity with himself and at peace with his neighbour and the cosmos, it is inescapable that this primal condition of integrity emerges again as restored in the goal of the justification event – whether it is restored as law, or as cosmos, or as man's original condition as being the image of God. A primal era balanced against the End-time is a pattern that is familiar from apocalyptic eschatology: τὰ ἔσχατα ὡς τὰ πρῶτα. It has parallels in the Greek idea of world aeons. Considered in the context of this pattern, the justification of the sinner would be the restoration of that original condition of being made in the image of God against which the sinner sinned.

> What meaning therefore has the divine righteousness or the forgiveness of sins? . . . Its meaning is that the original relationship of creation will be restored, that the complex of sin in which I still stand, the complex of being-flesh, or being-world, will be ended, that the ancient revelation will be again made visible.[36]

Man has set himself in contradiction to God and because of this has lost himself. 'God's contradiction calls him back to himself, to that which he really is.' This is an age-old mythological scheme which is not demythologized simply by talking about 'authentic existence' instead of heaven, and 'alienation' instead of hell – that is to say, by subjectivizing objective notions about the world-picture, as Bultmann does:

> No light shone in Jesus other than the light that always shone in creation. In the light of the revelation of redemption, man does not have to understand himself any differently from the way he was always supposed to understand himself in the face of revelation in creation and law: as God's creation.

In the event of justification and in faith self-deifying and hence self-alienated man finds his way back to himself again, to his authentic existence. He had lost himself through sin, yet his vocation to be his true self in the form of remembrance cannot be lost by man and is the question of who he really is. In this scheme, moreover, the victory of Christ over the forces of this world which are hostile to God would make it possible for Christians again to live in the cosmos, once more understood as creation. Sin distorts the true being of man, justification restores it again. Sin darkens creation, grace brings it to light again in its primal form. Here the goal of the Christ event is understood as restitution, and restitution is presupposed as being present, and as not having been lost in spite of all distortion. It is the positive thing with which sin is contrasted as the thing that is negative. The forgiveness and overcoming of sin therefore restores what was originally positive, being the negation of the negative. The 'new thing' in the justificatory event is then only new for sinning and perverted man: it is not new in itself.

It is noticeable however, that in the promise of the future world and the new creation, Paul avoids the accusatory 'authorities' that impeach man for his sin – the accusers named in Romans 1–3: the cosmos, the law and the conscience.[37] His statements about the creative actions of God are contained in his resurrection kerygma. It is the God 'who gives life to the dead and calls into existence the things that do not exist' (Rom. 4.17). They are also contained in his doctrine of justification: man is dead because of sin. He is made alive by Christ. Resurrection and justification are therefore a creative quickening – indeed 'life from the dead' (Rom. 11.15). If justification interprets the event of Christ's resurrection, it also conveys the life-giving spirit of the resurrection; 'the power of his resurrection' (Phil. 3.10). The expressions used to visualize the future and the new being of man do not go back to some presupposd primal condition; they explain the 'new thing' of the raising of the crucified Jesus by promising his lordship over everything, the dead and the living: 'The city has no need of sun or moon to shine upon it, for the glory of God is its light, and its lamp is the Lamb' (Rev. 21.23). The person who is justified finds his path to life in the community of Christ. Through his death he comes under the rule of the crucified Jesus even in this transitory world. His future and his true life are hid with Christ in God, which is why he expects his own liberty from the future glorification of Christ

(Col. 3.2–4). Justification is therefore not a restoration of man springing from his beginning; it is the new beginning of his becoming man at his end. Faith in justification is therefore bound up with eschatological hope, not with memory of the beginning. Justification is not the adoption of man's lost origin, but the anticipation of his new future. This is not only new for perverted man; it is new in itself. It is not merely new in fact, but new in principle. That is why it finally transforms not man alone, but all things. The event of justification in man is part of a universal transfiguration of the passing world, and is to be understood as its beginning. Consequently there is not only a *usus resurectionis* in man's justification. There is another in the eschatological transformation of the passing world through glorification. Sin and suffering cannot simply be overcome through man's new understanding of them and new attitude towards them. They can only be surmounted by the new reality of righteousness and life.

This is finally clear when we add to the statements about the resurrection of the dead and the *creatio ex nihilo* in the justifying gospel statements that are 'socially critical' and ecclesiological. If the gospel of Christ justifies the godless and the God-forsaken, the poor and the despised, then this is conspicuously and polemically directed against all the self-righteous, the self-assured and the great:

> He has put down the mighty from their thrones,
> and exalted those of low degree;
> he has filled the hungry with good things,
> and the rich he has sent empty away
> (Luke 1.50–53).

God chose what is foolish in the world to shame the wise, God chose what is weak in the world to shame the strong, God chose what is low and despised in the world, even things that are not, to bring to nothing things that are... Let him who boasts, boast of the Lord (I Cor. 1.27–31).

The connections show the goal of justification clearly. The dialectic of transformation aims at eschatological glory. The dialectic of faith in justification – 'righteous and yet a sinner' – is hence not paradoxically closed, but telelogically open: *'peccator in re – justus in spe.*

7. *Summary*

Creation is oppressed by Nothingness. In the justification of the godless and in faith we see the beginning of the transformation and the creation of the whole for the glorification of God.

The gospel becomes restorative in the notion of the restoration of the original creation, which was said to be good.

If it is only taken by itself as healing power for sinners and the miserable, without criticism of what is and and what considers itself of importance, the gospel becomes the uncritical compensation for existing evil.

Its liberating power only becomes manifest when it is based on the resurrection of the crucified Jesus, and when it is directed critically towards the eschatological transformation of the unjust world, which has been reduced to misery and is sinking into Nothingness. Then what Albert Camus supposed would happen will be impossible: that Christianity will insist on letting the virtue of rebellion and protest against suffering be torn from it – the virtue that once belonged to it a long time ago. Then its faith and its hope for the divine righteousness 'in heaven and on earth' will enter into dialogue with the movements for righteousness on earth, with the philosophy of the cross (Camus) and the philosophy of the resurrection (Bloch). Justifying faith will then belong entirely to the others, because it belongs entirely to the crucified liberator, Jesus Christ. The doctrine of the creative righteousness of God revealed in the resurrection of the crucified Jesus is the *articulus stantis et cadentis hominis*.

ABBREVIATIONS

BEvTh	Beihefte zur Evangelischen Theologie, Munich
CD	Karl Barth, *Church Dogmatics*, ET T. & T. Clark, Edinburgh and Eerdmans, Grand Rapids, Michigan 1936–69
CIOMS	Council for International Organisations of Medical Sciences
ET	English translation
EvKomm	*Evangelische Kommentare*, Stuttgart
EvTh	*Evangelische Theologie*, Munich
KiZ	*Kirche in der Zeit*, Düsseldorf
KuD	*Kerygma und Dogma*, Göttingen
NThT	*Nederlandsche theologisch tijdschrift*, Wageningen
NTQ	Ernst Käsemann, *New Testament Questions of Today*, ET of *Exegetische Versuche und Besinnungen* II, SCM Press and Fortress Press, Philadelphia 1969
NTS	*New Testament Studies*, Cambridge
RGG	*Die Religion in Geschichte und Gegenwart*, 3rd ed., Tübingen 1956–65
SBT	Studies in Biblical Theology, SCM Press and Allenson, Naperville
StZ	*Stimmen der Zeit*, Freiburg
TDNT	*Theological Dictionary of the New Testament*, ET Grand Rapids, Michigan 1964–76
ThB	Theologische Bücherei, Munich
ThEx	Theologische Existenz heute, Munich
ThF	Theologische Forschung, Hamburg
ThSt	Theologische Studien, Zürich
TLZ	*Theologische Literaturzeitung*, Leipzig
VuF	*Verkündigung und Forschung*, Munich
WA	Martin Luther, *Werke*, Weimarer Ausgabe, 1883ff.
WCC	World Council of Churches
ZdZ	*Zwischen den Zeiten*, Munich
ZThK	*Zeitschrift für Theologie und Kirche*, Tübingen

NOTES

I The Future as a New Paradigm of Transcendence

1. Here I am adopting Paul Tillich's term 'boundary'. Cf. also G. D. Kaufmann, 'On the Meaning of "God"; Transcendence without Mythology' in *New Theology* 4, ed. M. E. Marty, New York 1967, pp.69–98. On the definition of transcendence and immanence, cf. G. Stammler, 'Ontologie in der Theologie', *KuD* 4, 1958, p.143ff.

2. For this theological approach in Karl Barth cf. H.-G. Geyer,' Gottes Sein als Thema der Theologie', *VuF* 2, 1966, pp.3–36, and E. Jüngel, *Gottes Sein im Werden, Verantwortliche Rede vom Sein Gottes bei Karl Barth*, Tübingen 1965. On the philosophical problem cf. D. Henrich, *Der ontologische Gottesbeweis*, Tübingen 1960.

3. Aristotle, *Metaphysics* XII, ed. W. Jaeger, Oxford 1957, 1076a 34. With this quotation from *Iliad* II 204, Aristotle is adopting a political concept of unity. Cf. E. Peterson, 'Der Monotheismus als politisches Problem' in *Theologische Traktate*, Munich 1951, pp.49–164.

4. In what follows we are adopting the analyses of Karl Marx and Max Weber. For Marx the question was: why have circumstances become independent and opposed to men and women? Why has the power of their own life won the upper hand over them? Max Weber says of the this-worldly asceticism of modern Puritanism: 'Since asceticism undertook to remodel the world, material goods have gained an increasing and finally an inexorable power over the lives of men as at no previous period in history. Today the spirit of religious asceticism – whether finally, who knows? – has escaped from the cage' (*The Protestant Ethic and the Spirit of Capitalism*, ET Allen & Unwin and Scribner's, New York 1930, p.181).

5. C. Schmitt, *Politische Romantik*, 2nd ed., Leipzig 1925, p.227.

6. Cf. here H. Jonas, *Gnosis und spätantiker Geist* I, 2nd ed., Göttingen 1954, and 'Gnosticism and Modern Nihilism' in *Social Research* 19, New York 1952, pp.430–52.

7. Cf. R. Garaudy, 'Vom Bannfluch zum Dialog' in Garaudy, J. B. Metz and K. Rahner, *Der Dialog*, Hamburg 1966, p.91. This question about transcendence has since been taken up by many Marxists.

8. A. Gehlen first pointed to this ambivalence about alienation (*Entfremdung*) and release (*Entlastung*): see 'Die Geburt der Freiheit aus der Entfremdung' in *Studien zur Anthropologie und Soziologie*, Neuwied 1963, pp.232ff. and *Urmensch und Spätkultur*, Bonn 1956.

9. I am unable to see anything other than this in the hippie movement,

the transcendental-meditation trend, drug-taking and similar tendencies. One does not have to be a Puritan to come to this conclusion. As Harvey Cox has rightly perceived, a new 'post-industrial religiosity' is growing up here. But we ought rather to 'remain true to the earth' as Nietzsche puts it, even if the earth threatens to become uninteresting.

10. Dietrich Bonhoeffer, 8 June 1944, *Letters and Papers from Prison*, ET, 3rd enlarged edition, SCM Press and Macmillan, New York 1971, p.325.

11. G. W. F. Hegel, *The Phenomenology of Mind*, ET, 2nd ed. revised, Allen & Unwin and Macmillan, New York 1931, p.81.

12. Cf. G. Rohrmoser, *Subjektivität und Verdinglichung. Theologie und Gesellschaft im Denken des jungen Hegel*, Gütersloh 1961.

13. Cf. the title essay in my collection *Hope and Planning*, ET SCM Press and Harper & Row, New York 1971, pp.178–99.

14. I therefore think that R. Shaull uses the modern concept of 'transcending' rightly. Cf. his essay on 'Revolutionary Change in Theological Perspective' in *Christian Social Ethics in a Changing World*, ed. John C. Bennett, SCM Press and Association Press, New York 1966, pp.23–43 (one of the preparatory volumes for the WCC Conference on 'Christians in the Technical and Social Revolutions of our Time' held in Geneva later that year). H. E. Tödt takes a different view in his contribution to *Theologie der Revolution*, ed. Tödt and T. Rendtorff, Frankfurt 1968, pp.23ff. But we ought not to level down the concept of transcendence historically as Garaudy does, but should keep the 'qualitative alteration' in mind. It is this that makes it impossible for history to be perfected under history's conditions and makes revolution 'permanent revolution' unless it betrays itself.

15. Cf. T. W. Adorno, *Minima Moralia. Reflexionen aus dem beschädigten Leben*, Frankfurt 1963, p.333: 'The only way philosophy could be justified in the face of despair would be if it were the attempt to view all things in the way in which they present themselves from the standpoint of redemption. Knowledge has no light except the light that shines from redemption in the world. Everything else exhausts itself in imitation and remains a piece of technology.'

16. J. L. Austin, *How to Do Things with Words*, Oxford University Press 1965, investigates language in the sphere of moral philosophy but not as yet in the sphere of practical philosophy.

17. Did Luther have something like this in mind when he wrote, in reference to Rom. 8.19: 'Aliter Apostolus de rebus philosophatur et sapit quam philosophi et metaphysici. Quia philosophi oculum ita in praesentiam rerum immergunt, ut solum quidditates et qualitates earum speculentur, Apostolus autem oculos nostros revocat ab intuitu rerum praesentium, ab essentia et accidentibus earum et dirigit in eas secundum quod futurae sunt. Non enim dicit "essentia" vel "operatio" creaturae seu "actio" et "passio" et "motus", sed novo et miro vocabulo et theologico dicit "expectatio creaturae" ut eo ipso, cum animus audit creaturam expectare, non ipsam creaturam amplius, sed quid creatura expectat, in-

tendat et quaerat' (*Vorlesung über den Römerbrief* 1515/1516, ed. J. Ficker, Leipzig 1908, p.198; WA 56, p.371)?

18. This is a critical point in the theory that Marxism is transcendence. This theory is upheld by J. Krejči, 'Ein neues Modell des wissenschaftlichen Atheismus' in *Internationale Dialog-Zeitschrift*, Vienna, Freiburg and Basel 1968, Heft 2, pp. 191ff., especially pp. 197ff.

19. L. Landgrebe, 'Das philosophische Problem des Endes der Geschichte' in *Kritik und Metaphysik. Festschrift für H. Heimsoeth*, Berlin 1966.

II Trends in Eschatology

1. J. Weiss, *Die Predigt Jesu vom Reiche Gottes*, Göttingen 1964, p.236. This is a reprint of the 2nd, completely revised edition of 1900 (of 214pp.), with an appendix containing important sections of the 1st ed. of 1892 (of only 67pp.), ed. F. Hahn, with an introduction by R. Bultmann. (cf. ET of the 1st edition, *Jesus' Proclamation of the Kingdom of God*, SCM Press and Fortress Press, Philadelphia 1971, p.114).

2. Ibid., p.246 (cf. ET of 1st ed., p.135).

3. See here the typological interpretation in W. Kreck, *Die Zukunft des Gekommenen*, Munich 1961, pp.14ff., and G. Sauter, *Zukunft und Verheissung*, Zürich 1965, pp.84ff.

4. On Bultmann's eschatology cf. H. Ott, *Geschichte und Heilsgeschichte in der Theologie Rudolf Bultmanns*, Tübingen 1955; J. Körner, *Eschatologie und Geschichte. Eine Untersuchung des Begriffs des Eschatologischen in der Theologie R. Bultmanns*, ThF 13, 1957; also the critical discussions in Kreck, op. cit., pp.50ff., J. Moltmann, *Theology of Hope*, ET SCM Press and Harper & Row, New York 1967, pp.58ff., and Sauter, op. cit., pp. 115ff.

5. O. Cullmann, *Christ and Time*, ET of 3rd ed., SCM Press and Westminster Press, Philadelphia 1962, and *Salvation in History*, ET SCM Press and Harper & Row, New York 1970.

6. E. Brunner, *Eternal Hope*, ET Lutterworth Press and Westminster Press, Philadelphia 1954, pp.59f.: 'This paradox appears in the fact that exegetes hold contradictory views about the relationship of present and future in the primitive community. Some speak of a "realized eschatology" and see in the event of Pentecost the Parousia proclaimed by Christ (Dodd), while others relate the primitive community to the framework of contemporary Judaism and its purely futuristic apocalyptic (A. Schweitzer); others, again, see the decisive fact in what happened once for all in Christ but none the less regard the expectation of what is to be as the culminating moment of the Christian faith (Cullmann, E. Schweizer, Kümmel, etc.), and others yet again view this orientation towards the future as a purely mythological expression of what is really meant – the new character of the present (Bultmann).'

7. It is true that in his book Kreck has spoken out against 'cheap harmonizations' of different New Testament theologies and against the

harmonizations of contrasting understandings of eschatology today (pp. 118f.). But he is really seeking for 'the eschatology of the Bible' and would like to relativize the differing views of a Christian eschatology as being merely different emphases. For a critical view of this cf. P. Stuhlmacher, *Gerechtigkeit Gottes bei Paulus*, Göttingen 1965, p.206 n.2, and K. Linke, 'Grundprobleme der Eschatologie', *KiZ* 18, 1963, pp.299–305.

8. Op. cit. pp.50, 80, 82 et passim. The possible adoption of the Lutheran *simul* must not of course overlook the fact that in Luther's formula *res* and *spes* are confronted with one another and that in faith in justification the future of righteousness gains the upper hand over the condition of our transient sins. If we were to stabilize this non-simultaneous 'at once' as a simultaneous paradox, we should be overlooking the character of 'process' in this real dialectic. I do not understand what a 'paradox' is whose 'conceptual possibility can only be grasped pneumatically' (W. Kreck, op. cit., appendix). Christ's cross and resurrection are no paradox if Christ died and rose again *for the purpose* of being 'Lord both of the dead and of the living' (Rom. 14.9).

9. Cf. K. Rahner, *Theological Investigations* IV: *More Recent Writings*, ET Darton, Longman & Todd, and Seabury Press, New York 1966, p. 337: 'Biblical eschatology must always be read as an assertion based on the revealed present and pointing towards the genuine future, but not as an assertion pointing back from an anticipated future into the present. To extrapolate from the present into the future is eschatology, to interpolate from the future into the present is apocalyptic.'

H. Berkhof has made this observation the methodological criterion for eschatology in general: 'The future is an extrapolation of what has already been given in Christ and the Spirit' ('Over de Methode der Eschatologie', *NThT* 19, 1965, pp.480ff.). But if the present is not the already efficacious '*Einstand*' or beginning (E. Jüngel) of the future, no efficacious future can be extrapolated and claimed from it either.

10. This difference also appears in the Johannine exegesis that follows Bultmann. Cf. L. van Hartingsveld, *Die Eschatologie des Johannesevangeliums*, Assen 1962, p.154: 'The statements of presentative eschatology are only possible on the basis of the statements of futurist eschatology. . . Without an eschatological future, an eschatological present is impossible.' Also J. Blank, *Krisis. Untersuchungen zur johanneischen Christologie und Eschatologie*, Freiburg 1964, p.353: 'For John the precise opposite is true: without the eschatological present there is no eschatological future.'

11. P. Althaus, *Die letzten Dinge*, Gütersloh 1922, pp.16f.

12. Kreck, op. cit., pp.40ff.

13. Sauter, op. cit., p.98.

14. Althaus, *Dinge*, Gütersloh ⁷1957, p.18: 'In distinguishing between statements about remaining and statements about coming, I believe the truth to lie in the earlier distinction between "axiological" and "teleological" eschatology.' (From now on, quotations are from the 7th ed.)

15. Op. cit., p.45.

16. Op. cit., p.48.

17. G. Hoffmann, *Das Problem der letzten Dinge in der neueren evangelischen Theologie*, Göttingen 1929, p.84. In n.66 (contrary to Althaus's two statements) he lays down the propositions: '1. Hope is already inherent in faith, in its wider sense of faith in salvation *per se*. 2. Faith in the narrower sense as justifying faith or faith in the present always already stands in the light of hope.'

18. Op. cit., pp.73, 88. Cf. also the discussion on Hoffmann's views in Althaus, op. cit., pp.43ff. Apart from quotations from Paul and John, however, no new systematic viewpoints are offered.

19. P. Althaus, *Die Christliche Wahrheit. Lehrbuch der Dogmatik*, 6th rev. ed., Gütersloh 1963, pp.659ff.

20. G. Hoffmann, op. cit., p.84 n.66.

21. Althaus, *Dinge*, pp.49f.

22. Sauter, op. cit., pp.123ff.; Moltmann, op. cit., pp. 50ff.

23. K. Barth in *ZdZ*, 1931, p.460. Cf. also his *Weihnacht* (Kleine Vandenhoeck-Reihe 48), Göttingen 1957, p.39.

24. Sauter, op. cit., pp.157 and 257ff., has developed these ideas further. H. Gollwitzer's criticism in *EvTh* 26, 1966, pp.166ff., is directed against this very point. In my *Theology of Hope* I have tried to describe Christ's significance for the promise of the future with the idea of βεβαίωσις, confirmation, liberation, putting in force. W. Kreck's criticism is levied against this particular point (op. cit., 2nd ed. 1966, pp. 203–09).

25. H. Ott views this positively; cf. his *Eschatologie*, ThSt 53, Zürich 1958, pp.12f.: 'This view of the eschatological to which we are forced by the existential postulate is inherent in the concept of ἀποκάλυψις. For this means that the future in the striking eschatological sense is nothing other than the being revealed, the unveiling of the meaning of the present.' In the preface (p.4) Ott writes that his insight into the meaning for eschatology of the idea of apocalypse is due above all to Karl Barth. For a critical view see U. Hedinger, *Unsere Zukunft*, ThST 70, Zürich 1963, pp.30ff.: 'Future as Revelation and new Creation', pp.36ff.: 'But beyond apocalypse we understand the eschatological future as being also the creative-ontic happening.' For another, positive view see Kreck, op. cit., pp.83ff. and 100: 'It is true that the fulfilment cannot really be anything other than the unveiling of what is already reality in Jesus Christ: but it is this very unveiling which will now be looked for and waited for as something in the future.' Sauter is critical (op. cit., pp.123ff.): 'The suggestion of the apocalypse motif for an eschatology which must ultimately do away with the contradictions of an allocation of revelation and history which is determined on principle is even more pronouncedly noticeable in Barth [i.e., more than in Althaus].' Cf. also J. Moltmann, op. cit., pp.228f.

26. K. Barth, *CD* IV/3, p.489. Cf. here Hedinger, op. cit., pp.31ff. Kreck tries to get beyond this by adding to the paired concepts of 'hiddenness – revelation' and 'law – gospel' the other, Old Testament pair, 'promise – fulfilment' (op. cit., pp. 91ff.). In the appendix to the 2nd edition he puts it even more clearly: 'The expected revealing of the lordship of Jesus Christ, which is already valid now, implies a newly creating divine

activity, which has not yet taken place.' But how are these three pairs of concepts related to one another?

In the dogmatic appeal to I John 3.2, the 'it does not yet appear' is often related to the previously mentioned fact that we are God's children now, in the present; and this is interpreted as if the passage read: 'It does not yet appear what we already are.' Cf. Kreck, op. cit., p.123; H. Wenz, *Die Ankunft unseres Herrn am Ende der Welt*, Arbeiten zur Theologie I/21, Stuttgart 1965, p.29. But according to the passage 'it does not yet appear what we shall be': 'The state of being the child of God will become the state of being like God.' Cf. here W. Schrage in *Göttinger Predigtmeditationen* 20, 1, 1965, p.35.

27. *CD* III/2, p.490.

28. *CD* IV/3, pp.326f., 329.

29. Cf. here the criticism by M. Josuttis, *Die Gegenständlichkeit der Offenbarung. Karl Barths Anselm-Buch und die Denkform seiner Theologie*, Abhandlungen zur evangelischen Theologie 3, Bonn 1965, p.153: 'What is decisive is what is reported by testimony; because it is localized as a unique event beyond testimony and beyond faith, all synergistic vulnerability but also all eschatological rigour is removed from these two.' R. Bohren made a similar point earlier in 'Bemerkungen zu Karl Barths Predigtweise an Hand seiner Predigten aus den Jahren 1954–1959' in*VuF*, 1962, pp.141–9.

30. E. Käsemann, 'Principles of the Interpretation of Romans 13', *NTQ*, pp.196–216, esp. pp.205–7.

31. *CD* IV/1, pp.327ff. H. Ott took this up in *Eschatologie*, pp.10ff. Similarly Kreck, op. cit., pp.90f.

32. Käsemann, 'On the Subject of Primitive Christian Apocalyptic', op. cit., p.133.

33. *CD* IV/1, p.324.

34. Similarly Ott, *Eschatologie*, p.10: 'Just because he is the Lord, he is by his nature the eschatologically future one . . . Eschatology as dogmatic "discipline" is concerned with the unsurpassability and the sovereignty of God in the context of time.' For a provocatively critical and opposing view see T. Stadtland, *Eschatologie und Geschichte in der Theologie des jungen Karl Barth*, Beiträge zur Geschichte und Lehre der Ref. Kirche XXII, Neukirchen 1966.

35. E. Peterson, *Theologische Traktate*, Munich 1951, p.334.

36. So A. Oepke, with his article παρουσία (*TDNT* V, 865) may be said to be right in his opposition to Barth's idea of the threefold parousia, when he writes: 'Primitive Christianity waits for the Jesus who has come already as the One who is still to come. The hope of an imminent coming of the exalted Lord in Messianic glory is, however, so much to the fore that in the NT the terms are never used for the coming of Christ in the flesh, and παρουσία never has the sense of return. . . . A basic prerequisite for understanding the world of thought of primitive Christianity is that we should fully free ourselves from this notion, which, so far as the NT is concerned, is suspect both philologically and materially.' Kreck replies: 'We may be

certain that what Barth wants to say does not depend on the New Testament use of the term parousia; but it can hardly be denied that Jesus Christ's threefold coming is talked about in the New Testament' (*Zukunft*, p.83).

37. E. Käsemann, 'Rudolf Bultmann. Das Evangelium des Johannes', review in *VuF* 1942–46 (1947), pp.197f.: 'For the expectation of the first Christians was really directed towards the end of all history, towards the parousia of the End-time. It is only in the light of this final liberation that this End acquires its meaning, that Christ already liberates me today; it is only in the light of the redemption of the body and the gift of the spiritual body in the resurrection of the dead that I can understand that Christ already calls me physically to his service today: it is only in the light of the general proskynesis of the cosmos that the End acquires its meaning – that faith already worships the Kyrios today. For the end of history is not merely history's final point; it is its key, the very foundation for the understanding of it.'

38. The development of God's eternity and sovereignty in talk about God's pre-temporeity, contemporeity, or post-temporeity, or in the designations: the one who has come, the one who is present, the one who is to come (and accordingly in the doctrine of Christ's threefold parousia) has a remarkable correspondence – the correspondence of a mirror image – to the existential interpretation of eschatology as futurity, in the sense of the prolongation of existence into time. In the one we hear, 'God is the future'; in the other, 'faith is future'. For both aspects of the interpretation, 'resurrection' becomes the cipher. Cf. Bultmann's criticism of Barth's *The Resurrection of the Dead* (1924, ET 1933), in *Faith and Understanding: Collected Essays*, ET SCM Press and Harper & Row 1969, p.81: 'It is not allowable to explain away the components of this world-view . . . as simply figurative; or to by-pass them by a reinterpretation.' This criticism, however, also applies to the critic himself.

39. Cf. here P. Stuhlmacher, *Gerechtigkeit*, p.232: 'God's divinity, however, is in accordance only with a new world in which death has been overcome and destroyed.'

40. This has been finely stressed recently by W. Pannenberg. Cf. 'Der Gott der Hoffnung' in *Ernst Bloch zu ehren*, ed. S. Unseld, Frankfurt 1965, pp.209ff.

41. E. Käsemann, *NTQ*, p.133; P. Stuhlmacher, op. cit., p.209.

42. Cf. E. Käsemann's review of E. Jüngel, *Paulus und Jesus*, Tübingen 1964, in *TLZ* 90, 1965, p.187.

43. I am taking over this formulation of the question from Kreck, *Zukunft* (in what follows I quote from the 2nd ed. of 1966).

44. Kreck, op. cit., p.118.

45. Ibid., p.120.

46. Ibid.

47. Ibid., p.108.

48. E. Käsemann in *The Future of our Religious Past, Essays in honour of R. Bultmann*, ET ed. J. M. Robinson, SCM Press and Harper & Row 1971, pp.49–62; here p.51.

49. Ibid., p.56.

50. Ibid., p.64.

51. E. Käsemann, ' "The Righteousness of God" in Paul', *NTQ*, pp. 168–82; here pp.171f.: 'But our particular problem is to identify the unitary centre from which he [Paul] managed to combine present and future eschatology, "declare righteous" and "make righteous", gift and service, freedom and obedience, forensic, sacramental and ethical approaches.'

52. The quotations which Kreck takes over in his book from H. W. Iwand's meditations make it obvious that Iwand's eschatology was really of a somewhat different kind. Cf. *Die Gegenwart des Kommenden*, 1955, p.37: 'For Jesus Christ is the one who is to come. He encounters everyone whom he truly encounters in the light of the future, as the life to come, as the Lord of the coming world. Otherwise he cannot be our Lord . . . He is only the one who has come and the one who is to come . . . What Jesus wants to say is: as the one who is to come, I am in the midst of you now. And as the one who has already come, I will come to you. The one who will come again remains the one who has already come.'

53. As far as I know E. Brunner was the first to point out this historical linguistic distinction (*Eternal Hope*, p.25 and note, pp.221f.). A. Rich (*Die Bedeutung der Eschatologie für den christlichen Glauben*, Zürich 1954, p.5) and Sauter (op. cit., p.154) have both developed it further. I have used it myself in my essay 'Die Zukunft Christi' in *Radius*, Stuttgart 1966, p.3, applying it to the ambiguity of the use of the word 'future' in E. Bloch. If one wants to extend the distinction between *Zukunft* and *Futur* further beyond the purely linguistic field, one could not say with E. Jüngel: 'God's being is in the becoming' (*Verantwortliche Rede vom Sein Gottes bei Karl Barth. Eine Paraphrase*, Tübingen 1965); it is rather 'in coming'. See now the 'Epilegomena 1975' to the 3rd ed. Nor could one say God is God 'with the future tense as his constitutive character' (E. Bloch, *Das Prinzip Hoffnung* II, Frankfurt 1959, p.1458), although by this Bloch means specifically the God of the exodus and the hope for the kingdom. But his concept of God also changes to the Greek *physis*, to mater-materia, for which the future tense gives every reason.

54. W. Pannenberg is quite right in giving this priority to the resurrection, which is not merely the apocalypse of the cross (H. Ott, op. cit., p.18) but can only be that in universality, if it is understood in its own context as the beginning of the general resurrection of the dead. But he should not underestimate the fact that even in the early Christian traditions, in the face of the contradiction between eschatological faith and experience (the delay of the parousia), faith in the resurrection could only hold its ground as faith in the mediation of the resurrection through the crucified Jesus.

55. J. Habermas, *Theorie und Praxis. Sozialphilosophische Aufsätze*, Politica 11, Neuwied 1963, p.181.

56. T. W. Adorno, *Zur Metakritik der Erkenntnistheorie. Studien über Husserl und die phänomenologischen Antinomien*, Stuttgart 1956, p.49.

57. H. Gollwitzer, *EvTh* 26, 1966, p.167.

58. J. B. Metz, *Welterfahrung im Glauben*, Mainz 1965.

59. H. E. Cox, *The Secular City*, Macmillan, New York 1965, SCM Press 1966.

60. Cf. here T. W. Adorno, 'Blochs Spuren' in *Noten zur Literatur* II, Bibl. Suhrkamp 71, Frankfurt 1961.

61. R. Bultmann in *Kerygma and Myth*, ET SPCK 1957, p.5.

62. W. Pannenberg, *Jesus – God and Man*, ET Westminster Press, Philadelphia and SCM Press 1968, pp.107f.

63. Ibid., p.107.

64. Ernst Bloch frequently expressed these ideas, giving his reasons. Cf.*Verfremdungen* I, Frankfurt 1962, p.216.

65. W. Pannenberg, 'Hermeneutik und Universalgeschichte' in *ZThK* 60, 1963, p.116.

66. Barth, *CD* IV/3, p.331.

67. Kreck, *Zukunft*, p.89.

68. Ott, *Eschatologie*, pp.25f.

69. W. Trillhaas, *Dogmatik*, Sammlung Töpelmann I/3, Berlin 1962, pp.471ff. Cf. also G. Sauter, *Zukunft*, p.157.

70. With particular emphasis in A. A. van Ruler, *Die christliche Kirche und das Alte Testament*, BEvTh 23, Munich 1955.

71. Althaus, *Dinge*, p.309.

72. Ibid., pp.309, 313.

73. For the following passage cf. H. W. Bartsch, 'Early Christian Eschatology in the Synoptic Gospels', *NTS* 11, 1965, pp.387–97, and *Das Auferstehungszeugnis, sein historisiches und sein theologisches Problem*, ThF 41, 1965.

74. H. J. Iwand, *Nachgelassene Werke* IV, Munich 1964, p.217.

75. K. Barth, *The Resurrection of the Dead*, ET Hodder & Stoughton and Revell, New York 1933, pp.212f. (altered).

III Methods in Eschatology

1. H. Berkhof, 'Over de method der eschatologie', *NThT* 19, 1965, pp.480–91.

2. *Christelijk Geloof*, Nijkerk 1973, pp.511, 544.

3. Ibid., p.545.

4. Ibid., p.546.

5. Ibid., p.547.

6. Cf. the article 'Extrapolation' in *Historisches Wörterbuch der Philosophie*, ed. J. Ritter, vol. II, Darmstadt 1972, p.879.

7. Cf. here the distinction between future as *futurum* and as *adventus*, (cf. pp. 29f. above) and the distinction between extrapolation and anticipation in *Diskussion über die 'Theologie der Hoffnung'*, Munich 1967, pp.201ff.

8. Rahner, *Theological Investigations* IV, ET 1966, p.337.

9. Ibid.

10. On the following passage see the article 'Antizipation' in *Historisches Wörterbuch der Philosophie*, ed. J. Ritter, vol. I, 1971, pp.419–25.

11. The Message of the Assembly, quoted from K. Slack, *Uppsala Report*, SCM Press 1968, p.v.

12. The Dogmatic Constitution on the Church (*Lumen Gentium*), VII, § 48, quoted from *The Documents of Vatican II*, ed. W. J. Abbott, SJ, Geoffrey Chapman, Dublin, and Herder & Herder, New York 1966, p.79.

13. Franz Rosenzweig, *Der Stern der Erlösung*, Part II, Book III, 2nd ed., Frankfurt 1930, pp.169f.

V The Theology of the Cross Today

The ideas expressed in this essay are developed more fully in my book *The Crucified God*, ET SCM Press and Harper & Row, New York 1974.

1. H. U. von Balthasar, 'Mysterium Paschale' in *Mysterium Salutis. Grundriss einer heilsgeschichtlichen Dogmatik* III, 2, 1969; H. Mühlen, *Die Veränderlichkeit Gottes als Horizont einer zukünftigen Christologie. Auf dem Wege zu einer Kreuzestheologie in Auseinandersetzung mit der altkirchlichen Christologie*, Münster 1969 (see also the review by H.-G. Link, 'Auf dem Weg zu einer zukünftigen Kreuzestheologie' in *EvTh* 33, 1973, pp.424ff.; K. Rahner, *Theological Investigations* IV, ET 1974, pp. 137ff.; H. Küng, *Menschwerdung Gottes. Eine Einführung in Hegels theologisches Denken als Prolegomena zu einer zukünftigen Christologie*, Freiburg 1970.

2. E. Jüngel, 'Vom Tod des lebendigen Gottes. Ein Plakat', *ZThK* 65, 1968, pp.93ff.; H.-G. Geyer 'Atheismus und Christentum', *EvTh* 30, 1970, pp.255–74; R. Weth, 'Heil im gekreuzigten Gott', *EvTh* 31, 1971, pp.227ff. Cf. also the older books by A. Schlatter, *Jesu Gottheit und das Kreuz*, 2nd ed., Gütersloh 1913; B. Steffen, *Das Dogma vom Kreuz. Beitrag zu einer staurozentrischen Theologie*, Gütersloh 1920; P. Althaus, 'Das Kreuz Christi' in *Theologische Aufsätze*, Gütersloh 1929, pp.5ff.

3. M. Kähler, 'Das Kreuz. Grund und Mass der Christologie' (1911) in *Schriften zur Christologie und Mission*, ThB 42, 1971, pp.292–350.

4. For more detail see Moltmann, *The Crucified God*, pp.7ff.

5. K. Barth, 'The Word of God and the Task of the Ministry' in *The Word of God and the Word of Man*, ET Hodder & Stoughton and Pilgrim Press, Boston 1928, p.186: 'As ministers we ought to speak of God. We are human, however, and so cannot speak of God. We ought therefore to recognize both our obligation and our inability and by that very recognition give God the glory.'

6. K. Rahner, art. 'Theologia crucis', *Lexikon für Theologie und Kirche*, ed. M. Buchberger et al., 2nd ed., Freiburg 1957–65, vol. X, col. 61.

7. J. W. Goethe, *Die Geheimnisse. Ein Fragment*.

8. *Wilhelm Meisters Wanderjahre* II, 1: ET *William Meister's Travels*, Bell 1882, p.156.

9. F. Nietzsche, *Beyond Good and Evil*, III, 46 (ET, *Collected Works* 12, Foulis, Edinburgh, and Macmillan, New York 1909, p.65, altered).

10. M. Heidegger, *Phänomenologie und Theologie* (1928), Frankfurt 1970, 18.

11. F. Viering, *Der Kreuzestod Jesus. Interpretation eines theologischen Gutachtens*, Gütersloh 1969.

12. P. Althaus, op. cit., p.23.

13. K. Rahner, *Theological Investigations* IV, p.113, and 'Der Tod Jesu als Tod Gottes' in *Sacramentum Mundi* II, Freiburg, Basle and Vienna 1968, pp.951f.

14. *Sacramentum Mundi*, pp.951f.

15. Op. cit., p.951.

16. Op. cit., p. 952.

17. Ibid.

18. Karl Barth, *CD* II/2 and IV/1–4; B. Klappert, *Die Auferweckung des Gekreuzigten. Der Ansatz der Christologie Karl Barths im Zusammenhang der Christologie der Gegenwart*, Neukirchen-Vluyn 1971.

19. *CD* II/2, p.123.

20. B. Klappert's correct judgment, op. cit., p. 180.

21. Cf. here G. C. Berkouwer, *Der Triumph der Gnade in der Theologie Karl Barths*, 1957, p.277; and similarly B. Klappert, op. cit., p.182 n.58.

22. Cf. *CD* II/2, pp.155, 163, 165, 169f.

23. Luther, WA 23, 141, 28, quoted in E. Wolf, 'Die Christusverkündigung bei Luther' in *Peregrinatio* I. *Studien zur reformatorischen Theologie, zum Kirchenrecht und zur Sozialethik*, Munich 1954, p.56.

24. K. Kitamori, *Theology of the Pain of God*, ET SCM Press and John Knox Press, Richmond, Va. 1966; see also review of the German translation (1972) by R. Weth in *EvTh* 33, 1973, pp.431ff.

25. H. Gollwitzer, *Krummes Holz – aufrechter Gang*, Munich 1970, p.258.

26. T. Haecker, *Tag- und Nachtbücher*, Munich 1947, p.245.

27. Goethe himself interpreted this saying as follows, however: 'These people cannot be defeated by anything except the universe itself, with which they began their struggle . . . and that strange but tremendous saying may well have arisen from such observations.' Cf. E. Spranger, 'Nemo contra Deum nisi Deus ipse' in *Philosophie und Psychologie der Religion, Gesammelte Schriften*, vol. 9, Tübingen 1974, pp.315–31.

28. C. Schmitt, *Politische Theologie* II, Berlin 1970, p.123.

29. Op. cit., p.118; cf. pp.116 and 123: 'If every unity is a duality, so that a potential rebellion, a *stasis*, is immanent, then theology seems to become "stasiology".'

30. T. Rüther, *Die sittliche Forderung der Apatheia in den beiden ersten christlichen Jahrhunderten und bei Klemens von Alexandrien*, Freiburg 1949.

31. Aristotle, *Metaphysics* XII, 1073a 11.

32. This is rightly criticized by W. Elert in *Der Ausgang der altkirchlichen Christologie*, Berlin 1957, p.95, and by K. Kitamori, op. cit., pp.46ff.

33. Origen, *Homilies on Ezekiel*, 6.6. Hans Urs von Balthasar kindly drew my attention to this passage.

34. A. Heschel, *Die Prophetie*, Berlin 1936, and *The Prophets*, Harper & Row, New York 1962.

35. *The Prophets*, pp.232ff.

36. Quoted ibid., pp.251f.

37. P. Kuhn, *Gottes Selbsterniedrigung in der Theologie der Rabbinen*, Munich 1968.

38. Ibid., p.90.

39. E.g. in A. von Harnack, *What is Christianity?*, ET, 3rd ed. 1904, reissued Harper Torchbooks, New York 1957, esp. pp. 63ff.: 'God the Father and the Infinite Value of the Human Soul'.

40. Steffen, op. cit. (n.2 above), p.152; cf. Mühlen, op. cit. (n.1 above), p.33.

41. W. Kramer, *Christ, Lord, Son of God*, ET, SBT 1.50, 1966.

42. Käsemann, 'On the Subject of Primitive Christian Apocalyptic', *NTQ*, p.133.

43. W. Popkes, *Christus traditus. Eine Untersuchung zum Begriff der Dahingabe im Neuen Testament*, Zürich 1967, pp.286f.

44. Mühlen, op. cit., p.36.

45. So J. Schniewind, *Nachgelassene Reden und Aufsätze*, Berlin 1952, p.130; H. Schwantes, *Schöpfung der Endzeit*, Berlin 1962, pp.88f.

46. Contrary to Melanchthon's famous statement in the *Loci Communes* of 1521: 'We adore the mysteries of the Godhead. That is better than to investigate them' (*Melanchthons Werke* II, ed. R. Stupperich, Gütersloh 1952, p.7).

47. J. B. Metz ('Erlösung und Emanzipation', *StZ* 98, 1973, pp.181f.) has objected to the attempt 'to absorb the non-identity of our human history of suffering into the trinitarian history of God by way of God's *kenosis* in Jesus Christ', claiming that the painfully experienced non-identity of suffering is not identical with that negativity which belongs to a dialectically understood historical process, even if it be the trinitarian history of God. He would like to avoid any confusion between the negativity of *suffering* and the negativity of the dialectically communicated *concept of suffering*. But in a trinitarian theology of the cross what is at stake is not the communication of facticity and conceptuality, but the mediation of two histories: the human history of suffering and Jesus Christ's history of suffering. If this were not so, only a dialectical theology of the cross without the Jesus crucified under Pontius Pilate would emerge. But if the doctrine of the Trinity is understood as 'the shortened version of the *history* of Christ's passion', then his objection is unfounded. Through its inevitably paradoxical aspects, the dialectical doctrine of the Trinity is itself narrative and also points into the history of Christ and the history of the believer. But if by his distinction Metz really means the distinction between the negative in the dialectical process and the nothingness itself which remains outside (a distinction which is to be found in Hegel and Bloch, and which only goes a little way beyond the ancient world's distinction between the μὴ ὄν and the οὐκ ὄν) this would merely fortify Christology's traditional hint of docetism and confirm soteriology's familiar combination with moralism. If this is not intended, then the passion of Jesus must be capable of being related in such a way that all the

godless and God-forsaken recognize themselves in it, and can find in it the salvation which has grown out of their doom, and the hope that has sprung out of their misery. But this presupposes that in principle no pit of nothingness is unreachable by Christ's passion. The essential question is then not argumentative as opposed to narrative Christology, but 'salvation in the crucified God' as opposed to the inhuman God and godless man.

48. Dorothee Sölle's view in *Christ the Representative*, ET SCM Press and Fortress Press, Philadelphia 1967, p. 94.

49. From the presuppositions of his *Systematic Theology* Paul Tillich came to similar conclusions. In the idea of the suffering of God and 'his participation in existential estrangement and its self-destructive consequences', as this has become manifest in the cross of Christ, 'the doctrine of the living God and the doctrine of the atonement coincide' (*Systematic Theology* II, 1957, reissued SCM Press 1978, pp.174f.). Then the Christian doctrine of the atonement is the doctrine of God's participation in the world's suffering in the crucified Christ; and conversely the Christian doctrine of God is the doctrine of the event of reconciliation, provided in the cross of Christ. If one starts from this and if one keeps the point of coincidence in view, however, then Tillich's remarks about the dialectical negativity in the divine life process (op. cit. I, 1951, reissued 1978, pp. 177, 185, 241) ought to turn out less speculative than they appear.

50. K. Rahner, 'Remarks on the Dogmatic Treatise *De Trinitate*', *Theological Investigations* IV, pp.87 and 96.

51. Tillich, op. cit. vol. I, pp.179ff.

52. Quoted in W. Capelle, *Die Vorsokratiker*, Stuttgart 1958, pp.217f.

53. Aristotle, *Metaphysics* II, 1000b 5.

54. *Nicomachean Ethics* VIII, 1155a 3. *Magna Moralia* II, 1208b.

55. F. W. J. Schelling, *On Human Freedom*, ET Open Court Co., Chicago 1936, p.50.

56. E. Bloch, *Tübinger Einleitung in die Philosophie* II, Frankfurt 1964, p.16.

VI The Trinitarian History of God

Lecture delivered to the theological faculty of the University of Oslo on 16 January 1975, and in the University of Oxford on 9 May 1975.

1. K. Rahner rightly complains of this in 'Remarks on the Dogmatic Treatise *De Trinitate*', *Theological Investigations* IV, ET 1966, pp.77–102.

2. P. Melanchthon, *Loci Communes*, 1521 (see ch. V n.46 above).

3. I. Kant, *Der Streit der Fakultäten*, A 50, 57.

4. For more detail see J. Moltmann, *The Crucified God*, ET 1974, and *The Church in the Power of the Spirit*, ET SCM Press 1977 and Harper & Row, New York 1977.

5. K. Barth, 'Vergangenheit und Zukunft' in J. Moltmann (ed.), *Anfänge der dialektischen Theologie*, ThB 17/I, Munich 1962, p.41.

6. Cf. here Barth, 'Der Christ in der Gesellschaft' (op. cit., pp.9ff.), where he describes knowledge of God in the movement of, and the being moved by, the history of God as being 'like the flight of a bird' and therefore 'without any fixed abode'.

7. J. Pohle and J. Gummersbach, *Lehrbuch der Dogmatik* I, Paderborn 1952, p.464. Cf. here also H. Mühlen, *Der Heilige Geist als Person*, Münster 1966, pp.201ff. On the following passage cf. also A. M. Aagaard, *Helliganden sendt til Verden*, Aarhus 1973, and 'Missio Dei in katholischer Sicht', *EvTh* 34, 1974, pp.420–33.

8. So K. Rengstorf, *TDNT* I, p.398.

9. Attention might be drawn to Luke 4.18ff. and Matt. 11.5 as a reminder of the realistic and all-embracing character of messianic mission for Jesus and the church. Matt. 10.7f. reads: 'Preach as you go, saying, "The kingdom of heaven is at hand." Heal the sick, raise the dead, cleanse lepers, cast out demons. You received without pay, give without pay.'

10. A. M. Aagaard, 'Missio Dei', pp.423f.

11. Details in N. A. Nissiotis, *Die Theologie der Ostkirche im ökumenischen Dialog. Kirche und Welt in orthodoxer Sicht*, Stuttgart 1968, pp.28ff.

12. Barth, *CD* IV/2, p.342.

13. *CD* I/1, p.448.

14. *CD* I/1, p.383.

15. So also according to the Orthodox presentation. Cf. G. Wagner, 'Der Heilige Geist als offenbarmachende und vollendende Kraft', in C. Heitmann and H. Mühlen (eds.), *Erfahrung und Theologie des Heiligen Geistes*, Hamburg 1974, p.220: 'The rejection of the *filioque* implies that in the conception of the East the Trinity remains essentially "open" – open in order to reveal itself in the coming of the Spirit.' On the interpretation of the term *Dreifaltigkeit* cf. M. Kähler, *Die Wissenschaft der christlichen Lehre*, 1966, pp.325ff.

16. In the following passage I am deliberately taking into account a shift in meaning compared with the traditional and frequently abstract use of the term 'protology', which is often difficult to support theologically.

17. For what follows see the article δόξα by G. Kittel in *TDNT* II, pp. 237, 242ff.; H. U. von Balthasar, *Herrlichkeit. Eine theologische Asthetik*, I–III/2, 1961–67; J. Moltmann, *Theology and Joy*, SCM Press and Harper & Row, New York 1973, pp.58ff. For the exegetical foundation cf. W. Thüsing, *Per Christum in Deum. Studien zum Verhältnis von Christozentrik und Theozentrik in den paulinischen Hauptbriefen*, 2nd ed., Münster 1968.

18. Cf. E. Stauffer, article ἵνα, *TDNT* III, pp.324ff., here p.329.

19. Cf. Adrienne von Speyr, *The Word. A Meditation on the Prologue to St John's Gospel*, ET Collins and McKay, New York 1953, p. 26.

20. See H. Mühlen's critical comments in *Der Heilige Geist als Person*, pp.318ff. For the Eastern church, on the other hand, the unity of the Trinity lies in the person of the Father, who is seen as *fons divinitatis* and as the origin both of the Son and of the Spirit.

21. F. Rosenzweig, *Der Stern der Erlösung*, III, 3rd ed. 1954, pp.192–4.

22. I am here adopting some of Adrienne von Speyr's ideas and insights.

I was surprised to discover subsequently the close similarity between the theology of 'the crucified God' and her Easter Eve mysticism. Cf. B. Albrecht, *Eine Theologie des Katholischen. Einführung in das Werk Adrienne von Speyrs*; vol. I: *Durchblick in Texten*; vol. II: *Darstellung*, Einsiedeln 1973. Cf. especially vol. II, pp.155ff.: 'Die Sendung der Liebe und ihre Rückwirkung auf Gott.'

23. Lady Julian of Norwich, *Revelations of Divine Love*, ch.31, quoted in K. J. Woollcombe, 'The Pain of God', *Scottish Journal of Theology* 20, Edinburgh 1967, pp.129ff.

24. R. Bohren points expressly to this in *Fasten und Feiern*, Neukirchen 1973, pp.11ff. and n.2.

VII The Hope of Resurrection and the Practice of Liberation

1. This is the revised form of a lecture I delivered in the spring of 1972 in Singapore, Manila, Kyoto and Tokyo. It makes use of material which I treated at the last Christian–Marxist dialogue in Marienbad, Czechoslovakia, in 1968, under the title 'Die Revolution der Freiheit'. Cf. *Perspektiven der Theologie* I, 1968, pp.189–211.

2. Cf. M. Susman, *Das Buch Hiob und das Schicksal des jüdischen Volkes*, 2nd ed., Basle 1948, p.223.

3. The fact that a partnership of this kind can also be considered theoretically and scientifically is exemplified by, for example, *Humanökologie und Umweltschutz*, *Studien zur Friedensforschung* 8, Munich 1972.

4. I developed these ideas further in my book *The Crucified God*, ET 1974, because I had the impression that there cannot be a liberating 'theology of liberation' without a new doctrine of God. It is essential to overcome the classic doctrine of God's *apatheia*.

5. See here M. M. Thomas, 'Die Bedeutung des Heils heute' in *Das Heil der Welt heute. Dokumente der Weltmissionskonferenz Bangkok 1973*, Stuttgart 1973, pp.31–44.

6. Cf. H. Marcuse, *Das Ende der Utopie*, Berlin 1967, p.38.

7. In Christian terms, reconciliation cannot well be set against liberation or liberation against reconciliation. Reconciliation with the God of liberation means struggle against oppression in the world, just as peace with God means discordancy with a world without peace.

8. B. Brecht, *The Good Person of Szechwan*, scene 10 (ET, *Plays* II, Methuen 1962, p.307).

9. Cf. M. Susman, op. cit., p.238.

10. Here I am following the New Testament studies of K. Niederwimmer, *Der Begriff der Freiheit im Neuen Testament*, Berlin 1966; H. Schlier, 'Über das vollkommene Gesetz der Freiheit' in *Die Zeit der Kirche*, 4th ed., Freiburg 1963, pp.133–8; E. Käsemann, 'The Cry for Liberty in the Worship of the Church' in *Perspectives on Paul*, ET SCM Press and Fortress Press, Philadelphia 1971, pp.122–37.

11. R. Garaudy points this out in *L'Alternative*, Paris 1972, pp. 125f., making use of the 'Theology of Hope'. Cf. also, more recently, the last chapters of his autobiography, *Parole d'homme*, Paris 1975, pp.225ff.

12. Käsemann, op. cit., p.135.

13. Quoted from the Akademieausgabe, Series II, Vol. 3, Stuttgart 1971, p.183. Cf. M. Welker, *Der Vorgang Autonomie*, Neukirchen 1975.

14. R. Bultmann, *The Gospel of John*, ET Blackwell, Oxford, and Westminster Press, Philadelphia 1971, p. 437.

15. Here I am taking up ideas developed in connection with *The Theology of Hope* by Paul Ricoeur, *Le Conflit des interprétations. Essais d'herméneutique*, Paris 1969, pp.395ff.

16. M. Susman, op. cit., p.223.

17. K. Niederwimmer, op. cit., p.78.

18. Cf. J. Moltmann, *Die Sprache der Befreiung*, 2nd ed., Munich 1972.

19. The Confessing Church showed this clearly in Germany by means of the Barmen Declaration of 1934.

20. Cf. here R. Schutz, *Festival*, ET SPCK 1974, pp. 130f.

21. D. Bonhoeffer, 'Stations on the Road to Freedom' in *Letters and Papers from Prison*, ET, revised edition, 1971, p.370.

22. Cf. here E. Käsemann, 'Ministry and Community in the New Testament' in *Essays on New Testament Themes*, ET, SBT 1.41, 1964, pp.63–94; E. Schweizer, 'Zur Ekklesiologie des Neuen Testaments' in his collected essays, *Neotestamentica*, Zürich 1963, pp.239ff.; A. M. Aagaard, *Helliganden sendt til Verden*, Aarhus 1973; H. Berkhof, *The Doctrine of the Holy Spirit*, ET John Knox Press, Richmond 1964, Epworth Press 1965.

23. Here I agree entirely with F. Herzog, *Liberation Theology*, Seabury Press, New York 1972. This book's strength lies in the way it teaches us to understand anew liberation in the light of the Bible, and the Bible in the light of liberation.

24. Ernst Bloch, as a humanist Marxist, always insisted on this point. Cf. *Naturrecht und menschliche Würde*, Frankfurt 1961.

25. Cf. G. Gutierrez, *A Theology of Liberation*, Orbis Books, New York 1973, SCM Press 1974. It seems to me, however, that he understresses the democratic side of socialism. This is understandable in his particular situation, but it is not really possible.

26. The elements of liberation from racialism are presented best by J. Cone, *Black Theology and Black Power*, Seabury Press, New York 1969. But its problem seems to lie in the economic differentiation within the self-conscious black community. The interdependence between racialism and capitalism ought to be analysed more precisely.

27. Women's liberation has found a solid theological mode of expression in R. R. Ruether, *Liberation Theology*, Paulist Press, New York 1972, and L. M. Russell, *Human Liberation in a Feminist Perspective – A Theology*, Westminster Press, Philadelphia 1974. At the same time there is a threat of ideological fixation here too, as there is everywhere. The writer's vision of Christianity transformed from a Constantinian to a prophetic religion is a demand which is made of Christianity by all liberation movements today;

and it is everywhere shared by the theologians sympathetic to the uprisings of the sixties.

VIII Creation as an Open System

1. Cf. A. Koyré, *From the Closed World to the Infinite Universe*, ET Johns Hopkins Press, Baltimore 1968.

2. F. Gogarten and R. Bultmann incline to these solutions. For a critical view, cf. C. J. Dippel and J. M. de Jong, *Geloof en Naturwetenshap*, 1, The Hague 1965.

3. Cf. K. Barth, *CD* III/1, Preface. But as the anthropology he develops in this volume shows, he himself did not keep to this peaceful division between theology and science. On this point cf. C. Link, *Die Welt als Gleichnis. Studien zum Problem der natürlichen Theologie*, Munich 1976.

4. In his orientation towards an eschatological doctrine of creation I agree with Pannenberg. See his *Erwägungen zu einer Theologie der Natur*, Gütersloh 1970, and *Theology and the Kingdom of God*, ET Westminster Press, Philadelphia 1969. But in my view his account of the being of God as 'the power of the future', which is in accord with the 'theology of hope', is one-sided, because it overlooks the power of 'God's suffering'. Cf. my book *The Crucified God*, ET 1974.

5. M. Eliade, *The Myth of the Eternal Return*, ET Routledge & Kegan Paul and Pantheon Books 1955; W. F. Otto, *Die Gestalt und das Sein*, Munich 1955; E. Hornung, *Die Geschichte als Fest*, Darmstadt 1966.

6. Thomas Aquinas, *Summa Theol.* I, qu. 90, art. 3.2, and *Comm. in Sent.* I, distinct. 14, qu. 2, art. 2. Also the comment by M. Seckler, *Das Heil in der Geschichte. Geschichtstheologisches Denken bei Thomas von Aquin*, Munich 1964.

7. R. Bultmann, *Glauben und Verstehen* III, Tübingen 1960, pp.29, 26.

8. G. von Rad, *Old Testament Theology* I, ET (1962) SCM Press and Harper & Row 1975, pp.136ff.; W. H. Schmidt, *Die Schöpfungsgeschichte*, Neukirchen 1967. There is also a more recent attempt in Old Testament research to find an approach to belief in creation – no longer now by way of 'salvation history', but by way of 'Wisdom'. Cf. von Rad, *Wisdom in Israel*, ET SCM Press and Abingdon Press, New York 1972; H. H. Schmid, 'Schöpfung, Gerechtigkeit und Heil. "Schöpfungstheologie" als Gesamthorizont biblischer Theologie', *ZThK* 70, 1973, pp.1–19; C. Westermann, *Genesis* (Biblischer Kommentar. Altes Testament I), Neukirchen 1974; G. Liedke, 'Selbstoffenbarung der Schöpfung', *EvKomm* 7, 1975, pp.298–400. I understand this approach as a supplement rather than as an alternative to the salvation-history approach to belief in creation.

9. G. von Rad, *Old Testament Theology* I, p.139.

10. L. Köhler, *Old Testament Theology*, ET of 3rd ed., Lutterworth Press 1957, and Westminster Press, Philadelphia 1958, p. 88.

11. H. D. Preuß, *Jahweglaube und Zukunftshoffnung*, Stuttgart 1968, pp.97f.

12. L. Köhler, op. cit., p.143.

13. On necessity, chance and pleasure in the theory of play cf. J. Moltmann, *Theology and Joy*, ET 1973.

14. By the openness of a system I mean: (1) that the system has different possibilities of alteration; (2) that its future behaviour has not been totally determined by its previous behaviour; (3) that it can communicate with other systems; (4) that the final condition of the system is different from its initial state. Viewed scientifically, the 'closed system' is only a hypothesis, set up so that we may arrive at statements that can be expressed in terms of quantity. In itself there is no such thing as a 'closed system'; at least no statements can be made about closed systems, because they elude all observation. Statements can only be made about open systems, with which an exchange of information is possible. Every exchange of information needs carriers, in terms of material or energy. But a closed system would be, by definition, a system which had no exchange of material with the environment. Cf. E. von Weizsäcker (ed.), *Offene Systeme I. Beiträge zur Zeitstruktur von Information, Entropie und Evolution*, Stuttgart 1974; H. Wehrt, 'Über Zeitverständnisse und die Problematik von Möglichkeit und Offenheit' in A. M. Müller (ed.), *Zukunftsperspektiven zu einem integrierten Verständnis der Lebenswelt*, Stuttgart 1976, pp.144–208, in relation to the 'theology of hope'.

15. Cf. W. Pannenberg, *Theology and the Kingdom of God*, pp.78f.

16. Cf. Moltmann, *The Crucified God*, pp.267ff.

17. H. Schwantes, *Schöpfung der Endzeit*, Stuttgart 1962.

18. Käsemann, 'Primitive Christian Apocalyptic', *NTQ*, pp.132ff. My expression 'the concept of *aparche*' is intended to bring out the positive aspect of what Käsemann calls 'the eschatological reservation'.

19. Contrary to E. Brunner, *Eternal Hope*, ET 1954, pp.198ff., esp. p.203: 'The negative point is sharp and definite – that "the form of this world passeth away", that death and transience will no longer be. But, apart from what directly concerns the new life of man and humanity, the positive side is left almost completely vague.' Cf. also J. B. Metz, *Theology of the World*, ET Burns & Oates and Herder & Herder, New York 1969, p.97: 'Christian eschatology is not an omniscient ideology about the future, but a *theologia negativa* of the future.' But Metz sees the positive bond between present and future in love for 'the least of our brothers'.

20. On this point cf. G. Liedke, 'Von der Ausbeutung zur Kooperation. Theologisch-philosophische Überlegungen zum Problem des Umweltschutzes', in E. von Weizsacker, ed., *Humanökologie und Umweltschutz*, Stuttgart 1972, pp.35–65.

21. W. Heisenberg, *The Physicist's Conception of Nature*, ET Hutchinson and Harcourt Brace, New York 1958, p. 29; similarly also C. F.von Weizsäcker, *Die Einheit der Natur*, Munich 1971, pp.279ff.

22. K. Marx, *Frühschriften*, ed. S. Landshut, Stuttgart 1953, p.237; cf. *Early Writings*, ed. T. B. Bottomore, Watts 1963, p.155. But in *Capital* he takes a pessimistic view of the achievability of a unity between man and nature. Cf. A. Schmidt, *Der Begriff der Natur in der Lehre von Marx*, 2nd

ed.,Vienna 1971; E. Roeder von Diersburg, *Zur Ontologie und Logik offener Systeme - Ernst Bloch vor dem Gesetz der Tradition*, Berlin 1967.

23. The Bucharest Consultation of the WCC on 'Science and Technology for Human Development' held in June 1974; see *Anticipation* 18, August 1974 (published by the Department on Church and Society of the WCC, Geneva).

IX Ethics and Biomedical Progress

1. This question was raised several times at the Ciba Symposium in London in 1962. See *Man and his Future: A Ciba FoundationVolume*, ed. G. Wolstenholme, J. & A. Churchill and Little, Brown & Co., Boston 1963. Cf. also R. Jungk and J. Mundt, eds., *Das umstrittene Experiment: Der Mensch*, Munich 1966.

2. Julian Huxley, 'The Future of Man, - Evolutionary Aspects', in *Man and his Future*, pp. 1–22.

3. Ibid., pp.3f., 6.

4. On the problem of genetic control, which is quite new in kind, see now A. Etzioni, *Genetic Fix*, New York 1973. In his book Etzioni refers among other things to a lecture which I gave at the 7th CIOMS Round Table Conference in 1972 in Paris. We are in agreement about the importance of political responsibility for biological power. Cf. *Recent Progress in Biology and Medicine - its social and ethical implications*, CIOMS, Paris 1972, pp.68–81.

5. F. Böckle, 'Ethische Aspekte der Organtransplantation beim Menschen' in *Studium Generale* 23, Berlin 1970, pp.444–59.

6. J. Hersch, *Proceedings of the Symposium on Science Policy and Biomedical Research*, No. 16, UNESCO, Paris 1969, p.75.

7. M. Marlet, 'Medizinische Experimente am Menschen?' in *Orientierung* 33, Pfaffenhofen 1969, pp.21ff.

8. Cf. here A. Gierer, *Die physikalischen Grundlagen der Biologie und des Selbstverständnis des Menschen*, Munich 1969.

9. R. Musil, *The Man without Qualities*, ET Secker & Warburg 1953–60, vol. I, p.175. Similarly E. Fromm, *The Revolution of Hope*, Harper & Row, New York 1968, pp.38ff., 82ff.

10. J. Hersch, *The Challenge of Life*, Basle 1972, p.351.

11. F. Böckle, op. cit., p.457. Cf. also E. Jüngel, *Tod*, Stuttgart 1971.

12. J. Moltmann, *Perspektiven der Theologie*, Munich 1968, pp.51ff.,and 'Resurrection as Hope', Ingersoll Lecture, in *Harvard Theological Review* 61, 1968, pp.129ff.

X Justification and New Creation

1. H. J. Iwand, *Glaubensgerechtigkeit nach Luthers Lehre*, ThEx 75, Munich 1941; E. Bizer, *Fides ex auditu*, Neukirchen 1958; G. Gloege, *Gnade für die Welt. Kritik und Krise des Luthertums*, Göttingen 1964.

2. E. Wolf, 'Die Rechtfertigungslehre als Mitte und Grenze reformatorischer Theologie' in *Peregrinatio II, Studien zur reformatorischen Theologie, zum Kirchenrecht und zur Sozialethik*, Munich 1965, pp.11ff.

3. M. Luther, *Schmalkaldische Artikel 1537, 2. Hauptartikel*, in *Die Bekenntnisschriften der Evangelisch-Lutherischen Kirche*, 2nd ed., Göttingen 1952, pp.415f.: 'De hoc articulo cedere aut aliquid contra illum largiri aut permittere nemo piorum potest, etiamsi coelum et terra ac omnia corruant. Non enim est aliud nomen hominibus datum, per quod salvari possimus, inquit Petrus Actorum 4. Et per vulnera ejus sanati sumus, Es. 53. Et in hoc articulo sita sunt et consistunt omnia, quae contra papam, diabolum et mundum in vita nostra docemus, testamur et agimus. Quare oportet nos de hac doctrina esse certos et minime dubitare, alioquin actum est prorsus et papa et diabolus et omnia adversa jus et victoriam contra nos obtinent.'

4. *Confessio Augustana* IV, *Bekenntnisschriften*, p.56: 'Item docent, quod homines non possint justificari coram Deo propriis viribus, meritis aut operibus, sed gratis justificentur propter Christum per fidem, cum credunt se in gratiam recipi et peccata remitti propter Christum, qui sua morte pro nostris peccatis satisfecit. Hanc fidem imputat Deus pro justitia coram ipso, Rom. 3 et 4.'

5. Luther (*Disputatio de homine*, 1536, WA 39 I, pp.175ff.) saw in the doctrine of justification – 'homo justificatus fide' – the anthropological fundamental definition, but he himself developed no corresponding theological anthropology. Cf. here E. Wolf, 'Menschwerdung des Menschen?' in *Peregrinatio* II, op. cit., pp.119ff.; W. Dantine, *Die Gerechtmachung des Gottlosen*, Munich 1959: E. Jüngel, 'Der Gott entsprechende Mensch. Bemerkungen zur Gottebenbildlichkeit des Menschen als Grundfigur theologischer Anthropologie' in *Neue Anthropologie*, ed. H.-G. Gadamer and P. Vogler, VI, Stuttgart 1974, pp.342ff.; J. Moltmann, *Man*, ET Fortress Press, Philadelphia 1974, esp. pp. 105ff.

6. This questionability is documented by the new study volume of the theological committee of the Vereinigten Evangelisch-Lutherische Kirche Deutschlands, *Rechtfertigung im neuzeitlichen Lebenszusammenhang. Studien zur Interpretation der Rechtfertigungslehre*, ed. W. Lohff and C. Walter, Gütersloh 1974.

7. Cf. G. Gloege, 'Die Grundfrage der Reformation – heute' in *Verkündigung und Verantwortung, Theologische Traktate* II, Göttingen 1967, pp.11ff.

8. Cf. G. Ebeling, 'Reflexions on the Doctrine of the Law' in *Word and Faith*, ET SCM Press and Fortress Press, Philadelphia 1963, pp.247ff.

9. S. Kierkegaard, *Gesammelte Werke. Die Tagebücher*, vol. 5, Düsseldorf, Cologne 1974, p.374f. The context runs: '. . . in the same way, it can happen in Protestantism that worldliness is honoured and valued as – piety. And this cannot happen in Catholicism – or so I would maintain. But why can't it happen in Catholicism? Because Catholicism has as its premise the general proposition that we men and women are a society of rascals. And why can it happen in Protestantism? Because the basic prin-

ciple of Protestantism is linked with a particular premise: a man who sits in mortal terror, in fear and trembling and much temptation – and there are not many people like this in any generation.'

10. Cf. the collection of writings illustrating the history of exegesis in E. Jüngel, *Paulus und Jesus*, 2nd ed., Tübingen 1964, pp.5ff.; and P. Stuhlmacher, *Gerechtigkeit Gottes bei Paulus*, Göttingen 1965, pp.11ff.

11. W. Dilthey, *Weltanschauung und Analyse des Menschen seit Renaissance und Reformation, Gesammelte Schriften* II, p.59.

12. So e.g. P. Althaus, *Die christliche Wahrheit*, 6th ed. Gütersloh 1962, pp.43ff.

13. Quoted in E. Jüngel, op. cit., p.13.

14. R. Bultmann, 'The Significance of the Historical Jesus for the Theology of Paul', *Faith and Understanding*, ET 1969, pp.220ff.

15. Ibid., p.232.

16. Ibid., p. 238.

17. Ibid., p.244.

18. So also G. Bornkamm, article 'Paulus', *RGG*, 3rd ed., V, pp.175ff.

19. G. Ebeling, 'Jesus and Faith' in *Word and Faith*, pp.201ff., esp. p.242.

20. E. Käsemann, 'Blind Alleys in the "Jesus of History" Controversy', *NTQ*, p.40.

21. U. Wilckens, *Die Missionsreden der Apostelgeschichte, Form- und traditionsgeschichtliche Untersuchungen*, 2nd ed., Neukirchen 1963.

22. Cf. E. Lohse, *Märtyrer und Gottesknecht. Untersuchungen zur urchristlichen Verkündigung vom Sühnetod Jesu Christi*, 2nd ed., Göttingen 1963. For critical comments on the doctrine of reconciliation, cf. Käsemann, 'Some Thoughts on the Theme "The Doctrine of Reconciliation in the New Testament" ' in *The Future of our Religious Past*, ET 1971, pp. 49–64. For criticism of Käsemann's view, cf. now P. Stuhlmacher, 'Jesus als Versöhner. Überlegungen zum Problem der Darstellung Jesus im Rahmen einer Biblischen Theologie des Neuen Testaments' in *Jesus Christ in Historie und Theologie. Festschrift für H. Conzelmann*, Tübingen 1975, pp.87–104.

23. Cf. Lohse, op. cit., pp.113ff.; W. Kramer, *Christ, Lord, Son of God*, ET, SBT 1.50, 1966, pp.19ff.

24. Käsemann, 'On the Subject of Primitive Christian Apocalyptic', *NTQ*, pp.108ff.; W. Schrage, 'Ekklesia und Synagoge', *ZThK* 60, 1963, pp.178ff.

25. Cf. P. Stuhlmacher, *Gerechtigkeit Gottes bei Paulus*, pp.187ff.

26. The following remarks relate especially to Käsemann's great essay ' "The Righteousness of God" in Paul', *NTQ*, pp. 168ff. Cf. also U. Wilckens, *Rechtfertigung als Freiheit, Paulusstudien*, Neukirchen 1974.

27. I am deliberately reversing Hegel's final sentence in his *Glauben und Wissen*, 1802 (Philos. Bibliothek 62b, Hamburg 1962, p.124).

28. A. Camus, 'L'incroyant et les chrétiens', *Actuelles* I, Paris 1950, p.213.

29. A. Schlatter, *Luthers Deutung des Römerbriefes*, Gütersloh 1917,

p.53. Correctly from an exegetical and systematic point of view, Schlatter criticized the interpretation of the act of justification as being merely the forgiveness of sins, seeing this as the expression of a solely negative divine will and a solely retrospectively directed act. He saw the new and positive element in the event of justification as being the new obedience, the new powers of the Spirit, and the new church. His criticism of the Reformed doctrine of justification is not always historically sound, but it can be a help in overcoming Protestant one-sidedness.

30. Augustine, *Enchiridion*, cap.52: 'nihil autem aliud mortem Christi crucifixi, nisi remissionis peccati similitudinem, ut . . . quemadmodum in illo vera resurrectio, ita in nobis vera justificatio.'

31. So Luther, *Enarr. Ps. 51*, WA 40 II, p.328, 19f.

32. Barth, *CD* IV/1, p.527. If one wanted to be precise one must first of all say: it is not the article about the forgiveness of sins with which the church stands and falls, for in the Apostles' Creed this follows the article about the church, and has the same structure; it is the article *credo in Spritum Sanctum*, for that is the presupposition for the *credo ecclesiam* and the *credo remissionem peccatorum*.

33. H. J. Iwand, *Rechtfertigungslehre und Christusglaube*, 1927, ThB 14, 2nd ed. 1961.

34. Käsemann, *NTQ*, p.180.

35. Cf. C. Müller, *Gottes Gerechtigkeit und Gottes Volk. Eine Untersuchung zu Röm. 9–11*, Göttingen 1964, p.89: 'The idea of the eschatological creation [is] the root of the doctrine of justification.' For 'new creation is the realization of God's right to creation in creation.'

36. R. Bultmann, *Glauben und Verstehen* III, p.26; cf. also II, p.120; ET, *Essays Philosophical and Theological*, SCM Press and Macmillan, New York 1955, p.136.

37. Cf. H. Sasse, article κόσμος, *TDNT* III, p.885; W. Schrage, op. cit., p.130.

INDEX OF NAMES